IGBO Linguistics

An Expanded Guide to Igbo Orthography
Phonology, Morphology and Lexicology

Elisha O. Ogbonna

Igbo Linguistics: *An Expanded Guide to Igbo Orthography, Phonology, Morphology & Lexicology*

by Elisha O. Ogbonna

This book is written to provide educational and Igbo language learning information for linguistic and advanced learners.

Copyright © May 2024 by Elisha O. Ogbonna

All rights reserved. No part of this book may be reproduced, transmitted, or distributed in any form by any means, including, butnot limited to, recording, photocopying, or taking screenshots of parts of the book, without prior written permission from the author or the publisher. Brief quotations for noncommercial purposes, suchas book reviews, permitted by Fair Use of the Canada Copyright Law, are allowed without written permissions, as long as such quotations do not cause damage to the book's commercial value. Forpermission, write to the publisher, whose address is stated below.

ISBN:
978-1-7781320-8-7 (Hardcover)
978-1-7781320-7-0 (Paperback)
978-1-7781320-6-3 (eBook)

Produced by:

Prinoelio Press
For Igbo Learning Hub
E-mail: Igbolearninghub@gmail.com
https://www.Igbo learninghub.com

Dedication

To my daughters,

Amanda and **Rebecca**
Without whom this book would have been completed months earlier.

Table of Contents

Dedication 3
Table of Contents 5
    Introduction 13
    Guide to Pronunciation.. 14
Part One: 17
    Igbo Orthography (Ederede Igbo) 17
Chapter 1 19
    Orthography 19
        1.1 Introduction to Orthography (Okwu Mmalite Usoro Odide Asụsụ) 19
        1.2 Layers of Igbo Orthography 21
        1.3 Three Phases of Learning to Read 22
        1.4 Orthography Mapping 23
        1.5 Orthography and Language Diversity 23
        Exercise 25
Chapter 2 27
    Development of Igbo Orthography 27
        2.1 Development of Igbo Orthography (Nkwalite Usoro Odide Asụsụ Igbo) 27
        2.2 Nsibidi System of Writing.. 27
        2.3 Abịdịị System of Writing 29
        2.4 The Standard Igbo Writing 36
        2.5 Letters of Igbo Alphabet... 38
        2.6 Divisions of Alphabet (Nkeji nke Abiidii Igbo dị ụzọ abụọ): 39
        Exercise 41
Chapter 3 43
    Igbo Vowels (Ụdaume Igbo)... 43
        3.1 UDAUME (Vowels) 43
        3.2 Types of Vowels Sounds in Igbo Syllable.. 43

3.3 Vowel Harmony 45

3.4 Vowel Assimilation (Olilo udaume): 46

3.5 Vowel Elision (Ndapu Ụdaume) 51

3.6 Tonal Accent Marks (Diacritics) 51

Exercise 53

Chapter 4 55

Igbo Consonants (Mgbochiume Igbo) 55

4.1 MGBOCHIUME (Consonants) 55

4.2 Types of Consonants sounds: 55

4.3 Igbo Syllable 56

4.4 Syllabic consonants harmony (Ndagba myiriudaume): 56

4.5 Consonant Elision (Ndapu Mgbochiume) 57

4.6 Pseudo/Nasalized Vowels 58

4.7 Tonal Accent Marks (Diacritics) 58

Exercise 60

Chapter 5 61

Spelling and spelling rules (Nsupe na Iwu Nsupe) 61

5.1 *Letter starting Igbo words:* 61

5.2 *Successive Use of Consonants* 62

5.3 *Letter ending Igbo words.* 62

5.4 *Successive use of vowels:* 63

5.5 *Successive use of pseudo-vowel:* 63

5.6 *Pseudo-vowels preceding other consonants.* 64

5.7 *Use of "na" in a sentence:* 64

Exercise 66

Chapter 6 67

Punctuation in Igbo Language 67

6.1 Full-stop (Kpom) 67

6.2 Comma (Rikom) 67

6.3 Question Marks (Akara ajuju) 68

6.4 Semi-colon (Kpom Rikom) 68

6.5 Colon (kpomkpom) 68

6.6 Apostrophe (Rikom elu) 68

6.7 Hyphen (Akara uhie) 69

6.8 Quotation Marks (Rikom Ngwu) 69

6.9 Parentheses (Akara Nkudo) 69

6.10 Exclamation Mark (Akara Mkpu) 69

6.11 Slash (Akara oke) 70

6.12 Ellipsis (Nsepụokwu) 70

Exercise 71

Part Two:

Phonology & Phonetics (Ọdịdị ụdaasụsụ na Amụmàmụ Ụdaasụsụ) 73

Chapter 7

Introduction to Phonology 75

7.1 Definition and Scope of Phonology 75

7.2 Igbo Phonetics (Amụmàmụ Ụdaasụsụ) 75

7.3 Classification of Phoneme (Nkèụdị Mkpụrụụdaasụsụ): 80

7.4 Segmental Phonemes 81

Exercise 82

Chapter 8

Syllable Structure 83

3.1 What is syllable? 83

3.2 Classification of Igbo syllable: 83

3.3 Syllable Weight 84

3.4. Syllable Structure: 85

3.5 Syllable Structure Constraints 85

Exercise 87

Chapter 9

Prosody 89

9.1 Supra-segmental Phonemes 89

9.2 Rhythm 96

9.3 Pitch Accents 97

5.4 Phrase Boundaries 99

Exercise 102

Chapter 10 103

The organ of speech 103

10.1 Organ of Speech (Njiakpọ Okwu) 103

10.2 The Tongue (Ire): 105

10.3 The lips (Egbugbere Ọnụ): 106

10.4 The lungs (Ngụ): 106

10.5 The Uvular (Àshà/Nkọlọ): 106

10.6 The teeth (Eze): 106

Exercise 107

Chapter 11 109

Place of Articulation (Ebe Mkpọpụta Ụda) 109

11.1 Structure of Place of Articulation diagram 110

11.2 Place of Vowel Articulation (Ebe Mkpoputa Udaume) 111

11.3 Place of consonants articulation (Ebe Mkpoputa Mgbochiume) 114

11.4 Consonants Phoneme's chart 115

11.5 Consonants Alphabet's chart 116

Exercise 119

Chapter 12 121

Articulatory Phonetics (Amụmàmụ Mkpọpụta Ụdaasụsụ) 121

12.1 The Manner of consonant articulating: 123

12.2 The process of speech production: 124

12.3 Phonetic Transcription (Ndepụtagharị Mkpụrụụdaasụsụ Igbo) 128

12.4. IPA in Igbo Phonetics 128

12.5 Application of the Transcription and usage 130

Exercise 131

Chapter 13 133

Phonological Variation and Change.. 133

   13.1 Dialectal Variation.. 133

   13.2 Sociolinguistic Factors Influencing Variation 135

   13.3 Sound Change and Its Mechanisms... 136

   13.4 Historical Phonology 137

   Exercise 139

Part Three: 141

   Morphology of Igbo Linguistic (Amụmàmụ Mkpụrụasụsụ nke Mmụta Asụsụ Igbo) 141

   Chapter 14 143

   The nature of Igbo Morpheme 143

      14.1 Definition of Morphology 143

      14.2 Morpheme... 143

      14.3 Morpheme and Phoneme differences 144

      14.4 Identification of Igbo morphemes (mkpụrụasụsụ): 144

      14.5 Characteristics of Igbo morpheme (mkpụrụasụsụ):................................. 146

      Exercise 148

   Chapter 15 149

   Types of Igbo Morpheme 149

      15.1 Types of Igbo Morpheme 149

      15.2 Free Morpheme... 149

      15.3 Bound Morphemes 150

      15.4 Affixes 151

      Exercise 157

   Chapter 16 159

   Morphological Process of Igbo Word 159

      16.1 Inflectional Morphology... 159

      16.2 Derivational morphology:.. 161

      16.3 Extentional Morphology 164

      16.4 Enclitic (Nsokwụnye) 165

      Exercise 167

Chapter 17 169

Allomorphs in Igbo Language 169

17.1 Definition of Allomorphs 169

17.2 Participles (Òmekàngwaà) 169

17.3 Infinitives (Mfinitiivu) 170

17.4 Gerund (Jerọndụ) 171

17.5 Noun agent (Ahaomee/Omee) 173

17.6 Noun instrument (Ahammee/Mmee) 173

Exercise 176

Part Four: 177

Lexicology in Igbo Linguistics (Amụmàmụ Ụdịdị, Nghọta na Itinye Mkpụrụokwu Igbo N'ọrụ) 177

Chapter 18 179

Introduction to Lexicology 179

18.1 Definition of Lexicology 179

18.2 Lexicology interrelation in linguistics 179

18.3 Lexicography 180

18.4 Basic Concepts: Lexeme, Word Formation, Semantics 181

Exercise 185

Chapter 19 187

Word Formation Processes 187

19.1 Word Formation Process 187

19.2 Formal Word Formation Methods 187

19.3 Informal Word Formation Methods 196

Exercise 204

Chapter 20 205

Semantic Relations 205

20.1 Synonyms (Myìrì mkpụrụokwū): 205

20.2 Restrictions in Igbo Synonyms 207

20.3 Antonnyms (Okwu Mmegide) 219

20.4 Hyponymy 226

20.5 Homonymy 226

20.6 Polysemy 227

20.7 Multiple Taxonomies 228

Exercise 229

Chapter 21 231

Lexical Category of Word 231

21.1 Mkpoaha/ Aha (Noun) 231

21.2 Nnochiaha (Pronoun) 232

21.3 Verbs (Ngwaa) 235

21.4 Conjunction (Njikọ) 237

21.5 Adjective (Nkowaha) 237

21.6 Adverb (Nkwuwa) 242

21.7 Preposition (Mbuuzo) 248

21.8 Interjection (Ntimkpu) 249

Exercise 251

About the Author 252

Other Books 253

Index 257

Introduction

For many years, I was asked by someone who learned that I taught the Igbo language in school to start an online class to teach people who would be interested to in learning language. But I brushed it off because I was too busy with work and another self-help book I was writing at that time. I did not consider it as something too necessary because of the dwindling and disappearing usage of the language due the popular embrace and preference of learning to speak and write in English by many Igbo speakers.

Then, the Covid-19 pandemic hit and I was forced to stay at home as much as everyone else when lockdown was authorized. That long time of unemployment got me into looking at Igbo language as Igbo language YouTube channels were on the increase and many people were showing interest on getting to know their ancestry and the language. It hit me. I wanted to use that time to start something.

I decided to start with writing Igbo language books. This was the best option for me since many of my zoom meetings and online programs that I was having at the time were frequently interrupted by my kids who were also forced to stay home by the pandemic. I then, picked up my pen and started writing. That led to the publishing of my first book, "Comprehensive Igbo Language;" which was for beginners and intermediate learners.

Two years later, I thought to myself that I need to move up higher to produce a resource for people who already have the skill of speaking and writing the language and train teachers of the language. An advanced book came to my mind. I, without much hesitation, decided to put forward another book that would serve as a textbook to learners in both high and tertiary institutions worldwide.

Today, you have in your hand, a clear, detailed, and most-up-to-date Igbo language book that gives a straightforward description and greater knowledge on Igbo language orthography, spelling rules, solution to linguistic ambiguities, word formation, class changing and maintaining, organ of speech, place of articulation and many more.

Guide to Pronunciation

Igbo language pronunciation is a reflection of spelling and tonal markings. The pronunciation of each letter is subject to have precise and consistent rules of identifying the sound associated with that particular letter. Words are pronounced by adding together the sounds of each individual letter.

Vowels

Letter	Pronounced like	Examples
a	the *a* in apple and again	aka, akpa, Amerika
e	the *e* in essay and eternal	ekwe, eke, egbe
I	the i in elise and *e* in easy	igbe, ikpere, imi
ị	the *i* in iguana and *i* in inch	ịgba, ịchafụ, ịsha
o	the *o* in orange and owner	okwe, oke, okwu
ọ	the *or* in organ and corn	ọka, ọkwa, ọma
u	the *u* in rule and *oo* in tool	ukwe, ukwu, ugo
ụ	the *u* in furrow and church	ụkwa, ụka, ụgba

Diagraphs

Letter	Pronounced like	Examples
ch	the *ch* in ouch and chum	ọcha, chukwu, ichie
gb	the *gb* is a linguistic letter	gbanye, ịgba, agbo
gh	the *gh* is a linguistic letter	aghara, agha, ghọta
gw	the *gui* in linguine	gwongworo, egwu
kp	the *kp* is a linguistic letter	ekpere, ikpere, Akpa
kw	the *que* in queenie	ekwe, akwa, okwa
nw	the *w* in winter	enwe, anwụ, onwụ
ny	the *ny* in new (BrE)	anya, anyanwu, enyi
sh	the *sh* in shampoo	isha, ọsha, ashiri

The pronunciation of diagraphs like gb, gh, and kp, whose English phonetic equivalent I could not provide, may be learned by listening to the sound of their pronunciations from my audiobook. You may also ask a proficient Igbo language speaker to help you with them.

Other consonants sound

Letter	Pronounced like	Examples
b	the *b* in bitter	ọbịa, ọbara, boọlụ
d	the *d* in dig	ụdara, ọdachi, dabanye

f	the *f* in fish and fire	fọdụrụ, fopu, fecha
g	the *g* in give and gate	gaa, ụgụrụ, gawa
h	the *h* in heat and height	ọha, hapụ, ohụrụ
j	the *j* in jam and jean	jụrụ, jaachi, juputara
k	the *k* in kernel and keep	kedụ, onyeka, kasara
l	the *l* in latch and lean	laawa, lee, leta
m	the *m* in milk and mean	maka, mụrụ, ọmụmụ
n	the *n* in never and now	nọrọ, ọnọdụ, nnụnnụ
ṅ	the *ng* in strong and song	aṅụrị, aṅụ, ọṅu
p	the *p* in pillar and party	pụrụ, pụta, oporo
r	the *r* in reach and rain	racha, rụrụ, rie, họrọ
s	the *s* in salt, self and sight	soro, sịrị, jisịke
t	the *t* in tea and attach	taa, teta, tinye
v	the *v* in invite and vent	mvọ (isi), nwanvo
w	the *wea* in weather	kụwaa, were, wụrụ
y	the *y* in year and yield	yịri, ya, yọro,
z	the *z* in zebra and zion	zara, zụru, zoro

Tonal Marking (Akara Ụdaolu)

Tonal marking, also referred to as diacritical marks, are extra symbols that are placed above or below a letter to modify the pronunciation or to clarify the meaning of a word.

Igbo language is a tonal language with three distinctive tones: the high, mid and low. The following are the list of Igbo alphabets with their tonal accent marks, both in capital and small letters.

Examples:

Letter	Acute (High tone)	Macron (Mid tone)	Grave (Low tone)
a	Á á	Ā ā	À à

Examples:

ákwá	-	cry	[high tone – high tone]
àkwá	-	egg	[low tone – high tone]

Here are five tips that should help you perfect your pronunciation of words in Igbo language:

1. Begin with learning the alphabet's sounds.
2. Practice as many times as you can.
3. Try pronouncing three-letter words starting from breaking the Igbo word down into sounds: Example, [a] + [k] + [a] = aka and so on.
4. Say it out loud and exaggerate the sounds until you can consistently produce them.
5. If possible, record yourself saying the word in full sentences, then watch yourself and listen.

According to Greg Thomson, *"The only way to begin speaking a new language is to begin speaking badly."*

Part One:

Igbo Orthography (Ederede Igbo)

Chapter 1
Orthography

1.1 Introduction to Orthography (Okwu Mmalite Usoro Odide Asụsụ)

Research has shown that there are at least 6,000 spoken languages in the world today. These spoken languages are expressed by a variety of writing systems to help in conveying written messages. The term that denotes this writing system is called "orthographies." The term "orthographic" comes from Greek, which means to have correct writing. Over 400 orthographies exist today.

Orthography is the study of a language's standard spelling system and rules governing the representation of sounds in written symbols. The rules of spelling, punctuation, capitalization, and other characteristics of written language are all included in orthography. A standardized orthographic system ensures uniformity and clarity in written communication, allowing readers to correctly perceive and comprehend written texts. Orthography is essential for literacy, education, and language preservation because it creates a link between spoken and written language.

Orthographies are the symbols used to represent spoken language. It is a system of visually representing a language in a written form. Thus, a written language that uses symbols for entire words is called a logographic orthography. Orthographies differ in the size of the sound unit that is represented by each symbol. Each of these orthographies can be classified as alphabetic or non-alphabetic.

1.1.1 Alphabetic orthographies

In alphabetic orthographies, each symbol represents an individual sound called a phoneme (e.g., the /b/ sound in "book" is one phoneme). There are several different alphabets that are used to create written languages. For example, English uses the Latin alphabet, and 26 symbols (letters), to represent the spoken language. Norwegian and Slovak also use the Latin alphabet, with extra three vowels not used in English (å, æ, ø). Slovak uses an added series of accent marks to indicate how a letter is spoken (for example, ó or š), resulting into 46 symbols to represent the Slovak spoken language.

Igbo language, our subject of study, uses the Latin alphabet with an additional diacritical mark that alters the pronunciation of duplicated symbols or letters, resulting into 36 symbols to represent the Igbo spoken language. It uses three accent marks to indicate tone not sound. This makes it 10 symbols less than Slovak. Slovak 46 symbols (letters) make it the longest Slavic and European alphabet. Most European languages, including Czech, Danish, Dutch, English, Finnish, French, German, Hungarian, Icelandic, Italian, Norwegian, Polish, Portuguese, Slovak, Spanish, Swedish, Turkish, and Welsh use the Latin alphabet.

Other alphabetic orthographies include Cyrillic, Devanagari, Greek, Hangul alphabet, etc. and a combination of Latin and Cyrillic. Cyrillic alphabet is the type of alphabet that uses different sets of symbols to represent the spoken language, but at the level of the phoneme, it still codes the spoken language. The Cyrillic alphabet is used for Bulgarian, Russian, and Ukrainian spoken languages. The Devanagari alphabet is used for Hindi, one of the official languages of India. The Greek alphabet is only used for the Greek language. The Hangul alphabeti is used for the Korean language. Some languages, such as the South Slavic language spoken in Serbia, Croatia (Serbo-Croat), use the combination of Latin and the Cyrillic alphabets. Hebrew and Arabic are sometimes classified as abjads. It is a symbol used to represent a spoken language that only contains consonants, and not vowels. It is called an "abjad", because generally vowels are not included when writing them. However, a lot has changed from the past in the representation of "abjad." Nowadays, the use of accent marks to show where a vowel should has led to many people to classify both Hebrew and Arabic written symbols as alphabets, not abjads.

In alphabetic languages, the smallest meaningful contrastive unit in a writing system (graphemes) represents phonemes or individual sounds. This is evident in alphabetic language, like English, other European languages such as French, German, Italian, Spanish, as well as in Arabic, Hebrew, and Korean Hangul. On the contrary, Japanese kana or Cherokee use a syllabic writing system in which each grapheme represents a syllable. Whereas, Chinese, Japanese Kanji, and Korean Hanja use a morphographic writing system in which each grapheme represents a morpheme or a unit of meaning.

In alphabetic orthographies, when each letter is pronounced the same way, the mapping is said to be "consistent" and the orthography is called "shallow." There is always a match up in how the phonemes (sounds) and the graphemes (symbols or letters) are presented. In German, Igbo, Italian, Spanish, almost every letter represents only one sound which makes their mapping consistent. On the other hand, when each letter is pronounced in more than one way, the mapping is said to be "inconsistent" and the orthography is called "deep." There is no match up in how the phonemes (sounds) and the graphemes (symbols or letters) are presented. A letter can have many pronunciations, such as the two different/a/sounds in "apple" and "aid." In English and Danish, many letters represent more than one sound which makes their mapping inconsistent. As a result, researchers for the most part agree that Finnish, German, Greek, Italian, Korean, Serbo-Croat, Spanish, and Turkish are relatively shallow or consistent orthographies, while Danish, French, Portuguese, etc. contain more inconsistent mappings in phonemes and graphemes match up. English is the most inconsistent language in the world because it has 26 letters against 44 graphemes. That is 18 more additional smallest meaningful contrastive units in a writing system.

1.1.2 Non-alphabetic orthographies

Non-alphabetic orthographies represent either the syllable or a one-syllable unit of meaning with each symbol. A unit of spoken language is represented by a symbol, in a similar fashion as the alphabetic orthographies, but unlike alphabetic orthographies, that unit of spoken language is larger than just a phoneme. For example, people often referred to Chinese as a pictograph (a language made up of pictures), because the characters are pictures of the words they represent. In reality, very few Chinese characters are actually pictures of the words they represent.

Cherokee, Tamil, or Japanese Kana orthographies represent their syllable while Chinese, Japanese Kanji symbol represent a unit of pronunciation (a syllable) that is also a unit of meaning. Chinese orthography and writing system is considered a morpho-syllabic system. This is because about 80–90% of Chinese characters contain what is called a phonetic radical. A phonetic radical is just one part of the character that provides a clue as to how to say the word.

1.2 Layers of Igbo Orthography

Orthography is governed by a number of rules and guidelines that control how words, sounds, and grammatical constructions are represented in written language. Phonemic representation, morphological transparency, etymological considerations, and grammatical rules are some of these guiding concepts. Language-specific orthographic systems can differ in complexity and consistency due to historical, cultural, and linguistic influences. To promote clarity and accessibility in written communication, effective orthography strikes a compromise between the requirements for phonetic accuracy, morphological transparency, and conformity to established standards.

Igbo orthography is the system of writing conventions used to represent spoken Igbo in written form, allowing readers to connect the graphemes to sound and to meaning. It includes Igbo's norms of spelling, hyphenation, capitalization, word breaks, emphasis, and punctuation. There are three layers of Igbo orthography or spelling, namely the alphabet layer, the pattern layer, and the meaning layer.

Alphabet layer represents one-on-one correspondence between letter and sound. In this layer, students use the sound of individual letters to accurately spell words. In Igbo alphabetic orthographies, each letter is pronounced exactly the same way in all expression, the mapping is consistent. Since there is always a match up in how the phonemes (sounds) and the graphemes (symbols or letters) are presented, students would have to grapple with the number of sounds to learn and nothing more.

Pattern layer: As there are 44 sounds in English but only 26 letters in the alphabet, English learners would have to explore the combinations of sound spellings that form visual and auditory patterns associated with the 44 phonemes. In this layer, unlike English learners, Igbo students would have to learn the pattern of vowels combinations and the permissibility that is granted to word combination as well as loan words. All these will be discussed in detail in other following chapters.

Meaning layer: meaning layer is when Igbo students learn that groups of letters can represent meaning directly. This includes the derivations associated with prefixes, suffixes, and verb root in the formation of words from units or groups of morphemes. Morphemes are the smallest units of meaning in language.

1.3 Three Phases of Learning to Read

Phonetic inconsistencies, homophones, loanwords, dialectal variances, and technological improvements all provide obstacles for orthography. To overcome these obstacles and enhance the efficacy and efficiency of written communication, writers and language experts may suggest orthographic modifications or adjustments. Orthographic reforms can include adding diacritical marks to indicate pronunciation or identify homographs, modernizing punctuation rules, or standardizing spelling standards. The goal of orthography adaptations is to maintain linguistic legacy and cultural identity while improving written texts' readability, uniformity, and accessibility.

Orthographic reading skills refer to the ability to identify patterns of specific letters as words, eventually leading to word recognition. With development of these skills, reading becomes an automatic process. When learning to read, one of the most fundamental processes for learners is the understanding of the relationships between printed text and spoken language. Orthography refers to the language-specific variations in these relationships.

The first phase can be considered a *pictorial stage*, when the learner's brain photographs words and visually adjusts to the shape of the alphabet's letters. The visual symbols that represent individual sounds in a spoken language known as phonemes are gradually identified and learned.

The second phase is the *phonological stage*, when the brain begins to decode the letters (graphemes) into sounds (phonemes). The visual symbols that represent individual sounds in a spoken language known as phonemes are gradually committed to memory. The students become more confident with letters arrangements.

The third phase is the *orthographic stage*, when the language learner is able to recognize words quickly and accurately. More confidence in spelling and pronunciation are the indicators of this phase. Reading material in the language becomes less worrisome as students continuously learn new words and build their vocabulary.

1.4 Orthography Mapping

Linnea Ehri coined the term "orthographic mapping". Orthographic Mapping is the process through which a reader can fully analyze sounds in spoken words and match those sounds to printed words. Kilpatrick (2015) describes orthographic mapping as 'the mental process we use to permanently store words for immediate, effortless retrieval.'

Orthographic mapping has been known about since the late 1970s, and was first described by Linnea Ehri, when her work in the 1980s provided evidence for her Orthographic Mapping Theory. Spelling becomes mapped onto pronunciations and these "mapping connections" serve as the glue to hold these words in memory.

It is the process we use to take an unfamiliar printed word and turn it into an immediately recognizable word'. Orthographic mapping (OM) involves the formation of letter-sound connections to bond the spellings, pronunciations, and meanings of specific words in memory. It explains how language learners learn to read words by sight, to spell words from memory, and to acquire vocabulary words from print.

1.5 Orthography and Language Diversity

Orthography helps to preserve and promote linguistic diversity by providing written representation for a wide range of languages and dialects. Orthographic systems can be adapted or created for previously unwritten or marginalized languages to aid literacy, education, and cultural revitalization activities. Orthographic diversity reflects the richness of human language and the variety of ways that writing systems, meanings, and sounds are conveyed and recorded within various societies and civilizations.

As language changes, technology advances, and societal factors impact the world, orthographic systems also change with time. The process of standardizing orthography includes establishing rules, guidelines, and reliable sources to control punctuation, spelling, and other characteristics of written language. Orthographic standards serve as resources for authors, editors, and educators and can be formalized in dictionaries, style manuals, or official language rules. The way that orthography has changed over time reflects both the dynamic character of language and the continuous efforts to keep written communication coherent, clear, and consistent.

We can learn more about the relationship between spoken and written language, the rules that govern written communication, and the difficulties and modifications associated with conveying linguistic diversity in written texts by studying orthography. Orthography shapes how languages are acquired, used, and perpetuated over generations and cultures. It is a fundamental component of literacy, education, and cultural expression.

Exercise

1. What is orthography and where does the term originate from?
2. Explain the term "alphabetic orthographies" and provide examples.
3. What are the three layers of Igbo orthography?
4. Explain the concept of the pattern layer in Igbo orthography.
5. Explain the significance of orthographic mapping in reading and spelling.

6. Cross match the following terms with their definitions:
   a) Phonemes   Visual symbols representing individual sounds.
   b) Graphemes   Mental process of analyzing sounds in spoken words
   c) Orthographic mapping Smallest meaningful contrastive units in a writing system.

7. Multiple Choice Questions:
   What is the primary goal of orthographic reforms?
   a) To complicate written texts.
   b) To standardize spelling and improve readability.
   c) To increase linguistic diversity.
   d) To eliminate orthographic systems altogether.

8. Multiple Choice Questions:
   What is the process of permanently storing words for immediate, effortless retrieval called?
   a) Orthographic mapping
   b) Orthographic reform
   c) Phonetic consistency
   d) Phonological awareness

9. Explain the term "morpho-syllabic system" and provide one example mentioned in the chapter.
10. Write down one implication of orthographic diversity discussed in the chapter.

Chapter 2

Development of Igbo Orthography

2.1 Development of Igbo Orthography (Nkwalite Usoro Odide Asụsụ Igbo)

Orthography is a set of conventions for writing a language. Igbo language has had two types of orthographies from inception until now. These orthographies could be classified as ancient orthography and modern orthography. The two types of Igbo orthography are: Nsibidi and Abịidịị. This chapter will look into the history of both orthographies and why modern orthography is preferable, predominant and premminent.

2.2 Nsibidi System of Writing

Nsibidi (also known as nsibiri, nchibiddi or nchibiddy) is a system of symbols or proto writing developed in the former eastern part of Nigeria prior to colonization. Proto writing consists of visible marks communicating limited information. Nsibidi systems emerged from earlier traditions of symbol systems in the early Neolithic, as early as the 7th millennium BC. The Neolithic period is the final division of the Stone Age. The Stone Age was a broad prehistoric period during which stone was widely used to make tools with an edge, a point, or a percussion surface. The period lasted for roughly 3.4 million years and ended between 4,000 BCE and 2,000 BCE, with the advent of metalworking.

Nsibidi used ideographic or early mnemonic symbols or both to represent a limited number of concepts, in contrast to true writing systems, which record the language of the writer. Ideographic is a graphic symbol that represents an idea or concept, independent of any particular language, and specific words or phrases. Some ideograms are comprehensible only by familiarity with prior convention; others convey their meaning through pictorial resemblance to a physical object, and thus may also be referred to as pictograms.

Mnemonic is any learning technique that aids information retention or retrieval (remembering) in the human memory for better understanding. Mnemonics make use of elaborative encoding, retrieval cues, and imagery as specific tools to encode information in a way that allows for efficient storage and retrieval. Mnemonics aid original information in becoming associated with something more accessible or meaningful—which, in turn, provides better retention of the information.

Nsibidi are classified as pictograms, though there have been suggestions that some are logograms or syllabograms. A logogram or logograph is a written character that represents a word or morpheme. Syllabograms, on the other hand, are signs used to write the syllables (or morae) of words. This term is most often used in the context of a writing system otherwise organized on different principles, three of which—alphabet symbols mostly represent phonemes, logographic script symbols represent morphemes—but a system based mostly on syllabograms is a syllabary (they represent the syllables or moras which make up words).

The use of the Nsibidi symbol system was first described in 1904.[1] Excavation of terracotta vessels, headrests, and anthropomorphic figurines from the Calabar region of southeast Nigeria, dated to roughly the 5th to 15th centuries, revealed "an iconography readily comparable" to nsibidi.[2] The origin of nsibidi is attributed to the Ejagham people in Northern Cross River. Nsibidi spread throughout the region and was adopted by other cultures and art such as the Igbo uri or uli graphic design.[3] In 1909 J. K. Macgregor who collected Nsibidi symbols claimed that nsibidi was formed by the Uguakima, Ebe or Uyanga subgroups of the Igbo people, which legend says were taught the script by baboons.[4]

However, the Nsibidi of the Ejagham people predates these events and it is believed that Macgregor had been misled by his informants.[5] There are several hundred nsibidi symbols. They were once taught in a school to children.[6] Many of the signs deal with love affairs; those that deal with warfare and the sacred are kept secret.[7] Nsibidi is used on wall designs, calabashes, metals

---

[1] Gregersen, Edgar A. *(1977). Language in Africa: An Introductory Survey*. CRC Press. p. 176. ISBN 0-677-04380-5.
[2] Slogar, Christopher *(2005). Eyo, Ekpo (ed.). Iconography and Continuity in West Africa: Calabar Terracottas and the Arts of the Cross River Region of Nigeria/Cameroon*. University of Maryland. pp. 58–62.
[3] Slogar, Christopher *(Spring 2007).* "Early Ceramics from Calabar, Nigeria: Towards a History of Nsibidi". African Arts. University of California. 40 (1): 18–29. doi:10.1162/afar.2007.40.1.18. S2CID 57566625.
[4] Diringer, David *(1953). The Alphabet: A Key to the History of Mankind*. Philosophical Library. pp. 148–149.
[5] West African journal of archaeology". *West African Archaeological Association. WAJA by Oxford University Press.* 21: 105. 1991.
[6] Isichei, Elizabeth Allo *(1997). A History of African Societies to 1870*. Nsibidi: Cambridge University Press. p. 357. ISBN 0-521-45599-5
[7] [sichei, Elizabeth Allo *(1997). A History of African Societies to 1870*. Nsibidi: Cambridge University Press. p. 357. ISBN 0-521-45599-5

(such as bronze), leaves, swords, and tattoes.[8] It is primarily used by the Ekpe Leopard Society (also known as Ngbe or Egbo), a secret society that is found across Cross River State among the Ekoi, Efik, Igbo people, Bahumono and other nearby peoples.

Before the colonial era of Nigeria history, nsibidi was divided into a sacred version and a public, more decorative version which could be used by women.[9] Aspects of colonial rule such as Western education and Christian doctrine drastically reduced the number of nsibidi-literate people, leaving the secret society members as some of the last literate in the symbols.[10] Nsibidi was and is still a means of transmitting Ekpe symbolism. Nsibidi was transported to Cuba and Haiti via the Atlantic slave trade, where it developed into the anaforuana and veve symbols.

2.3 Abịdịị System of Writing

Prior to Abịdịị system of writing, a form of writing called *nsibidi*, existed among the Igbo and neighboring groups before 15th centuries. It eventually fizzled out, probably because of evolution of alphabet system or its popular use among secret societies whose members limited its teachings and exposure to the younger generation who will end up not knowing that it was once a public system of communication and writing.

In 1904, T. D. Maxwell, Acting District Commissioner in Calabar, was the first European to learn about the existence of *nsibidi*. Apart from *nsibidi* writing, the Igbo acculturated themselves effectively by informal methods.[11]

There are five developmental periods of Igbo alphabetic system of writing, namely: the Isuawa Igbo studies, the union Igbo studies, the great orthography controversy period, the SPILC development period and the standard Igbo period. Each of these periods came after the extinction of Nsibidi and the inhuman slave trade that forced many Africans to migrate to North America and West Indies between 15th to q7th centuries.

2.3.1 The Isuama Igbo Studies period (1766-1900)

Between 1766-1900, Isuama Igbo studies period was the answer to the disappearing Nsibidi system. It was used as a type of dialect that represented a common standard dialect by emancipated

---

[8] Elechi, O. Oko (2006). *Doing Justice without the State: The Afikpo (Ehugbo) Nigeria Model*. CRC Press. p. 98. ISBN 0-415-97729-0.]; [Rothenberg, Jerome; Rothenberg, Diane *(1983)*. *Symposium of the Whole: A Range of Discourse Toward an Ethnopoetics*. University of California Press. pp. 285–286. ISBN 0-520-04531-9.
[9] Rothenberg, Jerome; Rothenberg, Diane *(1983)*. *Symposium of the Whole: A Range of Discourse Toward an Ethnopoetics*. University of California Press. pp. 285–286. ISBN 0-520-04531-9.
[10] Slogar, Christopher *(2005)*. Eyo, Ekpo (ed.). *Iconography and Continuity in West Africa: Calabar Terracottas and the Arts of the Cross River Region of Nigeria/Cameroon (PDF)*. University of Maryland. p. 155.
[11] Louis Nnamdi Oraka, **The Foundations of Igbo Studies** *(Onitsha: University Publishing Company, 1983 pp. 13, 17.*

slaves of Igbo origin that settled in Sierra Leone and Fernando Po (now part of Equatorial Guinea) in the 1800s. Around 1766, G. C. A. Oldendorp, a German missionary of the Moravian Brethren, went to their West Indies Caribbean mission.[12]

And by 1777, Oldendorp produced a book, **Geschichte der Mission der Evangelischen Bruder auf den Carabischen** (History of the Evangelistic Mission of the Brothers in the Caribbean). The book contained few Igbo words, numerals, 13 nouns, 2 sentences. As a result, he was the first person to publish a material that contains Igbo words and expression. As time progresses, in 1789, **The Life of Olaudah Equiano, or Gustavus Vassa The African** (London, 1789), written by a former slave, mentioned 79 Igbo words.[13] A good modern edition: London: Dawsons of Pall Mall, 1969 (2 vols; ed. by Paul Edwards).

By late 1700 and early 1800, Igbo language study transferred from the West Indies and London to Freetown, Sierra Leone, and Fernando Po, because freed slaves were settled there, the larger number in Freetown.[14]

In 1828, Mrs. Hannah Kilham, a Quaker mission teacher, published *Specimens of African Languages Spoken in the Colony of Sierra-Leone*. A material that included: Igbo numerals and some 50 Igbo nouns. Three years later, Mrs. Kilham started a girls' school at Charlotte village, Sierra Leone. Formal education in vernacular languages is begun. In 1837, MacGregor Laird published the wordlist he collected inside the Igbo homeland during his two-year Niger Expedition of 1832-1834. Six years later, in 1840, Jacob Friedrich Schon, German missionary, reported that he had collected 1600 words in the Igbo language. His report remained unpublished. A year later, in 1841, Edwin Norris, Assistant Secretary, Royal Asiatic Society, compiled wordlists from West and Central African languages to use in Niger expeditions. He used Laird's 70 words and others from two unknown sources (a manuscript, and an Igbo living in London).[15]

The same year, in another Norris expedition on the Niger, he took two missionary linguists from the staff of the CMS (Church Missionary Society) in Freetown, J. F. Schon and Samuel Ajayi Crowther (the latter a Yoruba-born ex-slave and teacher), along with twelve interpreters, including Igbo who came from emancipated slave families that settled in Freetown. John Christopher Taylor and Simon Jonas were among them. No permanent mission was founded. Schon was interested in

---

[12] Louis Nnamdi Oraka, *The Foundations of Igbo Studies* (Onitsha: University Publishing Company, 1983 p. 20.
[13] Louis Nnamdi Oraka, *The Foundations of Igbo Studies* (Onitsha: University Publishing Company, 1983 p. 21.
[14] Louis Nnamdi Oraka, *The Foundations of Igbo Studies* (Onitsha: University Publishing Company, 1983 p. 65.
[15] Louis Nnamdi Oraka, *The Foundations of Igbo Studies* (Onitsha: University Publishing Company, 1983 p. 22

Igbo and Hausa. At a stopover in Aboh, he tried to communicate in Igbo but was disappointed that people did not understand him. He then abandoned Igbo study for some twenty years.[16]

These missionaries continue in their quest to develop a common system of written communication. Between 1843 and 1848 Morrick (missionary in Fernando Po) and John Clarke, Baptist missionary, together collected vocabularies of African languages. Clarke published them in 1848, including 250 words and a few numerals written in Igbo. 24 Igbo dialects were represented, including Aro, Bonny, Ndoli and Agbaja. In 1854, Lepsius, German philologist, produced international "Standard Alphabet" for all world languages to use.[17]

Additional fifty words were added in 1854 by S. W. Koelle, a German missionary, who published Polyglotta Africana, with a vocabulary gathered from liberated slaves in Sierra Leone. His publication contained some 300 Igbo words representing five dialects: Isoama, Isiele, Agbaja, Aro, Mbofia (Oraka p. 23). Two years later, in 1856, Crowther and Jonas stayed together in Lagos, where Jonas taught his master Igbo. A year later, in 1857, Crowther produced his first book in Igbo, with Jonas's help. **Isoama-Ibo Primer** has 17 pages, with the Igbo alphabet, words, phrases, sentence patterns, the Lord's Prayer, the Ten Commandments, and translations of the first chapters of Matthew's Gospel. Thus, Crowther became the first to use the Lepsius "Standard Alphabet".[18]

It went fast after the publication of Lepsius "Standard Alphabet." In 1857, Dr. William Baikie's ship berthed at Onitsha. On board were Crowther and his missionary team, including Igbo speakers Simon Jonas and Rev. J. C. Taylor. Crowther established a mission and left it in Taylor's hands. In less than a week Taylor had opened a school for young girls. **Isoama-Ibo** Primer served as their textbook. In 1861, J. F. Schon picked up the tab and resumed Igbo studies, publishing his **Oku Ibo: Grammatical Elements of the Ibo Language**, written in the Isuama dialect, using Lepsius orthography. In 1870, Church Missionary Society (CMS) in London used Lepsius orthography to publish **An Ibo Primer**, by F. W. Smart, a catechist posted in 1868 to the first outpost of Christian Station in Niger Delta. Crowther, first Bishop of the Niger, posted him there with W. E. L. Carew. In the 1870s Smart and Carew each published an Igbo Primer and carried out translation works on church liturgy.[19]

In 1880, Crowther thought his Niger Mission was collapsing, since the Igbo dialect he chose was not a "living" dialect spoken by a particular group of the Igbo. The Church Missionary Society (CMS) realized its mistakes and decided to give up its effort to use one dialect only. In 1882 Crowther wrote **Vocabulary of the Ibo Language**, the first comprehensive dictionary in Igbo. In

---

[16] *Louis Nnamdi Oraka, **The Foundations of Igbo Studies** (Onitsha: University Publishing Company, 1983 p. 23.*
[17] *Louis Nnamdi Oraka, **The Foundations of Igbo Studies** (Onitsha: University Publishing Company, 1983 pp. 24, 25.*
[18] Louis Nnamdi Oraka, ***The Foundations of Igbo Studies*** *(Onitsha: University Publishing Company, 1983 pp. 23, 24, 25.*
[19] Louis Nnamdi Oraka, ***The Foundations of Igbo Studies*** *(Onitsha: University Publishing Company, 1983 pp. 25, 26.*

1883 Crowther and Schon jointly revised it and added more words. They finally came out with **Vocabulary of the Ibo Language, Part II**, an English-Ibo dictionary. By this time, Igbo had had some 50 books and booklets published in it.[20]

In 1882, Britain enacted the first education ordinance to control and direct educational activities of Christian missions in what later became her West African colonies. It provided grants-in-aid conditional on the teaching of reading and writing of the English language only. This caused a stalemate in the development of many West African languages. As a result, in 1885, Roman Catholic Mission (RCM) reached Igboland but did not seem to be interested in the study of the Igbo language.[21]

Sadly, in 1891, Bishop Crowther died (at over 80 years of age), and the Isuama-Igbo period died with him. By this time two young men, the Englishman T. J. Dennis and the Sierra Leonean Henry Johnson, had joined the mission. In 1892, Julius Spencer, an Onitsha-based Sierra Leonean missionary, published **An Elementary Grammar of the Igbo Language**. This was revised by Archdeacon Dennis in 1916.[22]

2.3.2 The Union Igbo Studies (1900-1929)

Between 1900 – 1929, Igbo orthography development entered into the Union Igbo Studies period. This period is commonly referred to as Igbo version developed by Church Missionary Society (CMS). It aimed at inclusiveness in binding or writing all Igbo dialects. As a result it used terms understood in Onitsha, Owerri, Unwana, Arochukwu and Bonny dialects, in its orthography keeping idioms and proverbs common to all. This version was intended to be a sort of "central" or "compromise" Igbo, playing the role of a literary medium for the Igbo people.

The most prominent work published in Union Igbo was the Holy Bible (Bible Nso). The Union Igbo period saw major translation works. Missionaries collected materials on Igbo culture, including proverbs, folktales, riddles and customs.[23] Within this period (1900-1929), Rev. Thomas J. Dennis was the best, most prolific student of Igbo and writer of his time. He used an Igbo Language Translation Committee, including Igbo indigenes, to translate **Pilgrim's Progress** and some catechisms into Igbo. He also translated the **Union Reader** and the **Union Hymnal**. In 1917, he died in a shipwreck.[24]

---

[20] Louis Nnamdi Oraka, *The Foundations of Igbo Studies* (Onitsha: University Publishing Company, 1983 p. 27.
[21] Louis Nnamdi Oraka, *The Foundations of Igbo Studies* (Onitsha: University Publishing Company, 1983 pp. 28, 29.
[22] Louis Nnamdi Oraka, *The Foundations of Igbo Studies* (Onitsha: University Publishing Company, 1983 pp. 27, 30.
[23] Louis Nnamdi Oraka, *The Foundations of Igbo Studies* (Onitsha: University Publishing Company, 1983 pp. 28, 29.
[24] Louis Nnamdi Oraka, *The Foundations of Igbo Studies* (Onitsha: University Publishing Company, 1983 p. 28.

A. Gabot, French missionary, produced a trilingual dictionary, **English-Ibo and French Dictionary** in 1904. A year later, in 1905, Niger Mission saw a need to adopt a compromise dialect if the Bible were to be translated into a generally understood Igbo. Church Missionary Society (CMS) sent Dennis from Onitsha to Owerri to see about locating the headquarters of Igbo language studies there. He went with Alphonsus Onyeabo, an Onitsha-born catechist who later became a bishop. Dennis reported that Egbu, near Owerri, would be the ideal site, because the purest Igbo dialect was spoken there. Church Missionary Society (CMS) approved it and Dennis, Onyeabo, and T. D. Anyaegbunam went to Egbu and opened a station. In 1907, P. C. Zappa, a French missionary, compiled a bilingual dictionary, **Essai de Dictionnaire Francais-Ibo ou Francais-Ika**, with the help of a catechist, Mr. Nwokeabia. Zappa rightly saw Ika as an Igbo dialect and not as a language in itself. And in 1909, Dennis and the others completed translation of the New Testament, the last part of their work. Lepsius orthography was used. Dennis replaced "ds," "ts" and "s" with "j," "ch" and "sh." Controversy ensued about the dialect used.[25]

In 1912, Rev. G. T. Basden published Niger Ibos, a collection of Igbo customs and traditions. Between 1913 - 1914, Northcote W. Thomas produced **Anthrological Report on the Igbo-Speaking People of Nigeria**, in 6 volumes. Part II and Part V were devoted to Igbo-English (based on Onitsha and Awka dialects) and English-Igbo (with many words from the western Igbo dialect of Asaba) dictionaries, respectively. In 1916, Archdeacon Dennis revised and enlarged Spencer's 1892 grammar. Four years later, in 1920 Phelps-Stokes Fund (American philanthropic organization interested in education of world's black people) sponsored two commissions to Africa. Subsequently (1922) it published **Report on Education in Africa: Study of West, South and Equatorial Africa**, recognizing the importance of the mother tongue in education of children. In 1923 Isaac Iwekanuno wrote the first historical essay in the Igbo language, **Akuko Ala Obosi**, in Obosi dialect. In 1925, The Phelps-Stokes Report prompted the British Colonial Office to set up an Advisory Committee on Native Education in its African colonies, stressing the importance of the vernaculars.[26]

In 1926, The Education Ordinance and Code was enacted, requiring that only the vernacular or English be media of instruction. The Board of Education in Nigeria was reorganized to conform to the provisions of the Ordinance. On June 29, 1926, linguists and others from Africa and Europe met in London and launched the International Institute of African Languages and Cultures (IIALC). In 1927, the International Institute of African Languages and Cultures (IIALC) published a pamphlet, **Practical Orthography of African Languages**. 8 vowels and 28 consonants, with "gw," "kw," and "nw" added for Igbo sounds. The pamphlet used some international phonetic symbols. This was a radical change from the Lepsius orthography used by Church Missionary

---

[25] Louis Nnamdi Oraka, *The Foundations of Igbo Studies* (Onitsha: University Publishing Company, 1983 pp. 29 30.
[26] Louis Nnamdi Oraka, *The Foundations of Igbo Studies* (Onitsha: University Publishing Company, 1983 pp. 30, 31.

Society (CMS) for nearly seventy years. It started a heated controversy that almost suspended Igbo studies for more than thirty years.[27]

2.3.3 The Great Orthography Controversy Period (1929-1961)

In 1929, the International Institute of African Languages and Culture (IIALC) member Prof. Westermann was invited to Nigeria to advise the Colonial Government on orthography for languages, including Igbo. He recommended the 1927 "Africa" orthography of the IIALC. The Board of Education agreed, and made efforts to replace the Lepsius orthography. The IIALC orthography became known as the "Adams-Ward" orthography because of two people in Eastern Nigeria who fought hard for its adoption: Mr. R. F. G. Adams, an Inspector of Education, and Dr. Ida C. Ward, a research linguist of the London School of Oriental and African Studies. Also, the Protestant missions (except for the Methodists), led by the CMS (Anglican) and conservatives, opposed the "new" orthography, while the government, the Roman Catholic and Methodist missions adopted it. Thus the old came to be dubbed "CMS" orthography and the new the "Roman Catholic" orthography.[28]

A year later, in 1930, an advisory committee that included members of the missions agreed to set up a Translation Bureau at Umuahia. In 1933, **Omenuko**, by Pita Nwana, was published after winning an all-Africa literary contest in indigenous African languages organized by the International Institute of African Languages and Culture. Nwana was the first Igbo to publish fiction in the Igbo language. The first edition was in the Protestant Orthography, but it was soon issued in the other orthographies. In 1963 Longman Nigeria published an "Official Orthography Edition" transliterated by J. O. Iroaganachi. See Ernest Emenyonu's **The Rise of the Igbo Novel** (Ibadan: Oxford University Press, 1978). In 1939, A research expedition led by Dr. Ward, to examine some dialects for possible use as a widely-accepted literary medium. She thought this might form the basis of a growing "standard" Igbo. Her "central" Igbo covered Owerri and Umuahia areas with special inclination toward Ohuhu dialect. It was gradually accepted by missionaries, writers, publishers, and Cambridge University.[29]

In 1944, Adams arranged a series of three meetings to urge the adoption of both Ward's "central' dialect and the new orthography. The first meeting was in Umuahia dated 6/13/44, attended by 24 scholars, teachers, missionaries, and government officials. Its recommendations included acceptance of Ward's alphabet from the **Ibo Dialects and the Development of a Common Language**. The reactions and results from that meeting was that: Anglicans stuck to the Union, Catholics insisted on the Onitsha dialect, Methodists embraced central dialect. Between June 26 and 27th of the same year, the Assistant Director of Education at Enugu convened another meeting

---

[27] Louis Nnamdi Oraka, *The Foundations of Igbo Studies (Onitsha: University Publishing Company, 1983 pp. 32, 33.*
[28] Louis Nnamdi Oraka, *The Foundations of Igbo Studies (Onitsha: University Publishing Company, 1983 pp. 30, 34.*
[29] Louis Nnamdi Oraka, *The Foundations of Igbo Studies (Onitsha: University Publishing Company, 1983 pp. 33, 35.*

at Onitsha, attended by 27 persons from the above groups. All interest groups again stuck to their ideal dialects. On Sept. 6 of the same year, another meeting, at Enugu, attended by 16 persons, presided over by the Assistant Director of Education. It resolved that the "central" dialect would be compulsory only for literature connected with government.[30]

Four years later, in 1948, The Owerri Diocese of the Roman Catholic Mission was carved out of Onitsha Ecclesiastical Province, giving impetus to the RCM's growing practice of issuing readers in the two dialects of Onitsha and Central. But CMS, while accepting Central dialect which Ward saw as her "Union Igbo" under another name, resolved never to adopt the new orthography.[31]

2.3.4 The Emergence of The SPILC (1948-1972)

The same year, in 1948, Frederick Chidozie Ogbalu, mission tutor at Dennis Memorial Grammar School, Onitsha, wrote a lengthy article in the Onitsha newspaper **The Nigerian Spokesman**, challenging the new orthography. Principal E. D. C. Clark of the DMGS reprimanded him for its nationalist flavor, a sensitive issue. Clark recommended that he produce books in Igbo to convince people that the old orthography was best. A year later, in 1949, after his transfer to St. Augustine's Grammar School, Nkwerre, Ogbalu used an existing association he had formed (Society for Promoting African Heritage) as a nucleus for the Society for Promoting Igbo Language and Culture (SPILC). One of his purposes was to fight the new orthography. Membership was at first limited to staff and students of St. Augustine's, but through its activities it was soon making an impact on Igbo people and led to a great turning point in the development of Igbo Studies.[32]

In 1950, Society for Promoting Igbo Language and Culture (SPILC) was formally inaugurated by a large percentage of the few educated Igbo men meeting at Dennis Memorial Grammar School chemistry lab, Onitsha. Officers appointed were Dr. Akanu Ibiam (President); Dr. S. E. Onwu (First Vice President); Bishop John Cross Anyogu (Second Vice President); Mr. D. C. Erinne (Chairman); F. C. Ogbalu (Secretary). The Central dialect was seen as an attempt to impose the white man's will. A new battle line was drawn between Government, RCM, and Methodist Mission on one side and SPILC and CMS on the other. SPILC acquired a public character.[33]

By the early fifties, precisely 1952, many patriotic Igbo worried about unresolved orthography question. The Government convened another conference at Aba. Mr. R. I. Uzoma, Eastern Nigeria Minister of Education, presided. SPILC strongly opposed the "new" orthography. No decision was reached. A year later, in August 25, 1953, a select committee, chaired by Dr. S. E.

---

[30] Louis Nnamdi Oraka, *The Foundations of Igbo Studies* (Onitsha: University Publishing Company, 1983 pp. 35, 36.
[31] Louis Nnamdi Oraka, *The Foundations of Igbo Studies* (Onitsha: University Publishing Company, 1983 p. 36.
[32] Louis Nnamdi Oraka, *The Foundations of Igbo Studies* (Onitsha: University Publishing Company, 1983 p. 36, 41.
[33] Louis Nnamdi Oraka, *The Foundations of Igbo Studies* (Onitsha: University Publishing Company, 1983 pp. 36, 37, 41, 42.

Onwu, met at Owerri to reach a compromise on an orthography. The four phonetic symbols in the new orthography were removed, but the suggestion to replace them with diacritical marks was rejected. All parties except SPILC were either satisfied or no longer interested in contesting the issue. In 1954, another committee meeting, headed by Mr. Alvan Ikoku. SPILC presented a "modified" orthography. It was rejected. SPILC members walked out on the meeting. In 1955, F. C. Ogbalu issued his "compromise" orthography. So many other suggested orthographies were issued at different times by different groups and individuals. Controversy lingered until 1961, when the Government set up another committee, the Onwu Orthography Committee, chaired by Dr. S. E. Onwu, Assistant Director of Medical Services for Eastern Nigeria.[34]

Finally, in September 13, 1961, eleven members of the Onwu Committee met at the W.T.C., Enugu. The Minister of Education warned them to reconsider use of diacritical marks, in line with SPILC recommendations. They produced a pacifying orthography using diacritical marks to distinguish "light" and "heavy' vowels which, with other recommendations, brought to an end the 32-year-old controversy. All parties were satisfied.[35]

In June, 1962, the Government ordered all school principals to see that tutors and students acquainted themselves with the new orthography as the official Igbo orthography. The order reads: "All must use it henceforth in the teaching and studying of the language."[36]

2.4 The Standard Igbo Writing

The Standard Igbo Period (1972 – Present): In 1972, Society for Promoting Igbo Language and Culture (SPILC) set up its Standardization Committee. Its main objectives were to adopt words from different dialects of Igbo, whether or not they belonged to the "Central" dialect areas, for the purpose of enriching the Igbo language. It was also liberal with the adoption of loan words where there were no Igbo equivalents. Thus, Standard or Modern Igbo was designed to be spoken and understood by all, because it was more flexible than Isuama, Union or "Central" dialect. It was a cross-pollination and diffusion of dialects.[37]

A year later, in August, 1973, SPILC approved the recommendation of its Standardization Committee about the spelling of Igbo words. The following year, in 1974, by intensive lobbying, SPILC brought about the establishment of the Dept. of Igbo Language and Culture at Alvan Ikoku College of Education. And in August, 1976, SPILC recommended the rearrangement of Igbo alphabet. In 1978, the Department of Igbo Language and Culture was started, with the opening of

---

[34] Louis Nnamdi Oraka, *The Foundations of Igbo Studies* (Onitsha: University Publishing Company, 1983 p. 39.
[35] Louis Nnamdi Oraka, *The Foundations of Igbo Studies* (Onitsha: University Publishing Company, 1983 pp. 34, 40.
[36] Louis Nnamdi Oraka, *The Foundations of Igbo Studies* (Onitsha: University Publishing Company, 1983 p. 40.
[37] Louis Nnamdi Oraka, *The Foundations of Igbo Studies* (Onitsha: University Publishing Company, 1983 p. 56.

Anambra State College of Education at Awka, with F. C. Ogbalu as Head of Department. In September, another Department of Igbo was established at Federal Advanced Teachers College, Okene, Kwara State.[38]

Nonetheless, till date Mazi Ọnwụ committee remains the widely accepted and used orthography in Igbo language. It is the orthography used in writing this book. The challenge for computer users with Mazị Ọnwụ orthography is that, there is curremtly no Microsoft insert symbol that has both diacritic mark together with tonal mark for letters of Igbo alphabet.

Please note that the above series of events leading up to Onwu Committee of 1961 Orthography were extracted and coined from "*A History of the Igbo Language*" compiled by Frances W. Pritchett whose research on Louis Nnamdi Oraka, "*The Foundations of Igbo Studies*" helped put forward a summarized post on Columbia University website.[39]

The Ọ́nwụ́ Committee of 1961 Orthography alphabet and pronunciation as modified with revision of four letters to include 1976 Igbo Standardization Committee version which substituted c, ñ, ö and ü in Ọnwụ's orthography with ch, ṅ, ọ, ụ, are as follows:

Letter	*Pronunciation IPA*
A B Ch D E F G Gb	/a/ /b/ /t͡ʃ/ /d/ /e/ /f/ /g/ /g͡ɓ/
Gh Gw H I Ị J K Kp	/ɣ/ /gʷ/ /ɦ/ /i/ /ɪ/ /d͡ʒ/ /k/ /k͡p/
Kw L M N Nw Ny Ṅ O	/kʷ/ /l/ /m/ /n/ /ŋ/ /ŋʷ/ /ɲ/ /o/
Ọ P R S Sh T U Ụ	/ɔ/ /p/ /ɹ/ /s/ /ʃ/ /t/ /u/ /ʊ/
V W Y Z	/v/ /w/ /j/ /z/

The IPA (International Phonetic Alphabet) uses collection of characters to transcribe any human voice sound, from various languages of the world, in a way that people skilled in foreign languages and language enthusiasts across the globe can understand, regardless of their mother language or cultural background.

---

[38] Louis Nnamdi Oraka, **The Foundations of Igbo Studies** *(Onitsha: University Publishing Company, 1983 pp. 46, 47, 48.*
[39] http://www.columbia.edu/itc/mealac/pritchett/00fwp/igbo/igbohistory.html

2.5 Letters of Igbo Alphabet

There are thirty-six letters in Igbo alphabet. Igbo alphabet is called inn Igbo language Abịịdịị Igbo. The Abịịdịị Igbo used in this book is from Igbo Izugbe which is the central Igbo from Mazị Ọnwụ Committee. It has two forms: capital and small letters. See examples below.

Akara ukwu (capital letter):

A	B	CH	D	E	F	G	GB	GH	GW	H	I	Ị
J	K	KP	KW	L	M	N	Ṅ	NW	NY	O	Ọ	P
R	S	SH	T	U	Ụ	V	W	Y	Z			

Akara nta (small letter)

a	b	ch	d	e	f	g	gb	gh	gw	h	i	ị
j	k	kp	kw	l	m	n	ṅ	nw	ny	o	ọ	p
r	s	sh	t	u	ụ	v	w	y	z			

Igbo Alphabet and Their Inclusive Words

A	Aka (Hand)	**M**	Mmiri (Water)
B	Bọọlu (Ball)	**N**	Nkịta (dog)
CH	Chịnchị (Bedbug)	**Ṅ**	Nụọ (Drink)
D	Dee (Write)	**NW**	Nwa (Baby)
E	Enyi (Elephant)	**NY**	Nye (Give)
F	Fe (fly)	**O**	Osisi (Tree)
G	Gụọ (read)	**Ọ**	Ọka (Corn)
GB	Gbanye (Pour)	**P**	Pọpọ (Papaya)
GH	Ghe (fry)	**R**	Rie (eat)
GW	Gwa (Tell)	**S**	Saa (Wash)
H	Hụọ (Roast)	**SH**	Ịsha (Crab)
I	Ite (Pot)	**T**	Torotoro (Turkey)
Ị	Ịgba (Drum)	**U**	Unere (Banana)
J	Ji (Yam)	**Ụ**	Ụlọ (House)
K	Iko (Cup)	**V**	Mvọ isi (Comb)

KP	Kpakpando (Star)	**W**	Kụwaa (Break)
KW	Kwụọ (Grind)	**Y**	Ịnyịnya (Horse)
L	Leta (Letter)	**Z**	Azịza (Broom)

2.6 Divisions of Alphabet (Nkeji nke Abiidii Igbo dị ụzọ abụọ):

Igbo Alphabet is divided into the following:

1. Ụdaụme (vowel)
2. Mgbochiume (consonants)

Ụdaụme (Vowels): Unlike English language, there are eight vowels that make up the Igbo vowels. The letters that make up the Igbo vowels are:

a   e   i   o   u   ị   ọ   ụ

Igbo vowels are divided into Ụdamfe (Light vowels) and Ụdaarọ (Heavy vowels):

ỤDAMFE (Light Vowel):   e   i   o   u
ỤDAARỌ (Heavy Vowel):   a   ị   ọ   ụ

Ụdamfe (Light vowels) are vowels that do not have dot under the letters and include the letter 'e'; on the other hand, Ụdaarọ (Heavy vowels) are vowels with dot under the letters and include 'a'.

ỤDAMFE (Light Vowel):   e   i   o   u
ỤDAARỌ (Heavy Vowel):   a   ị   ọ   ụ

Mgbochiume (Consonants): there are twenty-eight consonants in Igbo Alphabet. The letters that make up the consonants in Igbo alphabet are:

b	ch	d	f	g	gb	gh	gw
h	j	k	kp	kw	l	m	N
ṅ	nw	ny	p	r	s	sh	T
v	w	y	z.				

The Igbo consonants are divided into two, namely mgbochiume mgị (ordinary consonants), and Mgbochiume mkpi (diagraphs).

Mgbochiume mgị (consonant of "gị" sound): These are consonants that are not Mgbochiume mkpi (diagraphs). There are nineteen letters that make up the consonant of "gị" sound which are:

b	d	f	g	h	j	k	L
m	n	ṅ	p	r	s	t	V
w	y	z.					

Mgbochiume mkpị (Diagraphs): These are consonants that are a combination of two consonant letters. There are two Latin consonants that form single letters in Igbo language. There are nine digraphs in Igbo alphabet. These are:

ch gb gh gw kp kw nw ny sh

It is of great importance to always remember that despite digraphs such as ch, gh, gb, kp, kw, and sh, do not count as double consonants and pronounced as a single sound.

Exercise
1. What are the two main types of orthographies that have been used for writing the Igbo language, and how do they differ?
2. Describe the Nsibidi system of writing, including its origins, symbols used, and its significance in Igbo culture.
3. What were the factors that contributed to the decline of the Nsibidi system of writing before the colonial era?
4. Explain the significance of the Isuama Igbo Studies period in the development of Igbo orthography, including key figures and milestones.
5. What were the major features of the Union Igbo Studies period, and how did it contribute to the standardization of Igbo orthography?
6. Detail the events and controversies surrounding the Great Orthography Controversy Period (1929-1961) in the development of Igbo orthography.
7. Who were the key players involved in the emergence of the Society for Promoting Igbo Language and Culture (SPILC), and what role did it play in standardizing Igbo orthography?
8. How did the SPILC contribute to the development of the Standard Igbo Writing period, and what were its main objectives?
9. Explain the significance of the Onwu Committee of 1961 Orthography in resolving the orthography controversy surrounding the Igbo language.
10. What are the key features of the Standard Igbo Writing period, and how does it differ from previous periods in Igbo orthography development?
11. How did the introduction of the International Phonetic Alphabet (IPA) influence the standardization of Igbo orthography during the Standard Igbo Writing period?
12. Describe the role of linguists and scholars in the ongoing development and refinement of Igbo orthography since the establishment of the standard writing system.
13. What are some of the challenges faced in implementing and promoting the use of standardized Igbo orthography in education, literature, and everyday communication?

Chapter 3

Igbo Vowels (Ụdaume Igbo)

3.1 UDAUME (Vowels)

Ụdaụme (Vowels): Unlike English language, there are eight vowels that make up the Igbo vowels. The letters that make up the Igbo vowels are:

      a   e   i   o   u   ị   ọ   ụ

Igbo vowels are divided into Ụdamfe (Light vowels) and Ụdaarọ (Heavy vowels):

    ỤDAMFE (Light Vowel):   e   I   o   u

    ỤDAARỌ (Heavy Vowel):   a   ị   ọ   ụ

Ụdamfe (Light vowels) are vowels that does not have dot under its letter and includes the letter 'e'; on the other hand, Ụdaarọ (Heavy vowels) are vowels with dot under its letter and include 'a'.

    ỤDAMFE (Light Vowel):   e   I   o   u

    ỤDAARỌ (Heavy Vowel):   a   ị   ọ   ụ

3.2 Types of Vowels Sounds in Igbo Syllable

Types of Vowels sounds in Igbo Syllable (Ụdịdị Mkpọpụta ụdaume na Nkejiokwu Igbo): There are two types of vowels in the Igbo syllable namely: monophthong and diphthong.

3.3.1 Monophthong (Ụdange): Monophthong also known as short vowel (ụdaume di nkenke) is a vowel that is spoken with exactly one tone and one mouth position. It is a single vowel articulated without change in quality throughout the course of a syllable. It is the only vowel sound produced in a word and it does not require other vowels to support in the production of sound of words that it is a part of.

Example of monophthong is as follows:

Word	*Monophthong*	*~ in a Sentence*
Chaa	aa	Chaa n'ụzọ ahụ dị njọ. *Avoid that bad road*
Chọọ	ọọ	Chọọ ewu ojii ahụ. *Find the black goat.*
Dọọ	ọọ	Dọọ ụmụ gị aka na ntị. *Warn your children.*
Kpeenụ	ee	Kpeenụ ya n'aka nne ya *Report him to her mom*
Kpọọrọ	ọọ	Kpọọrọ m ya n'ekwentị *Call him on the phone*
Kweere	ee	Dinta ahụ kweere ọnya. *The hunter set his trap*
Meere	ee	O meere ha ihe ọma. *She did him/her a favor.*
Mgbaaka	aa	Mgbaaka Ada dị ọcha. *Ada's bracelet is clean.*
Mịịrị	ịị	Osisi ahụ mịịrị mkpụrụ. *That tree has fruits.*

3.3.2 Diphthong (Ụdamkpị): This is a sound formed by the combination of two vowels in a single syllable, in which the sound begins as one vowel and moves toward another (as in coin, loud, and side). It is a sound that is made up of two separate vowel sounds within the same syllable.

It is important to note that having two consecutive letters, especially consonants do not result into a diphthong. Igbo consonants do not function as a diphthong, and they do not occur side by side in Igbo words. The only exception to this rule is semivowels which double as Igbo consonants. The alphabet (m, n) or sounds /m, n/ are permitted to reduplicate in a word, e.g. mma, nna, nne, nnu, mmadụ and so on.

There are six types of Igbo diphthong but there are eight in English language. The six types of Igbo diphthong are: ụo, io, ie, uo, ịọ and ịa. These diphthongs can be separated into *preceding* and *ending* diphthongs.

The *preceding vowels* refer to those vowel sounds that produced first in the pronunciation of diphthongs. There are four *preceding diphthong vowels* in Igbo language and they are: /i̩/, /i/, /u̩/ and /u/.

The *ending vowels* refer to those vowel sounds that produced first in the pronunciation of diphthongs. There are four *ending diphthong vowels* in Igbo language and they are: /a/, /e/, /o/ and /o̩/.

Example of the six types of diphthongs in Igbo language are as follows:

Word	*Monophthong*	*~ in a Sentence*
Hio	io	Ha Hio ya ụkwara ahụ.
		They infected him with cough.
Hịochapụ	ịo	Hịochapụ ya ọnụ ojọọ.
		Deal with his arrogant words.
kpụọrọ	ụo	Kpụọrọ ya Ụlọ aja.
		Build (form) a sand castle for him
Merie	ie	Merie onye owụwa ahụ.
		Overcome the tempter
Pịata	ịa	Pịara ya otito ahụ.
		Poop his bump/pimple.
Tigbuo	uo	Tigbuo ndị iro gị.
		Crush your enemies.

3.3 Vowel Harmony
Vowel harmony (Ndakọrịta Ụdaume Igbo) applies to heavy and light vowels syllabic combination inn words. It is a form of grammatical rule that Ụdamfe (Light vowels) usually consist of vowels of its own syllables (such as e, i, o and u) in a word. They do not combine with Ụdaarọ (heavy vowel: a, ị, ọ and ụ) unless it is a compound verb or word.

Translation to Igbo
Ụdamfe na ụdaarọ anaghi anoko onụ na otu mkpụrụ okwu. O bụrụ na ụdamfe di na mkpụrụ okwu o bụ nani mkpuru uda ya puru ịdị na mkpụrụ okwu ahụ na otu aka ahu ka ọ dị kwa na ụdaarọ. Nke a ka anakpọ iwu na achị ụdamfe na ụdaarọ.

Ọmụmaatụ:

Ụdamfe: Osisi (Tree), Iko (cup), Ukwe (song) etc.

Ụdaarọ: Ụlọ (house). Ụka (church), Ọka (corn)etc.

3.4 Vowel Assimilation (Olilo udaume):

Assimilation is a sound change, where some phonemes (typically consonants or vowels) change to more similar other nearby sounds. This happens during rapid speed pronunciation of two words.

For example:
    I don't know /I duno/
    Camera /kamra/

And this omission is often indicated in print by an apostrophe. For example: 'fish 'n' chips'.

In Igbo language, vowel Assimilation (Olilo udaume) is the process whereby two vowels of two words sitting beside each other harmonize and pronounce with one sound as though it was one vowel present in those compound words.

Igbo translation of the above definition: *Olilo ụdaume bụ otu ụdaume si eme ka udaume nodebere ya yie ya na mkpọpụta mkpụrụokwu abụọ nọdebere onwe ha.*

Examples:
English	Igbo (Normal)	Assimilation
Boss/Leader	Onye + isi	onyiisi
Health	Ahụ + ike	Ahiike
Peacemaker/seeker	Ọchọ + udo	Ọchuudo
Strong hand	Aka + ike	akiike
Welldone	jisi + ike	jiisike

During Vowel Assimilation, two words that have two vowels sitting beside each other experience a dropping of one: the condition is that the vowel which is "stronger" (greater pitch sound) will overide the sound pronunciation of the "weaker" (lower pitch sound) vowel sound before it.

There are five kinds of vowel Assimilation (Olilo udaume) in Igbo language. They are:

1. Progressive Assimilation (Olilo ihu)
2. Regressive Assimilation (Olilo azụ)
3. Coalescent Assimilation (Olilo mmakọ)
4. Conditional Assimilation (Olilo ndapụta)
5. Complete Assimilation (Olilo nlocha)

3.5.1 Progressive Assimilation (Olilo Ihu): Forward dropping happens when the first word ending in a vowel pitch overides the second word's first vowel, thereby replacing the vowel with its own vowel. It is uncommon to notice progressive assimiliation unlike regressive assimiliation.

Igbo translation: *A na-enwe olilo ihu mgbe nke mbụ gara n'ihu loo ụdaume dị n'okwu nke abụọ we me onwe ka ọ bụrụ ụdaime ahụ.*

It can be expressed in the form of:
Preceding vowel + Following Vowel = Preceding vowel reduplication.
V_P + V_F = $V_P V_P$ if V_F is /a/

For example:

Words	Merging of Elements	Pronunciation
eju + a	eju a	eju u
ekwe + a	ekwe a	ekwe e
elu + a	elu a	elu u
esu +a	esu a	esu u
nzu a	nzu a	nzu u
obe a	obe a	obe e
ogbe a	Ogbe a	ogbe e
oge + a	oge a	oge e

3.5.2 Regressive Assimilation (Olilo Azụ): Forward dropping happens when the first vowel of the second outrides the sound pitchword of the first ending vowel pitch.

Igbo translation: *A na-enwe olilo azụ mgbe ụdaume bidoro okwu nke abụọ loo mkpụrụokwu kwwụsịrị ụdaume nke mbụ.*

It can be expressed in the form of:
Preceding vowel + Following Vowel = Following vowel reduplication.
V_P + V_F = $V_F V_F$ if V_F is /a, e, o, ọ/

Compounnd word	Merged	Pronunciation

Nwa + eke	nweeke	nweke
Oke + anu	okaanu	okanu
Ada + obi	adoobi	adobi
Uso + ekwu	useekwu	usekwu
Ego + ọkụ	Egoọkụ	Egọkụ
Ome + ire	Omiire	Omire

3.5.3 Coalescent Assimilation (Olilo mmakọ): This process causes a sound to change by merging two contiguous vowel sounds (invariably adjacent) into another vowel sound different from the two coalesced sounds. This is usually the case when two words are pronounced with rapid speed.

This kind of assimilation often happens when that last word that is merging with the first word is the Igbo word "ya." The third person reflective or object pronoun "ya" would drop the consonant /y/ to either use the vowel /a/ or /e/. Otherwise, it would leave the word "ya" and change the vowel preceding it, "ya" or both the preceding vowel and the vowel after /y/.

It can be expressed in the following forms:

FORM 1: When "Following" vowel is any vowel of the same tone and vowel group (harmony) of /i/ or /ị/, the /i/ or /ị/ is substituted with the consonant "y" whose phoneme is /j/.

V_P = Preceding vowel and V_F = Following vowel
$V_P + V_F = $ 'y'V_S

Notice the introduction of 'y' is the phoneme /j/ as a replacement for V_P.

For example:

Compound words	Merging words	Coalescent A.
asị and ọcha	asị + ọcha	asyọcha
lie and white	*lie + white*	*white lie*
ụdịrị and azụ	ụdịrị + azụ	ụdịryazụ
Type and fish	*type + fish*	*type of fish*
enyi and oma	enyi + oma	enyyoma
friend and good	*friend + good*	*good friend*
ezi and omume	ezi + omume	ezyomume

good and behavior   good + behavior   good behavior

Notice the vowel harmony and the de-syllabification that is accompanied by the substitution of /i/ or /ị/ with consonant "y" whose grapheme is /j/.

FORM 2: When "Following is the pronoun "ya", the consonant "y" whose approximant is /j/, will drop out and the vowel "a" would remain or change following vowel harmony rule in terms of heavy or light vowel. The Igbo word "ya" is the pronoun for his, her, it or its in English.

V_P = Preceding vowel and "ya" = Following vowel
V_P + ya = ịya (heavy vowel)
V_P + ya = iye (light vowel)

Heavy vowel (Ụdaarọ):   a   ị   ọ   ụ
Light vowel (Ụdamfe):   e   i   o   u

For example:

Compound words			Coalescent A.	Vowel type
afọ	+	ya	afịya	heavy
aka	+	ya	akịya	heavy
akwa	+	ya	akwịya	heavy
anya	+	ya	anyịya	heavy
azụ	+	ya	azịya	heavy
ego	+	ya	egiye	light
ije	+	ya	ijiye	light
ike	+	ya	ikiye	light
imi	+	ya	imiye	light
mkpa	+	ye	mkpịya	heavy
ntị	+	ya	ntịya	heavy
nwanne	+	ya	nwanniye	light
oche	+	ya	ochiye	light
ọnụ	+	ya	ọnịya	heavy
uche	+	ya	uchiye	light
ụda	+	ya	ụdịya	heavy

3.5.4 Conditional Assimilation (Olilo ndapụta): This type of assimilation does not occur unless there is a rapid pronunciation of words. In the absence of rapid speed, there is no assimilation.

It can be expressed in the following forms:

FORM 1: When "Preceding" vowel is /u/ or /ụ/, the /u/ or /ụ/ is eclipsed by the "Following" vowel; which make the preceding adopt the phonetic sound of the "Following" vowel thereby producing a reduplication form of "Following" vowel. Note that this can only occur during rapid utterance.

V_P = Preceding vowel and V_F = Following vowel
$V_P + V_F = V_F V_F$ if V_P is /u/ or /ụ/ during rapid pronunciation.

For example:

Merging words	**Rapid utterance**	**Slow utterance**
Agụ + ọhịa	Agọọhịa	Agụọhịa
Leopard + Forest	*Wild Leopard*	*Wild Leopard*
Azụ + aka	Azaaka	Azụaka
Back + Hand	*back of hand*	*back of hand*
mkpụrụ + ọka	mkpụrọọka	mkpụrụọka
Seed + corn	*Corn seed*	*Corn seed*
Okwu + ego	Okweego	Okwuego
Talk + money	*Talk about money*	
Ọnụ + azụ	Ọnaazụ	Ọnụazụ
Mouth + fish	*mouth of fish*	*mouth of fish*

3.5.5 Complete Assimilation: (Olilo Nlocha): Complete assimilation happens when the preceding vowel (a, e, o and ọ) are eclipsed by the "Following" light vowel (i, e, u, o) which also reduplicates itself within the merged words.

It can be expressed in the form of:
Preceding vowel + Following Vowel = Following vowel reduplication.
$V_P + V_F = V_F V_F$ if V_P is /a, e, o, ọ/

Compounnd word	*Merged*	*Pronunciation*
Nwa + ike	nwaike	nwiike
Ude + isi	Udeisi	Udiisi
Aha + ihe	Ahaihe	Ahiihe
Ụlọ + Obi	Ụlọobi	Ụloobi

Ego + enwe	Egoenwe	Egeenwe

3.5 Vowel Elision (Ndapụ Ụdaume)

Vowel Elision is the omission of a vowel sound (a phoneme) in speech. Vowel elision often occurs in the Igbo compound words. Vowel elision happens when compound words with vowel ending and beginning siting side by side are spoken together faster than normal.

Igbo translation: *Ndapụ ụdaume bụ ọpụpụ otu ọdaume na mkpọpụta ụdaume abụọ nọkọtara ọnọ.*

The following are examples of elision of vowels that affect syllables because of the same pitch level they have. This is referred to as diachronic elision because it has affected two words.

English	Igbo (Normal)	Dropping
Male/man	nwa + oke	*nwoke*
Strong man	di + ike	*dike*
Stove	uso + ekwu	usekwu
Doctor	Di + ibia	*dibia*

3.6 Tonal Accent Marks (Diacritics)

Tone is a pitch accent. It is used in Igbo language to show the different meaning of words though they are spelt the same. Tone performs syllabic stress and semantic function in Igbo language.

Tonal marking, also referred to as diacritical marks, are extra symbols that are placed above or below a letter to modify the pronunciation or clarify the meaning of a word. In pronunciation, tone distinguishes pitch level of a syllable. These are examples of their usage in the Igbo language:

Letter	Acute (High tone)	Macron (Mid tone)	Grave (Low tone)
a	Á á	Ā ā	À à
e	É é	È è	Ē ē
i	Í í	Ī ī	Ì ì
ị	Ị́ ị́	Ī ī	Ị̀ ị̀
o	Ó ó	Ò ò	Ō ō
ọ	Ọ́ ọ́	Ō ō	Ọ̀ ọ̀
u	Ú ú	Ū ū	Ù ù
ụ	Ụ́ ụ́	Ū ū	Ụ̀ ụ̀
m	Ḿ ḿ	Ṁ ṁ	M̀ m̀
n	Ń ń	Ṅ ṅ	Ǹ ǹ

Examples:

ákwá	-	cry	[high tone – high tone]
àkwá	-	egg	[low tone – high tone]
àkwà	-	bridge/bed	[low tone – low tone]
ákwà	-	cloth	[high tone – low tone]
ísí	-	head	[high tone – high tone]
ìsì	-	blindness	[low tone – low tone]
ísì	-	smell	[high tone – low tone]
ìsí	-	to cook	[low tone – high tone]
óké	-	male	[high tone – high tone]
òkè	-	portion	[low tone – low tone]
ókè	-	boundary	[high tone – low tone]
òké	-	rat/mouse	[low tone – high tone]

Exercise

1. (a). What are the eight vowels that make up the Igbo vowel system?
   (b). How are Igbo vowels categorized based on their characteristics?
   (c). What distinguishes Ụdamfe (Light vowels) from Ụdaarọ (Heavy vowels)?

2. (a). Define syllabic nasal.
   (b). What are the two similarities between Igbo vowels and semi-vowels that you know.
   (c). Provide five examples of Igbo words that contain only monophthongs?

3. (a). Explain the concept of diphthongs in Igbo language with examples.
   (b). What role do diphthongs play in the pronunciation of Igbo words?

4. (a). What is vowel assimilation?
   (b). How does vowel assimilation occur in Igbo language?
   (c). Provide examples of progressive assimilation in Igbo words.

5. Explain any two of the following terms:
   (a). Vowel Harmony
   (b). Vowel Elision
   (c). Consonant Elision

6. What is the significance of vowel harmony in Igbo language?
7. Describe the process of vowel elision in Igbo compound words.
8. How do tonal accent marks affect the pronunciation and meaning of Igbo words?

9. Explain the difference between the following tones types in Igbo?
   (a). ụdaelu (acute),
   (b). ụdansụda (macron), and
   (c). ụdaala (grave)

10. How can you differentiate between words with similar spellings but different meanings?
11. Give examples of Igbo words where tonal accent marks change the meaning.
12. Why is it important to understand vowel harmony in Igbo language learning?
13. How do diphthongs contribute to the richness of Igbo phonology?
14. Can you discuss the role of vowel assimilation in natural speech communication in Igbo?
15. How do Igbo vowel sounds compare and contrast with those of other languages you are familiar with?

Chapter 4

Igbo Consonants (Mgbochiume Igbo)

4.1 MGBOCHIUME (Consonants)

Mgbochiume (Consonants): there are twenty-eight consonants in Igbo Alphabet. The letters that make up the consonanats in Igbo alphabet are:

b	ch	d	f	g	gb	gh	gw	h	j	k	kp
kw	l	m	n	ṅ	nw	ny	p	r	s	sh	t
v	w	y	z.								

4.2 Types of Consonants sounds:

The Igbo consonants are divided into two, namely mgbochiume mgị (ordinary consonants), and Mgbochiume mkpi (diagraphs).

4.2.1 Mgbochiume mgị (consonant of "gị" sound): These are consonants that are not Mgbochiume mkpi (diagraphs). There are nineteen letters that make up the consonant of "gị" sound which are:

| b | d | f | g | h | j | k | l | m | n | ṅ | p |
| r | s | t | v | w | y | z. | | | | | |

4.2.2 Mgbochiume mkpị (Diagraphs): These are consonants that are comprised of combination of two consonants letters. There are nine digraphs in Igbo alphabet. These are:

    ch   gb   gh   gw   kp   kw   nw   ny   sh

It is of great importance to always remember that despite digraphs such as ch, gh, gb, kp, kw, and sh, do not count as double consonants and pronounced as a single sound.

4.3 Igbo Syllable

A syllable is a unit of pronunciation having one vowel sound, with or without surrounding consonants, forming the whole or a part of a word; e.g., there are two syllables in *often*, three in *napkin* and one in *book*. Syllables usually contain a vowel and accompanying consonants.

There are two types of syllabic consonants: syllabic consonants and non-syllabic consonants.

4.3.1 Syllabic consonant or vocalic consonant: A syllabic consonant or vocalic consonant is a consonant that forms a syllable on its own, like the m, n and l in the English or m and n in Igbo language. A Syllabic Consonant in Igbo language are the two prominent pseudo-vowels also known as semi-vowel. The two vowels can replace the vowel in a syllable and produce a meaningful shorter syllable or word. They make it possible to make some short syllables shorter and simpler. For example: *ama* (neighbourhood) replacing /a/ with /m/ will become *mma* (beauty).

4.3.2. Non-syllabic consonant: M and N are the only syllabic nasal consonants in Igbo language. The rest of igbo consonants are non-syllabic. They cannot be seen sitting next to themselves in an Igbo word. Like in the example above, *mma* is a word but there is no such thing as *bba* in Igbo language. The same applies to the rest of the non-syllabic consonants.

4.4 Syllabic consonants harmony (Ndagba myiriudaume):

This refers to rules that apply when syllabic consonants and non-syllabic are combined together in words. It is a grammatical rule that all Igbo consonants follow when forming a word with a syllabic nasal consonant "m" and "n" in word spelling. The consonant that are allowed to combine with "m" are different from the consonants that "n" combines with.

4.4.1 "M" syllabic nasal harmony:

The syllabic nasal harmony rule shows that consonants that are allowed to combined with syllabic nasal consonant "m" are consonants that belong to Labial Velar (Mkpọnegbugbere Ọnụ) and labiodental (Mkpọnegbugbere Ọnụ na Eze). For example: b, f, gb, kp, m, p, v, w and y.

Word	*Meaning*	*Word*	*Meaning*
Mbe	*Tortoise*	Mbughari	*Carry Around*
Mfe	*Simple*	Mfepụ	*Fly out*
Mgbe	*When*	Mgbaaka	*Bracelet*
Mkpuchi	*Coverup*	Mkpo	*Vessel/container*

Mkpu	*Shout*	Mma	*Beauty*
Mmadu	*Human*	Mpiputa	*Press out.*
Mpụta	*Emergence*	Mpio	*Narrow door*
Mvọ isi	*Comb*	mvọcha	*Scrape out.*
Mwuli	*Motivation*	Mwetu	*Demoralization*
Mwapo	*Creep up*	Mwepu	*Subtraction*
Myọ	*Sieve*	Myocha	*Investigate*

4.4.2 "N" syllabic nasal harmony:

The syllabic nasal harmony rule shows that consonants that are allowed to combine with syllabic nasal consonant "n" are consonants that belong to Alveolar (Mkpọnanyụrụ na Akpo), Palatoaveolar (Mkpọnakpo ihu na akpo ime), Velar (Mkpọnegbugbere Ọnụ na Akpo) and Glottal (Mkpọekoapiri). For example: ch, d, g, gh, gw, h, j, k, kw, l, ṅ, n, nw, ny, r, s, sh, t, and z.

Igbo	***English***	***Igbo***	***English***
Ncha	*Soap*	Nche	*Security*
Nde	*Million*	Ndụ	*Life*
Nge	*Singular Item*	Nghaghari	*Stiring*
Ngwaa	*Verb*	Njụ	*Salad dressing*
Njepụ	*Outdoor walks*	Nhọpụta	*Choosing*
Njem	*Journey*	Nkewa	*Separate*
Nkịta	*Dog*	Nkwọ	*A Market Day*
Nlocha	*Devour*	Nna	*Father*
Nne	*Mother*	Nñomi	*Emulate*
Nnyetu	*Share*	Nrọ	*Dream*
Nshịpụ	*Slippery*	Nso	*Holy*
Nta	*Hunnting*	Ntọhapụta	*Liberation*
Nzapu	*Sweep Out*	Nzọpụta	*Salvation*

4.5 Consonant Elision (Ndapu Mgbochiume)

Consonant Elision is the omission of one or more consonant sounds (a phoneme) in speech. Consonant elision often occurs in the Igbo words with multiple consonant sounds. Consonant is heard when these words with one or more consonants sounds are spoken faster than normal.

For example:
Handbag drops (asimilates) the consonant letter /d/ when pronounced faster as *hanbag*.

Ndapu mgbochiume bu oge arapulu itinye mgbochiume ebe o kwersi idi maka na i na-akpoputa ya osiso.

English	Normal	Elision
Suffering	Afụfụ	Aụfụ
question	Ajụjụ	Aụjụ
Story	Akụkọ	Aụkọ
Side	Akụkụ	Aụkụ
Book	Akwụkwọ	Aụkwọ
Prophesy	Amụma	Aụma
Broom	Azịza	Aịza
Dress code	Ejije	Eije
Tree	Osiso	Oiso
Belief/Faith	Okwukwe	Oukwe
Chicken	Ọkụkọ	Ọụkọ
Morning	Ụtụtụ	Ụụtụ

4.6 Pseudo/Nasalized Vowels

Myiriudaume (semi-vowel, pseudo-vowels or nasalized vowel): These are consonants that are pronounced in similar manner in which vowels are pronounced. There are two letters that make up mgbochiume (nasalized vowels) and they are:

m and n

The Myiriudaume (nasalized vowels) function like vowels in the words with them. Note that you cannot treat "n" as a nasalized vowel when it is in the form of diagraph, for examples: ny, nw, or ñ.

ńnà	-	father
ńné	-	mother
ḿmā	-	good/beautiful
ḿmà	-	knife

4.7 Tonal Accent Marks (Diacritics)

Tone is a pitch accent. It is used in Igbo language to show the different meaning of words though they are spelt the same. Tone performs syllabic stress and semantic function in Igbo language.

Tonal marking, also referred to as diacritical marks, are extra symbols that are placed above or below a letter to modify the pronunciation or clarify the meaning of a word. In pronunciation, tone distinguishes pitch level of a syllable. These are examples of their usage in the Igbo language:

Letter	Acute (High tone)	Macron (Mid tone)	Grave (Low tone)
m	Ḿ ḿ	Ṁ ṁ	M̀ m̀
n	Ń ń	Ṅ ṅ	Ǹ ǹ

When "m" and "n" function as nasalized or pseudo-vowels in Igbo language, it means they can be expressed with tonal markings like other vowels. Therefore, they are pronounced with high, mid or low tones.

In Igbo grammar two consonants cannot follow each other unlike other languages where consonant clusters exist. As a result, "m" or "n" sitting in front of another consonant are given tonal marking which makes it function as a pseudo vowel.

Examples:

    ńnà   –   father [Acute – Grave]

    ńné   –   mother [Acute – Accent]

    ḿmā   –   good [Acute – Macron]

    ḿmà   –   knife [Acute – Grave]

If a word ends with a vowel sound, and the word after it begins with a vowel sound, then the later word with "stronger" vowel swallows the "weaker" vowel sound/the vowel sound before it.

Also, tonal marking helps to distinguish and disambiguate phrases, clauses and sentences that are otherwise similar in written expressions.

For example:

    Ọ dị mmā.   *It is good.* (Declarative)

    Ọ dị mmā?   *Is it good?* (Interrogative)

    Ọ dị mmā   *If it is good* (Conditional)

Exercise

1. (a). What is consonant (Mgbochiume)?
   (b). How many consonants are there in the Igbo alphabet, and what are they?
   (c). Differentiate between Mgbochiume mgị and Mgbochiume mkpị in Igbo consonants.

2. Provide examples of Mgbochiume mgị consonants?
3. Explain what Mgbochiume mkpị (diagraphs) are in Igbo language.
4. What is a syllable, and how does it relate to Igbo language?

5. (a). Describe the concept of syllabic consonants in Igbo, giving examples.
   (b). What distinguishes syllabic consonants from non-syllabic consonants in Igbo?
   (c). Explain the concept of syllabic consonant harmony in Igbo language.

6. (a). Which consonants are allowed to combine with the syllabic nasal consonant "m" in Igbo?
   (b). Give examples of words demonstrating "M" syllabic nasal harmony in Igbo.

7. (a). Which consonants combine with the syllabic nasal consonant "n" in Igbo?
   (b). Provide examples of words illustrating "N" syllabic nasal harmony in Igbo.

8. (a). What is consonant elision, and when does it occur in Igbo words?
   (b). Give examples of Igbo words where consonant elision takes place.

9. What are pseudo/nasalized vowels in Igbo, and how are they pronounced?

Chapter 5

Spelling and spelling rules (Nsupe na Iwu Nsupe)

Spelling is the forming of words from letters according to accepted usage. Igbo language like every other language orthography has spelling rules to follow for proper spelling and writing of words. The following five spelling and writing rules apply to any formation of Igbo words.

5.1 *Letter starting Igbo words:*
All consonants of Igbo alphabet (excluding "v" and "sh") can start a word but not end words. However, special consonants referred to as Pseudo-vowels are permitted.

Generally, Igbo words are not allowed to end with consonants. There are twenty-eight Igbo consonants. Among these twenty-eight consonants only consonants that are pseudo-vowels are exempted from this rule. Pseudo-vowels are "m" and "n". The most used pseudo-vowel in this case is "m." The following examples reveal the exempted condition which are majorly found in few names of animals, collective noun and figures of speech.

All	dum (collective noun)
Periwinkle	Ịsam (name of animal)
Innuendo	Ikpem (figure of speech)
Hippopotamus	Utobo/Akum
Lion	Ọdụm

Please be aware that most names of human beings that end with pseudo-vowels are often a phrase, clause or sentence. For example:

Chukwubuikem	*God is my strength.*
Ikem	*my strength*
Chinecherem	*My God thinks after me.*

Chidubem   *May God keeps leading me.*

5.2 *Successive Use of Consonants*

There is no successive use of consonants in Igbo words. Back-to-back use of consonants is not permitted in Igbo words formation. When consonants are in successive form, they follow or precede one another in the same word. And since diagraphs are considered as single entities and pronounced as single letters, they do not break the rule. The following examples show that this rule is followed.

Dabere	*lean on*
Kele	*greet/thank.*
Efere	*plate*
Ngajị	*spoon*
Ụlọ	*house*
Akara	*mark*

and so on.

Examples with diagraphs:

Akwa	*Egg*
Ugwu	*Mountain*
Akwụkwọ	*Book*
Nwatakịrị	*Child*
Agwọ	*Snake*

5.3 *Letter ending Igbo words.*

All Igbo words end with Igbo vovels or Pseudo-vowel. Igbo words in general usually end with vowels or Pseudo-vowels. There are eight Igbo vowels. Any of the eight Igbo vowels can be the last letter in Igbo words. This rule applies to Igbo nouns, verbs, adjectives, adverbs and so on. For example:

ihụnanya	*love*
udo	*peace*
nke onye	*private*
ihe nzuzo	*secret*
nchekwa	*security*

In Igbo morphology and lexicology, words whose spelling begins with a vowel must have at least another vowel in it. As a result, Igbo words do not permit vowel – consonant – VC- syllable structure as in English language. Another significant aspect of the Igbo writing and spelling system as it regards how spelling relates to phoneme is that, all sound in writable spelling must be pronounced.

5.4 *Successive use of vowels:*

Successive use of vowels are permitted. Back-to-back use of vowels is allowed in Igbo words formation. When vowels are in successive form, they must follow vowel harmony rule.

Vowel harmony applies to heavy and light vowels syllabic combination in words. It is a form of grammatical rule that Ụdamfe (Light vowels) usually consist of vowels of its own syllables (such as e, i, o and u) in a word. They do not combine with Ụdaarọ (heavy vowel: a, ị, ọ and ụ) unless it is a compound verb or word. Words that are imperative verbs in Igbo language often end with vowels written in a successive form. For example:

Ndeewo	-	*hello*
Nnọọ	-	*welcome*
Daluụ	-	*well-done*
Lee	-	*look/behold*
Ee	-	*yes*
Kpọọ	-	*call*

5.5 *Successive use of pseudo-vowel:*

Successive use of pseudo-vowel is allowed. Back-to-back use of pseudo-vowels is allowed in Igbo words formation. Although "m" and "n" are part of the twenty-eight Igbo consonants, they are special consonants and are referred to as pseudo-vowels because of their vowel's characteristics. This characteristic nature gives it the preference over other consonants. The example of successive use of pseudo-vowel is as follows:

ńnà	-	father
ńné	-	mother
ḿmā	-	good/beautiful
ḿmà	-	knife

5.6 Pseudo-vowels preceding other consonants.

Pseudo-vowels that precede fellow consonants in the formation of Igbo words are allowed to do so in the following two ways:

Sub-rule 1: Pseudo-vowel "m" must be ahead of the following nine consonants: b, f, gb, m, p, kp, v, w, y.

Sub-rule 2: Pseudo-vowel "n" must be ahead of the remaining nineteen consonants:

ch	d	g	gh	gw	h	j	k	kw
l	n	ṅ	nw	ny	r	s	sh	t	z

Examples with pseudo-vowel "m":

Mbara/Akiri	*Cricket*	Mbe	*Tortoise*
Mbuzu/Mgbaja/Nte	*Antelope*	Mfe	*Easy/Light*
Mgbada	*Antelope*	Mgbako	*Addition*
Mkpụrụ	*Seed*	Mma	*Knife*
Mpe	*Little/Small*	Mvọ	*Nail/Comb*
Mwepu	*Subtraction*	Myọ	*Sieve/Colander*

Examples with pseudo-vowel "n":

Igbo	*English*	*Igbo*	*English*
Ncha	*soap*	Nche	*security*
Ndida	*slope*	Ndidi	*patience*
Ngalaba	*branch*	Nganga	*pride*
Nhata	*equality*	Nhọpụta	*selection*
Njikọ	*union*	Nkọ	*sharp*
Nku	*wing*	Nchara	*Rust*
Nchị	*Grass cutter*	Nduru	*Dove*
Ngwere	*Lizard*	Nkapị/Nkakwụ	*Shrew*
Nkịta Ọhịa	*Wolf*	Nkwọ	*Kite*
Nshikọ	*Crab*	Nyanwuruede	*Fox*

5.7 Use of "na" in a sentence:
Construction and usage of "na" in written sentences.

In Igbo language "na" when used as a conjunction or preposition follows a specific construct that indicates what part of speech it expresses.

Subrule 1: when "na" is used in a sentence to express conjunction, it is written in full. Conjunction is a part of speech that connects words, phrases, clauses or sentences. For example:

    a) Anyanwụ na Ọnwa   *Sun and Moon*
    b) Ji na Ede   *Yam and cocoyam*
    c) Garri na Ofe dị ụtọ.   *Garri and soup is sweet*
    d) Ama m na ọ gara ahia   *I know he/she went to the market.*
    e) Echere m na ha bi ebe a.   *I thought they live here.*

Subrule 2: when "na" is used in a sentence to express preposition, which is followed by a vowel, there is omission of the vowel "a" as it becomes unstressed vowel allowing the vowel following it to take preeminence. The "na" is expressed as n'. For example:

    a) Mmiri zoro n'ụtụtụ   *It rained in the morning.*
    b) Ọjị dị n'ime akpa   *Kola nut is in the bag.*
    c) Nduru bere n'elu osisi.   *Dove perched on the tree.*
    d) Isi akwụ dara n'ala   *Palm Kernel fell (to the ground).*
    e) Ada no n'ulo akwụkwọ.   *Ada is at school.*

Subrule 3: when "na" is used in a sentence to express preposition, which is followed by a consonant, there is no omission of the vowel "a" as it remains stressed vowel in the sentence. The "na" is written in full as "na". For example:

    a) Mmiri zoro na mgbede   *It rained in the evening.*
    b) Azụ bi na mmiri   *Fishes live in water.*
    c) Zitara m ha na chi ọbụbọ   *Send them early (morning).*
    d) Isi akwụ dabara na nkata   *Palm Kernel fell into the basket.*

Exercise

1. (a). What are the rules regarding the starting letter of Igbo words?
   (b). Which consonants can start Igbo words, and which ones are exempted from the rule against ending words with consonants?
   (c). Can you provide examples of Igbo words where the starting consonant rule is applied?

2. Explain the rule regarding successive use of consonants in Igbo words.

3. Provide examples demonstrating the rule against ending Igbo words with consonants.

4. What are the permissible endings for Igbo words according to spelling rules?

5. (a). Describe the rule concerning successive use of vowels in Igbo words.
   (b). How does vowel harmony apply to successive use of vowels in Igbo words?
   (c). Give examples of Igbo words where successive use of vowels follows the vowel harmony rule.

6. (a). Are successive use of pseudo-vowels allowed in Igbo words? Explain.
   (b). Provide examples demonstrating successive use of pseudo-vowels in Igbo words.
   (c). What are the sub-rules concerning pseudo-vowels preceding other consonants in Igbo words formation?

7. Explain how the sub-rules differentiate the use of "m" and "n" as pseudo-vowels in Igbo words.

8. Can you give examples of Igbo words following the sub-rule for pseudo-vowels preceding other consonants?

9. How is the conjunction "na" used in Igbo sentences?

10. Describe the construction of "na" when used as a conjunction in Igbo sentences.

11. Provide examples demonstrating the usage of "na" as a conjunction in Igbo sentences.

12. What changes occur when "na" is used as a preposition before a vowel in Igbo sentences?

13. Explain the difference in the usage of "na" as a preposition before a vowel and before a consonant in Igbo sentences.

Chapter 6

Punctuation in Igbo Language

Punctuation (Akara Edemede di n'Asụsụ Igbo):
Punctuation is a special symbol used in writing to separate phrases, sentences and their elements and to clarify their meaning. They are also used to show that a sentence is a question, exclamation and so on. Examples of punctuations are full-stop/period, comma, question marks, parentheses, etc.

6.1 Full-stop (Kpom)
This type of punctuation is used at the end of a sentence or an abbreviation; a period. The punctuation mark or symbol for full-stop (kpom) is (.).
Examples:

English	Igbo
Mary went to the market.	Mary jere ahia.
Brian is my sibling.	Brian bu nwanne m.

6.2 Comma (Rikom)
This type of punctuation is used to indicate a pause between parts of a sentence. It is also used to separate items in a list and to mark the place of a thousand, and so on in a large numeral. The punctuation mark or symbol for comma (Rikom) is (,).

For example:

English	Igbo
Mary bought yam, bean and corn.	Mary zutara ji, agwa na oka.
Eze has school bag, book and pen.	Eze nwere akpa akwụkwọ, akwụkwọ na mkpịsị odide.

6.3 Question Marks (Akara ajuju)

This type of punctuation is used in a sentence to express doubt or uncertainty about something, or to indicate a question. The punctuation mark or symbol for question mark (Akara ajuju) is (?).

For examples:

English	Igbo
How are you?	Kedụ? Kedụ ka ịmere?
Do you speak English?	Ị na-asụ Bekee?
Do you speak Igbo?	Ị na-asụ Igbo?

6.4 Semi-colon (Kpom Rikom)

This type of punctuation is used in a sentence to indicate a pause, typically between two main clauses, and it is more pronounced than that indicated by a comma. The punctuation mark or symbol for semi-colon (kpom) is (;).

For example:

English	Igbo
Peter is rich; Paul is poor.	Peter bu ogaranyi, Paul bu ogenye.

6.5 Colon (kpomkpom)

This type of punctuation is used to precede a list of items, a quotation, or an expansion or explanation. The punctuation mark or symbol for colon (kpom-kpom) is (:).

Examples:

English	Igbo
You know what to do: practice.	I ma ihe I ga-eme: tinye omumu gi n'ọrụ.
I want the following items:	A choro m ihe ndi a: nchicha, eraser, paper and pen akwukwo na mkpisi odide.

6.6 Apostrophe (Rikom elu)

This type of punctuation is used in a vowel dropping to indicate the omission of letter. This is especially used when "na" functions as a preposition. The punctuation mark or symbol for apostrophe (Rikom elu) is (').

Examples:

English	Igbo
I love you.	A hụrụ m gi n'anya.
He is at home.	Ọ nọ n'ụlọ.

6.7 Hyphen (Akara uhie)

This type of punctuation is used in auxiliary verb, to join words to indicate that they have a combined meaning or are linked in the grammar of a sentence. It is also used to indicate the division of a word at the end of a line, or to indicate a missing or implied element. The punctuation mark or symbol for hyphen (Akara-uhie) is (-).

Examples:

English	Igbo
He will pay for everything.	Ọ ga-akwụ ụgwọ ihe nile.
Say it to me in Igbo.	Gwa mu ya na-asusu Igbo.

6.8 Quotation Marks (Rikom Ngwu)

This type of punctuation is used either to mark the beginning and the end of a title or quoted passage, or to indicate that the word or phrase is regarded as slang or jargon, or is being discussed rather than used within a sentence. The punctuation mark or symbol for quotation mark (Rikom Ngwu) is (' ') or (" ").

Examples:

English	Igbo
"I'm very tired," she said.	O siri, "Ike guru m."
"I work in Italy," said Ben.	Ben siri, "A na m aru—oru na obodo (mba) Italy."

6.9 Parentheses (Akara Nkudo)

This type of punctuation is a pair of brackets used to mark off a parenthetical word or phrase. It is also used to add extra information in a sentence. The punctuation mark or symbol for parentheses (Akara Nkudo) is ( ).

Examples:

English	Igbo
Yes (all is OK).	Ee (O di mma).
What are you called?	Gini ka anakpo g?i (aha eji mara gi).

6.10 Exclamation Mark (Akara Mkpu)

This type of punctuation is used with a word or phrase to indicate strong feelings (such as shock, surprise, anger or raised voice), or show emphasis, and often marks the end of the sentence. The punctuation mark or symbol for Exclamation mark (Akara mkpu) is (!).

Examples:

English	Igbo
Watch out!	Lee anya!
Go away!	Puo ebe a!
Leave me alone!	Hapu m aka!
Help!	Nyere m aka!
Fire!	Ọkụ!
Stop!	Kwụsi!
Call the police!	Kpoo ndi uwe ojii!

6.11 Slash (Akara oke)

Slash is also known as forward slash, slant, oblique dash or diagonal and is used to separate letters, numbers or words. It is also used to indicate "or". The punctuation mark or symbol for slash (Akara oke) is (/).

Examples:

English	Igbo
I'm good/fine.	a di m mm/O di mma.
Go straight.	gaba n'iru/ogologo.
Do you speak English/Igbo?	Ị na-asụ bekee/Igbo?

6.12 Ellipsis (Nsepụokwu)

This is a mark consisting of three dots (dot-dot-dot), that is used to indicate an intentional omission of a word, sentence, or whole section from a text without altering its original meaning. The punctuation mark or symbol for Ellipsis (Nsepụokwu) is (...).

Examples:

English	Igbo
My name is...	Aham bu ...
I'm from...	Esi m na ...

Exercise

1. What is punctuation, and what is its purpose in writing?
2. Describe the use of full stop (kpom) in Igbo language and provide examples.
3. How is a comma (rikom) used in Igbo sentences? Give examples.
4. Explain the function of question marks (akara ajuju) in Igbo sentences and provide examples.
5. What is the purpose of a semi-colon (kpom rikom) in Igbo writing? Give an example.
6. Describe how a colon (kpomkpom) is used in Igbo language and provide examples.
7. How is an apostrophe (rikom elu) used in Igbo writing? Provide examples.
8. Explain the function of a hyphen (akara uhie) in Igbo sentences and give examples.
9. Describe the use of quotation marks (rikom ngwu) in Igbo language and provide examples.
10. What is the purpose of parentheses (akara nkudo) in Igbo writing? Give examples.
11. How is an exclamation mark (akara mkpu) used in Igbo sentences? Provide examples.
12. Explain the function of a slash (akara oke) in Igbo language and give examples.
13. What is an ellipsis (nsepuokwu) and how is it used in Igbo writing? Provide examples.
14. Can you differentiate between the use of full-stop and comma in Igbo sentences?
15. How do question marks and exclamation marks differ in their usage in Igbo language?
16. Explain the difference between a colon and a semi-colon in Igbo writing.
17. Describe the purpose of quotation marks and parentheses in Igbo sentences.
18. When is it appropriate to use a hyphen in Igbo language, and when is it not?
19. How does the usage of punctuation marks vary between formal and informal Igbo writing?
20. Can you provide examples of sentences where multiple punctuation marks are used together in Igbo writing?

Part Two:

Phonology & Phonetics (Ọdịdị ụdaasụsụ na Amụmàmụ Ụdaasụsụ)

Chapter 7
Introduction to Phonology

7.1 Definition and Scope of Phonology

The field of linguistics known as phonology (Ọdịdị ụdaasụsụ) is focused on the orderly arrangement and structuring of sounds in human languages. It examines how sounds function within a language system, including their distribution, patterns, and usage norms. Phonology studies the physical manifestations of sounds in speech (phones) as well as the abstract, underlying patterns of sounds (phonemes). Linguists use phonological analysis to identify the principles underlying sound patterns and understand their significance in language communication.

Phonology is the study of linguistic sound systems. Whereas Phonetics is the study of physical properties of human's speech sounds. Phonology is the classification of the sounds within the system of a particular language or languages.

Phonology, the study of the sound patterns in languages, can be divided into two parts, namely:

- Phonemes (vowels and consonants)
- Prosody (stress, rhythm and intonation)

7.2 Igbo Phonetics (Amụmàmụ Ụdaasụsụ)

Phonetics is the study of human sounds. It is the study of physical properties of human's speech sounds. It is concerned with all aspects of the production, transmission, and perception of the sounds of language.

Speaking Igbo is not easy for the people whose mother tongue is not Igbo. This is because it is a tonal language. Most of the words of a phonographic language can be pronounced according to their spelling. But most of the words of a tonal language follow their spelling as well as tonal marking during pronunciation.

Unlike Igbo language, many speech sounds in English have several different spellings, e.g. 'go', 'bow', 'row', 'know', 'though' etc. and many "same spellings" have different sounds, e.g. <ough>: 'though', 'cough', 'enough', 'bough', 'through', etc. Therefore, learners of English language cannot rely solely on the spelling of a word when they try to pronounce it.

Native speakers of Igbo language are not spared from this problem when they are new to reading and writing in Igbo. Igbo scholars, teachers and those who have took time to master Igbo phonetics may face the opposite problem as many like schoolchildren took a lot of time to learn to read and write in Igbo.

In Igbo language, the standard Igbo has thirty-six phonemes comprisingtwenty-eight consonants and eight vowels *(see chapter one for more details)*. This is why learning Igbo language appears to be difficult because it is like asking someone to learn the 44 phonemes of English language rather than starting from the 26 letters of English alphabets.

By learning Igbo alphabets, you learn the 36 Phonemes and will not have any other thing to worry about. Since Igbo language is a tonal language, Igbo words may differ only in tone. A typical example of tonal marking exists in 'akwa' which can assume the meaning of the following: ákwá *"cry"*, àkwà *"bed"*, àkwá *"egg"*, and ákwà *"cloth"*. As tone is not normally written, these all appear as ⟨akwa⟩ in printed format.

There are three major branches of Igbo phonetics namely, acoustic, articulatory and audible.

7.2.1 *Acoustic Phonetics* (Amụmàmụ Ọdịdị Ụda): is the study of the hearing characteristics of speech. It includes an analysis and description of vocal expression in terms of its physical properties, such as frequency, intensity, and duration.

Acoustic phonetics investigates time domain features such as the mean squared amplitude of a waveform, its duration, its fundamental frequency, or frequency domain features such as the frequency spectrum, or even combined spectrotemporal features and the relationship of these properties to other branches of phonetics (e.g. articulatory or auditory phonetics), and to abstract linguistic concepts such as phonemes, phrases, or utterances.

7.2.2 *Articulatory Phonetics* (Amụmàmụ Mkpọpụta Ụda): Articulatory Phonetics is a branch of phonetics that deals with the motive processes and anatomy involved in the production of the sounds of speech. Articulatory phoneticians explain how humans produce speech sound through the interaction of different physiological structures. Generally, articulatory phonetics is concerned with the transformation of aerodynamic energy into acoustic energy. Aerodynamic energy refers to the airflow through the vocal tract. Its potential form is air pressure; its kinetic form is the actual dynamic airflow. Acoustic energy is variation in the air pressure that can be represented as sound waves, which are then perceived by the human auditory system as sound.

Respiratory sounds can be produced simply by expelling air from the lungs. However, to vary the sound quality in a way useful for speaking, two speech organs normally move towards each other to contact each other to create an obstruction that shapes the air in a particular fashion. The point of maximum obstruction is called the *place of articulation*, and the way the obstruction forms and releases is the *manner of articulation*. For example, when making a p sound, the lips come together tightly, blocking the air momentarily and causing a buildup of air pressure. The lips then release suddenly, causing a burst of sound. The place of articulation of this sound is therefore called *bilabial*, and the manner is called *stop* (also known as a *plosive*).

7.2.3 *Auditory Phonetics* (Amụmàmụ Anụmụda): is the branch of phonetics that deals with the hearing of speech sounds and with speech perception. It involves the study of the relationships between speech stimuli and a listener's responses to such stimuli as mediated by mechanisms of the peripheral and central auditory systems, including certain areas of the brain. It is one of the three main branches of phonetics along with acoustic and articulatory phonetics, though with overlapping methods and questions.

Auditory phonetics is concerned with both segmental (mostly vowels and consonants) and prosodic (such as stress, tone, rhythm and intonation) aspects of speech. Most research in sociolinguistics and dialectology has been based on auditory analysis of data and almost all pronunciation dictionaries are based on impressionistic, auditory analysis of how words are pronounced.

7.2.1 Phoneme (Mkpụrụụdaasụsụ): A phoneme (mkpụrụụdasụsụ) is a unit of sound that can distinguish one word from another in a particular language. It is represented by one or more grapheme. A grapheme is a letter or a number of letters that represent the sounds in our speech. So a grapheme will be the letter/ letters that represent a phoneme. English language has a complex written code and in English code a grapheme can be 1, 2, 3 or 4 letters. For example:

One letter grapheme – c a r	(c)	and	m a t	(m)
Two letter grapheme – t ea m	(ea)	and	sh i p	(sh)
Three letter grapheme – s igh	(igh)	and	n igh t	(igh)
Four letter grapheme – r ough	(ough)	and	eigh t	(eigh)

The complex nature can simply be seen by looking at the different ways various sounds are represented. For instance, some sounds (phonemes) can be spelled by different graphemes (spellings) e.g.:

- the sound /s/ can be spelled 's, se, ss, c, ce, se'
- the sound /k/ can be spelled 'c, k or ck, ch, cc, que'
- the sound /ee/ can be spelled 'ee, ea, ie, ei, e, e-e,
- the sound /o/ can be spelled 'o, a, au, aw, ough'

A digraph is a 2-letter grapheme e.g. 'ch' in 'chip', 'ss' in dress. A trigraph is a 3-letter grapheme (the clue is in 'tri') e.g. 'igh' in 'high' and 'que' in cheque. Igbo language has nine diagraph (ch, gb, gh, gw, kp, kw, nw, ny, sh) and do not have any trigraph in its grapheme.

In English, there are 44 phonemes, or word sounds that make up the language. They're divided into 19 consonants, 7 digraphs, 5 'r-controlled' sounds, 5 long vowels, 5 short vowels, 2 'oo' sounds, 2 diphthongs.

In Igbo language, phoneme is used to distinguish one word from another as well as their meanings. The 36 grapheme of Igbo phoneme which also represents the letters of Igbo alphabet can be shown to contain a pair of words that differs by one sound, thus *minimal pair*.

Minimal pairs (mkpịiche): are pairs of words that differ in only one phonological element, such as a phoneme, toneme or chroneme, and have distinct meanings. A minimally phonologically distinctive pair of words establishes a minimal distinctive linguistic sound, known as a *phoneme*, from among the acoustically distinguishable sounds in a language, known as the phones of the language.

A minimal distinctive sound is one which can distinguish one word from another when all other sounds are identical. These phones are said to be in *Contrastive Distribution*. To establish the phonemes of a language such MINIMAL PAIRS, two words differing in just one distinguishable sound (hence 'minimal'), must be found for all the phonemes. If you cannot find a minimal pair, the phones are said to be in non-contrastive distribution. They may be in *Complementary Distribution* or in *Free Variation*.

The rules for minimum pairs are:

1. The words must have the same *number* of sounds.
2. The words must be *identical* in every sound except for one.
3. The sound that is different must be in the same *position* in each word.

4. The words must have different *meanings*.

The following are examples of minimum pairs of Phoneme in Igbo language. For example:

	1st pair	2nd pair	Note
1.	**Akụ** *(wealth)*	**Akị** *(Nuts)*	*last vowel*
2.	**Ajị** *(body hair)*	**Ajọ** *(bad)*	*last vowel*
3.	**Bi** *(lives)*	**Bụ** *(is)*	*initial consonant.*
4.	**Chere** *(wait)*	**Chebe** *(protect)*	*middle consonant.*
5.	**Eze** *(teeth)*	**Ezi** *(Pig)*	*initial consonant*
6.	**Ọchị** *(maggot)*	**Ọcha** *(white)*	*last vowel*
7.	**Ọka** *(corn)*	**Ọba** *(barn)*	*middle consonant*
8.	**Ozi** *(message)*	**Ozu** *(corpse)*	*last vowel*
9.	**Ukwe** *(chorus)*	**Ukwu** *(waist)*	*last vowel*
10.	**Ụzọ** *(entrance)*	**Ụdọ** *(rope)*	*middle consonant*

Phoneme		**Grapheme(s)**		**Examples**	**English**
/b/	/tʃ/	/b/	/ch/	buru, churu	*carried, fetched*
/tʃ/	/d/	/ch/	/d/	cheta, deta	*remembered, write to*
/d/	/f/	/d/	/f/	dee, fee	*write, fly*
/g/	/ɓ~g͡ɓ/	/g/	/gb/	gawa, gbawa	*proceed, break apart*
/gʷ/	/ɦ/	/gw/	/h/	gwa, ha	*tell, them*
/dʒ/	/tʃ/	/j/	/ch/	ije, iche	*walk, difference*
/k/	/tʃ/	/k/	/ch/	kee, chee	*what, think*
/ɓ~k͡p/	/kʷ/	/kp/	/kw/	kpee, kwee	*pray, agree*
/l/	/m/	/l/	/m/	mee, lee	*do, look*
/n/	/ŋʷ/	/n/	/ŋʷ/	anwụ, añụ	*sun, bee*
/ɲ/	/ŋ/	/ny/	/ñ/	anyụ, añụ	*alligator, bee*
/ɔ/	/ʊ/	/o/	/u/	ọka, ụka	*corn, church*
/p/	/ɹ/	/p/	/r/	panye, ranye	*pass down, commit*
/s/	/ʃ/	/s/	/sh/	ịsa, ịsha	*to wash, crayfish*
/j/	/z/	/j/	/z/	ije, ize,	*journey, dodge*
/z/	/l/	/z/	/l/	ụzọ, ụlọ	*way, house*

7.2.2 Toneme: A toneme is a phonological element that uses pitch within spoken language as an indicator to the meaning words. English language is devoid of tonemes, but many African and

Asian languages do have toneme. Igbo language is a tonal language, thus toneme is an abundant phonological element. A refreshing example is shown below:

Igbo		English	Pitch/Tonal Marking
óké	-	male	[high tone – high tone]
òkè	-	portion	[low tone – low tone]
ókè	-	boundary	[high tone – low tone]
òké	-	rat/mouse	[low tone – high tone]

7.2.3 Chroneme: A chroneme is a phonological element that uses the duration of a syllable to determine the meaning of the word. Chroneme is not used in the English language, however, some European native languages use it. The two common examples are Latin and Italian languages. For example, the Italian word "vile" means "coward," while "ville" means "villas." In Igbo language, chroneme is not as predominate as toneme but it does exist as one of the phonological elements. For example:

1. asa *(epitome of beauty)*   asaa *(seven)*
2. be *(one's dwelling/home)*   bee *(cry)*
3. gbasa *(spread)*   gbasaa *(dismiss)*
4. isi *(head)*   isii *(six)*
5. mee *(do)*   mmee *(red)*
6. na *(and)*   nna *(father)*
7. ole *(how many/how much)*   olee *(where/when/how)*

7.3 Classification of Phoneme (Nkèụdị Mkpụrụụdaasụsụ):

A phoneme is a unit of sound in speech. A phoneme doesn't have any inherent meaning by itself, but when you put phonemes together, they can make words. On the other hand, you can segment, or break apart, any word to recognize the sounds or phonemes in that word.

In order to know how many phonemes a word has, it's best to say the word out loud to focus on the sounds that make up the word rather than looking at the letters on paper. For example, if you say the word 'akị,' you will hear that there are three sound units, or phonemes, in that word: /a/ /k/ /ị/.

The two divisions of phonemes are: segmental and suprasegmental phonemes.

7.4 Segmental Phonemes

Segmental Phonemes (Mkpụrụụdaasụsụ Ụdanke):
The ability to separate the sounds of a word is called "phoneme segmentation". Segment is the 'basic' units or 'simple sounds' which make up 'words'. It often corresponds to a written alphabetic letter in Igbo language, even if sometimes spelling doesn't correspond nicely with pronunciation in some languages. The articulation of a particular phonemic 'segment' can be analyzed into its beginning, middle and end, any of which would be segments within that phoneme.

Phoneme represents the minimal units or one of a small speech sound. This unit of speech sound is known as segment. To determine the status of a phoneme, a substitution test is carried out. This is a method of substituting one segment with another segment such that it produces a different word.

It is recommended that by using a substitution test, one can determine if an expression qualifies as a phoneme. When a segment is replaced (substituted) by another segment and it produces a different word, then the status of segmented phoneme is established, for example, the phoneme of /e/ and /a/ in pest and past. Any pair of words as in the above that differs in one sound only or one segment is referred to as minimal pair.

Segmental Phonemes are small speech sounds (the minimal units) of a particular language that represent differences in meaning. Segmental phoneme consists of two aspects of sound's unit namely: the consonant phonemes and vowel phonemes. Mkpụrụ Edemede or Abidịị is the 36-letter alphabet of Igbo language. It features 28 consonants (mgbochiume) and 8 vowels (ụdaume).

Exercise

1. What is the primary focus of phonology, and how does it differ from phonetics?
2. Explain the concept of phonemes in the study of language and provide examples.
3. How does phonology contribute to understanding the structure and organization of sounds in human languages?
4. Describe the distinction between segmental and suprasegmental phonemes.
5. What are the two main branches of phonology, and what aspects of language do they cover?
6. How does the study of phonetics relate to the production, transmission, and perception of speech sounds?
7. What challenges do learners of tonal languages like Igbo face in pronunciation compared to non-tonal languages?
8. How does Igbo phonology differ from English phonology, especially in terms of spelling and pronunciation?
9. What are the major components of Igbo phonetics, and how do they contribute to the understanding of speech sounds?
10. Explain the significance of minimal pairs in phonological analysis and provide examples from Igbo language.
11. How are phonemes represented in Igbo language, and how do they contribute to word meaning?
12. Describe the branches of Igbo phonetics and their respective focuses.
13. What role do tonemes play in Igbo language, and how do they affect word meaning?
14. Explain the concept of chronemes and provide examples from Igbo language.
15. How are phonemes classified in Igbo phonology, and what are the main categories?
16. What is meant by the term "segmental phonemes," and how do they contribute to linguistic analysis?
17. Describe the process of phoneme segmentation and its importance in understanding language structure.
18. How are substitution tests used to determine the status of phonemes, and what do minimal pairs indicate?
19. Discuss the significance of the Igbo alphabet (Mkpụrụ Edemede) in representing phonemes and language sounds.
20. In what ways does the study of phonology enhance our understanding of language communication and linguistic diversity?

Chapter 8
Syllable Structure

3.1 What is syllable?

Syllables are the fundamental units of speech. They function as the building blocks of individual words. In the Igbo language, a syllable is a segment of a word that can be spoken as a whole or in part and consists of a single vowel sound, either with or without a consonant. 'Nkejiokwu' is the Igbo word for syllable. Igbo as tonal language has each of its syllable arranged in a manner that conveys tone of words. This makes syllables an essential component of Igbo language.

Igbo syllables are made up of a central vowel sound called the nucleus, which may sometimes have consonant sounds preceding it (called the onset). Unlike English syllable, consonant sounds come after Igbo vowels. Therefore, the phonetic properties and structure of Igbo syllables are shaped by these vowel sounds.

3.2 Classification of Igbo syllable:

There are different kinds of syllable structure, each distinguished by its sounds and internal arrangement. Open and closed syllables are one common distinction. When a syllable ends with an open vowel, like in "go" or "be," the vowel stands alone without a consonant behind it. On the other hand, words like "cat" or "jump," where the consonant comes right after the vowel, are examples of closed syllables that end in a consonant sound. As earlier said, closed syllables do not exist in Igbo syllable. This is because every Igbo word ends with a vowel sound.

Syllables are classified according to their length and complexity. Monosyllabic syllables, which make up basic units like "cat" or "dog," have just one vowel sound. In contrast, polysyllabic syllables, like "banana" or "elephant," are made up of several vowel sounds.

3.2.1. Monosyllabic syllables: Monosyllabic syllables, as the term suggests, consist of only one vowel or pseudo vowel (syllabic nasal) sound. They are the simplest units of pronunciation and form the building blocks of words. Examples of monosyllabic words include vowles: "a", "e:", "I", "ị", "o", "ọ", "u", "ụ", ans pseudo vowels "m", "n". In each of these words, there is only one vowel sound, and it stands alone a single letter syllable.

3.2.2. Polysyllabic syllables: Polysyllabic syllables are comprised of multiple vowel sounds. Polysyllabic words are typically longer and more complex than monosyllabic words. Examples of polysyllabic words include:

1. "efe (clothes),"
2. "efere (plate),"
3. "akwụkwọ (book),"
4. "akaraaka (fte/destiny)," and
5. "agbamakwụkwọ (wedding)."

In these words, there are multiple vowel sounds, each forming the nucleus of a syllable. For example, in the word "efe (clothes)," there are two syllables, each containing a vowel sound: "e-FE." The first syllable contains the vowel sound "e," and the second syllable contain "FE." In the third example above, there are three syllables, each containing a vowel sound: A-KWỤ-KWỌ." The first syllable contains the vowel sound "a," and the second and third syllables contain the diphthong "KW." Similarly, in the word "agbamakwụkwọ (wedding)," there are six syllables, each containing a vowel sound: "EL-e-phant."

The presence of multiple vowels sounds in polysyllabic words adds complexity to their pronunciation and contributes to their longer length compared to monosyllabic words.

3.3 Syllable Weight

Syllable weight refers to the perceived heaviness or lightness of a syllable, often determined by the number and type of consonants and vowels it contains. In languages with weight-sensitive stress patterns, syllable weight can influence the placement of stress or prominence within words. Syllables may be classified as light (containing a short vowel and no coda) or heavy (containing a long vowel, diphthong, or coda consonant). Some languages also recognize superheavy syllables, which contain an additional consonant cluster in the coda. However, coda (consonant ending words) does not exist in Igbo language.

Here are examples of different syllable weights:

1. Light syllable: "gba (to shoot/kick)" (contains a short vowel and no coda)
2. Light syllable: "Daalụ (thank you)" (contains a long vowel and no coda)
3. Heavy syllable: "niile (all)" (contains a long vowel and no coda)
4. Light syllable: "kwuo (say)" (contains a diphthong and no coda)
5. Heavy syllable: "kwere" (contains a diphthong and no coda)

These examples demonstrate the variation in syllable weight based on the presence and nature of vowel length, consonant clusters, and other factors within syllable structures.

3.4. Syllable Structure:
3.4.1. Consonant-vowel (CV) syllable: In a CV syllable like "bi (lives)," the syllable structure consists of a consonant sound (C) followed by a vowel sound (V). In this case, the consonant sound "b" serves as the onset of the syllable, and the vowel sound "i" serves as the nucleus. There is no coda, as there is no consonant sound following the vowel. The syllable "bi" is relatively simple, containing only one consonant sound and one vowel sound.

3.4.2. Vowel-consonant-vowel (VCV) syllable: In a VCV syllable like "akwa (egg)," the syllable structure consists of a vowel sound (V) followed by a consonant sound (C) and then another vowel sound (V). In "akwa," the vowel sounds "a" serve as the nuclei of the three syllables, with the consonant sound (diphthong) "kw" forming the coda of the first syllable. The syllable "akwa" is characterized by its vowel-consonant-vowel sequence, where the consonant sound intervenes between two vowel sounds.

3.4.2. Consonant-vowel-consonant-vowel (CVCV) syllable: In a CVCV syllable like "gara (went)," the syllable structure consists of a consonant sound (C) followed by a vowel sound (V), then another consonant sound (C), and finally another vowel sound (V). In "gara (went)," the consonant sounds "g" and "r" form the onset, while the vowel sounds "a" and "a" form the nuclei of the two syllables. The syllable "gara (went)" is more complex than "bi" because it contains two consonant sounds and two vowel sounds, alternating in a consonant-vowel-consonant-vowel pattern.

The structure of syllables, including the arrangement of consonant and vowel sounds, helps in analyzing the phonological patterns of words and their pronunciation in Igbo. Linguists can better comprehend spoken language and its phonological patterns by being aware of these differences in syllable kinds and structures. Such knowledge makes it easier to analyze word development, pronunciation differences, and linguistic processes, resulting in a more complete understanding of language structure and usage.

3.5 Syllable Structure Constraints
Languages impose constraints on syllable structure, governing the permissible combinations of consonants and vowels within syllables. These constraints vary across languages and can influence syllable complexity, syllable shape, and phonotactic patterns. Common syllable structure constraints include onset and coda restrictions, limitations on consonant clusters, and rules governing vowel sequences. Syllable structure constraints contribute to the phonological

characteristics and rhythmic patterns of languages, shaping the syllabic organization of words and the distribution of sounds.

In Igbo language, unlike English, there are specific constraints on the structure of syllables. Here are four key syllable structure constraints in Igbo:

3.5.1. Onset restrictions: In Igbo, syllables typically begin with one or two consonants in the onset position. Words such as "Nga" (prison) and "Mvọ" (comb) exemplify this constraint, where only one or two consonants appear at the beginning of the syllable.

3.5.2. Syllable-final consonant restrictions: Igbo syllables do not allow all consonants to occur as the final element. Certain consonants, such as "ng" or "sh," cannot appear at the end of syllables in Igbo. This constraint affects the phonotactic structure of syllables in the language.

3.5.3. Phonotactic constraints: Some consonant combinations are prohibited in Igbo syllables. For example, combinations like "nm" or "mn" are not permitted due to phonotactic constraints. These restrictions influence the permissible combinations of consonants within syllables.

3.5.4. Onset gemination restrictions: Geminate or doubled consonants are generally not allowed in the onset position of Igbo syllables. This means that sequences such as "chch," "tt," "kpkp," or "kk" are rare or nonexistent in Igbo words. The absence of onset gemination contributes to the phonological characteristics of Igbo syllables.

These examples illustrate the various constraints and limitations imposed on syllable structure in Igbo, which influence the distribution and organization of sounds within words. These syllable structure constraints shape the phonotactic patterns and pronunciation rules of words. Understanding these constraints is crucial for analyzing the phonological structure and syllabic organization of Igbo words.

Understanding syllable structure, including syllable types, syllable weight, and syllable structure constraints, provides insights into the phonological organization of Igbo languages. Syllable structure influences speech production, perception, and phonological processes, shaping the rhythmic patterns and prosodic features of spoken language.

Exercise

1. What is a syllable, and why are they considered fundamental units of speech?
2. Describe the structure of an Igbo syllable and explain how it differs from English syllables.
3. What are the main classifications of syllables, and how are they distinguished?
4. Explain the difference between open and closed syllables and provide examples from Igbo and English languages.
5. How are monosyllabic and polysyllabic syllables differentiated, and what are examples of each in Igbo language?
6. What is syllable weight, and how does it influence stress patterns in languages?
7. Provide examples of light and heavy syllables in Igbo language and explain their characteristics.
8. Describe the syllable structure of consonant-vowel (CV), vowel-consonant-vowel (VCV), and consonant-vowel-consonant-vowel (CVCV) syllables in Igbo, with examples.
9. What are some constraints on syllable structure in Igbo language, and how do they impact phonological patterns?
10. Explain the concept of onset restrictions in Igbo syllable structure and provide examples.
11. What is meant by syllable-final consonant restrictions, and how do they affect Igbo syllables?
12. Discuss phonotactic constraints in Igbo syllable structure and provide examples.
13. Why are onset gemination restrictions important in understanding Igbo syllable structure?
14. How does syllable structure influence speech production and perception in Igbo language?
15. Describe the role of syllable structure in shaping the rhythmic patterns and prosodic features of Igbo speech.
16. Explain the significance of understanding syllable structure for analyzing phonological processes in Igbo language.
17. Compare and contrast syllable structure in Igbo and English languages, highlighting key differences.
18. How does knowledge of syllable structure contribute to the study of language development and acquisition?
19. Discuss the implications of syllable structure constraints for language learning and teaching in Igbo-speaking communities.
20. In what ways does syllable structure influence the overall phonological organization of Igbo language and its spoken form?

Chapter 9

Prosody

9.1 Supra-segmental Phonemes

Supra-segmental phonemes (mkpụrụụdaasụsụ ụda-nsokwasị nke): Supra-segmental phonemes (prosody) refer to a phonological property of more than one sound segment. As the unit of linguistic which operates above a single sound, it uses pitch, loudness, tempo, and rhythm in a speech to convey information about the structure and meaning of an utterance. Therefore, the supra-segmental phonemes features include stress (ikeolu), intonation (ndebeolu/njeolu), duration (oge) and tone (ụdaolu).

9.1.1. Stress (ikeolu):

Stress, also known as lexical stress or word stress, is the level of emphasis placed on a sound or syllable during speaking. When two words or sentences seem to mean the same thing, stress patterns can assist separate them. It is the intensity—that is, the relative loudness—that a speech syllable receives via extra effort during articulation.

For example:

    a) Ọ dị mmā.   *It is good. (Declarative)*

    b) Ọ dị mmā?   *Is it good? (Interrogative)*

    c) Ọ dị mmā   *If it is good. (Conditional)*

9.1.2. Intonation (ndebeolu/njeolu):

The term "intonation" describes the melodic patterns of speech, such as changes in pitch, pitch range, and pitch contour, that support language's expressive and communicative qualities. In spoken speech, intonation is essential for expressing grammatical structure, pragmatic meaning, and emotional tone. Pitch rises and falls during utterances, impacting how assertions, queries, demands, and other speech acts are understood. In English, for instance, a question mark is usually indicated by a rising intonation contour at the end of a sentence, whereas a declarative statement is suggested by a falling intonation contour.

In Igbo language, intonation is used to convey emotions such as surprise, anger, or delight), and other differences of expressive meaning. It can also serve a grammatical function. Intonation is primarily a matter of variation in the pitch of the voice. Intonation describes how the voice rises and falls in speech.

Examples of intonation patterns in prosody:

1. Rising intonation at the end of a question:
   "Ị gara ụlọ ahịa?" *"Did you go to the store?"*

2. Falling intonation at the end of a statement:
   "Agara m ụlọ ahịa." *"I went to the store."*

3. Falling intonation for commands or directives:
   "Sachapụ ọnụ ụlọ gị." *"Clean your room."*

4. Rising-falling intonation for polite requests:
   "Biko ị nwere ike ịnyefe nnu?" *"Could you please pass the salt?"*

5. Falling intonation for completion or finality:
   "Nke ahụ bụ njedebe nke akụkọ." *"That's the end of the story."*

6. Rising-falling intonation for contrast or emphasis:
   "Ekwuru m na achọrọ m nke na-acha anụnụ anụnụ, ọ bụghị nke obara obara."
   "I said I wanted the blue one, not the red one."

These examples demonstrate how intonation patterns can convey various meanings, attitudes, and functions in spoken language.

Tonal marking helps to distinguish and disambiguate phrases, clauses and sentences that are otherwise similar in written expressions.

For example:
1. Ọ dị mmā. *It is good.* (Declarative)
2. Ọ dị mmā? *Is it good?* (Interrogative)
3. Ọ dị mmā *If it is good* (Conditional)

9.1.3. Length/Duration (oge):
In prosody, length or duration is an important feature of speech sounds that distinguishes them based on their extended length or quantity compared to other sounds. Iit refers to the amount of time a particular sound occupies in spoken language.

Length or duration plays a significant role in the perception and interpretation of speech. Certain sounds, such as vowels and consonants, can vary in duration, and this variation contributes to the rhythmic patterns and cadence of speech. For example, longer vowels or consonants may carry greater emphasis or prominence within an utterance, while shorter sounds may serve as unstressed elements or transitional segments between more salient sounds.

The general rhythm and tempo of speech can be affected by the length of sounds. Shorter durations help to maintain the coherent and fluid flow of speech, whereas longer durations may suggest emphasis, pauses, or interruptions within an utterance. Additionally, changes in duration can reflect emphasis or emotion or distinguish between words that are identical in meaning.

Furthermore, length or duration is not only relevant at the level of individual sounds but also at the level of larger linguistic units, such as syllables, words, or phrases. In phonology, the concept of mora, which refers to the time unit equivalent to one beat in a rhythmic pattern, is closely related to the notion of duration. By examining the duration of different linguistic units, linguists can gain insights into the rhythmic structure and phonological organization of languages.

Overall, length or duration is a fundamental aspect of prosody that contributes to the rhythmic, expressive, and communicative qualities of spoken language. Its variation and modulation play a crucial role in shaping the perception and interpretation of speech, enriching the overall texture and meaning of linguistic communication.

9.1.4. Contour tone (ụdaolu ngwe):
contour describes speech sounds which behave as single segments, but which make an internal transition from one quality, place, or manner to another. These sounds may be tones, vowels, or consonants. Many tone languages have contour tones, which move from one level to another or shift from one pitch to another over the course of the syllable or word. There are two contour tones in Igbo—the rising and the falling tones.

9.1.5. Tones:

Igbo has three tones, high, mid, and low, which are phonemic, serving to make lexical, grammatical, and syntactical distinctions. The mid-tone can only follow a high-tone and, in consequence, is absent in monosyllables. For example:

    Acute (High tone)   Macron (Mid tone)   Grave (Low tone)
    /   -   \
    Á   Ā   À

In pronunciation, tone distinguishes pitch level of a syllable. These are examples of their usage in the Igbo language:

ákwá	-	cry	[high tone – high tone]
àkwá	-	egg	[low tone – high tone]
àkwà	-	bridge/bed	[low tone – low tone]
ákwà	-	cloth	[high tone – low tone]
ísí	-	head	[high tone – high tone]
ìsì	-	blindness	[low tone – low tone]
ísì	-	smell	[high tone – low tone]
ìsí	-	to cook	[low tone – high tone]
óké	-	male	[high tone – high tone]
òkè	-	portion	[low tone – low tone]
ókè	-	boundary	[high tone – low tone]
òké	-	rat/mouse	[low tone – high tone]
ḿmā	-	good/beautiful	[high tone – mid tone]
ḿmà	-	knife	[high tone – low tone]

Igbo Consonants:

In the alphabet system, consonants are a somewhat easier concept to represent than vowels. A consonant involves some part of the tongue or lips touching or coming close to some other part of the mouth — lips, teeth, roof of the mouth in various places. The consonant system of Igbo language has major features, namely: doubly articulated consonants and labialized Velars.

<u>*Doubly articulated consonants*</u>: these are consonants with two simultaneous places of articulation – *bilabial* and *velar*. Bilabial and velar are produced in the same manner. Both of them are

produced as stops. /k͡p/ and /g͡b/ are the two examples of bilabial and velar. One can pronounce these sounds, by trying to say [k] or [g], with close lips as one would for [p] or [b].

Labialized velar or labiovelar: is a velar consonant that is labialized, with a /w/-like secondary articulation. Secondary articulation occurs when the articulation of a consonant is equivalent to the combined articulations of two or three simpler consonants, at least one of which is an approximant. Maledo (2011) defines secondary articulation as the superimposition of lesser stricture upon a primary articulation. Common examples are [kʷ, gʷ, xʷ, ŋʷ], which are pronounced like a [k, g, x, ŋ], with rounded lips, such as the labialized voiceless velar plosive [kʷ]. The three labialized velars in Igbo language falls between voiced stop, fricative voiceless and nasals. They are /kʷ/, /gʷ/ and /ŋʷ/. To produce these sounds, one would need to try pronouncing [k], [g] or [ng] with rounded lips.

Upper case	*Lower case*	*Phoneme*	*English*	*Igbo*
B	b	/b/	*bat*	bia
CH	ch	/t͡ʃ/	*chop*	chi
D	d	/d/	*dot*	dee
F	f	/f/	*fat*	fee
G	g	/g/	*go*	gi
GB	gb	/g͡b/	*jaw*	agba
GH	gh	/ɣ/	*war*	agha
GW	gw	/gʷ/	*ling<u>u</u>ine*	gwa
H	h	/ɦ/	*happy*	ha
J	j	/d͡ʒ/	*job*	njem
K	k	/k/	*key*	kele
KP	kp	/k͡p/ -	*left (hand)*	ekpe
KW	kw	/kʷ/	*<u>q</u>ueenie*	kwere
L	l	/l/	*lie*	Lee
M	m	/m/	*me*	mu
N	n	/n/	*never*	nne
Ṅ	ṅ	/ŋ/	*song*	aṅụ
NW	nw	/ŋʷ/	*winter*	nwere
NY	ny	/ɲ/	*canyon*	nye
P	p	/p/	*pet*	pụta
R	r	/ɹ/	*rent*	rie
S	s	/s/	*sit*	sara
SH	sh	/ʃ/	*shop*	ịsha
T	t	/t/	*tell*	teta
V	v	/v/	*vet*	vum

W	w	/w/	*wet*	*were*
Y	y	/j/	*yet*	*ya*
Z	z	/z/	*zag*	*zaa*

Igbo Vowels:

The sound inventory of Standard Igbo consists of eight vowels. Igbo vowels are divided into two major mutual exclusive groups. Group "aịọụ" are referred to as light vowels, and group "a" while group eiou are known as heavy vowels and "e" group. The heavy vowels "eiou" occur with advanced tongue root (+ATR) while the light vowels "aịọụ" occur with retracted tongue root (-ATR).

The vowel segments in +ATR group /eiou/ harmonize among themselves and those in the –ATR class /aịọụ/ harmonize among themselves during simple word formation (especially in the formation of simple nouns).

The vowel segments in +ATR group /eiou/ in a harmonized form:

àbàdà	*(abada cloth)*	ábúzù	*(cricket)*
áhíhíá	*(grasses)*	àkpà	*(bag)*
Ákpúkpá	*(scabies)*	átúrú	(sheep)
Ákwúkwó	*(book)*	Àzù	*(fish)*
Ákwà	*(egg)*	Àzúzú	*(catarrh)*
Ánú	*(meat)*	bịá	*(come)*
Gòté	*(buy)*	Ọkpụkpụ	*(bone)*
Ókpùrùkpù	*(lump)*	Òkúkò	*(chicken/fowl)*
Ónwú	*(death)*	Ózúzú	*(training)*
Úlò	*(house)*		

The vowel segments in -ATR group /eiou/ in a harmonized form:

égō	*(money)*	ègwúsí	*(melon)*
élū	*(top, up)*	érímérí	*(food)*
éwú	*(goat)*	ézè	*(king)*
ézē	*(teeth)*	Ógólógó	*(long, tall)*
Ókpórókō	*(stock fish)*	ókwú	*(speech/talk)*
Ólùlù	*(pit)*	Órírí	*(feast)*
Ósísí	*(tree/stick).*		

Igbo Vowel Harmony in Verb form:

bàtáwá	*come in*	bèté	*cut off*
bùtá (gbutu e)	*uproot*	fèé	*fly*
gaa	*go*	gbàwá	*runaway*
gbúbìté	*cut out*	gbúpù	*cut out*
gbùté	*cut out*	jèé	*go*
kpòtéwé	*collect*	mèé	*do*
nyèwé	*give*	nyùá	*excrete*
ríé	*eat*	rìwé	*eat on*
sàcháá	*wash*	sìé	*cook*
tútúà	*pick up*	zùtá	*buy*

There are areas where vowel harmony rules in Igbo language are violated. As a result, there are two main exceptions from Vowel Harmony Rules in Igbo Language. They are: Loan or Borrowed Words and compound words.

A. Vowel harmony violation via borrowed words, Examples:

Akpati	*box* (Yoruba)	Agidi	*Corn food* (Yoruba)
Àsháwó	*prostitute* (Yoruba)	Sájìn	*sergeant* (English)
Sójà	*soldier* (English)	ịchàfú	*chiffon* (French)
Osikápá	*chinkafa* (Hausa)	Òbàsì	(abasi God) (Efik)

The above words through socioeconomic interaction were either borrowed or coined from words obtained in different languages and introduced into Igbo language vocabularies.

B. Examples of vowel harmony violation via Compound Words or Compounding: Compound words or compounding are words which are formed by combining two simple words to form one word in Igbo languages. These are words formed through morphological indigenous resources. Words from different vowel classes can combine to form compound words and such words can never harmonize. Let us examine the formation of the following proper nouns in Igbo language and with their violation of vowel harmony rules.

a) Àdá + Òbì   Àdáóbì *(First daughter)*
b) Àdá + Ézè   Àdáèzè *(Princess)*
c) Ífé + Ómá   Íféómá *(Goodies/Good thing)*
d) Ísì + àkú   Ísíàkú *(head of wealth)*
e) Èké + ḿmā   Èkéḿmā *(good market day)*

9.2 Rhythm

Rhythm in speech refers to the temporal arrangement of syllables and stress patterns within spoken utterances, influencing the overall cadence and flow of language. It plays a crucial role in shaping the musicality and expressiveness of speech. Languages exhibit diverse rhythmic patterns, categorized into different types based on the organization of syllables and stress.

In stress-timed languages like English, syllables are organized around regular intervals of stressed beats. This means that stressed syllables occur at relatively uniform intervals, while unstressed syllables may vary in duration. English speakers tend to emphasize certain syllables within words and phrases, creating a rhythmic pattern characterized by alternating stressed and unstressed beats. This rhythmic structure contributes to the distinctive cadence and pacing of English speech.

Mora-timed languages, such as Japanese, base their rhythmic patterns on the duration of morae, which are units of time that may encompass a single syllable or a portion of it. In mora-timed languages, the timing of speech is determined by the duration of these morae rather than by stress patterns or syllable counts. This results in a rhythmic structure that is distinct from both stress-timed and syllable-timed languages, characterized by the rhythmic alternation of long and short morae.

Syllable-timed languages like Igbo and French distribute syllables more evenly in time, with each syllable occupying a relatively equal duration. This results in a smoother and more uniform rhythm compared to stress-timed languages. In syllable-timed languages, there is less variation in the duration of syllables, leading to a more consistent pace of speech.

Igbo language is classified as a syllable-timed language because it exhibits the characteristic of maintaining consistent timing or duration for each syllable during speech. This means that regardless of the complexity of the syllable in terms of the number of consonants or vowels it contains, each syllable tends to receive roughly equal time during pronunciation.

One of the key reasons for Igbo's classification as a syllable-timed language is its rhythmic structure. In Igbo, there's a tendency to pronounce each syllable with a consistent rhythm, without elongating or shortening individual syllables based on their internal complexity. This rhythmic consistency contributes to the syllable-timed nature of the language.

To further support the syllable-timed characteristic of Igbo, consider its very simple phonological structure, which consists of a few numbers of consonant-vowel (CV) and absence vowel-consonant (VC) pairs. Igbo has a more consistent rhythm throughout syllables than stress-timed languages, where timing is determined by word and phrase stress patterns.

Overall, Igbo language's rhythmic consistency and relatively basic syllable structure lead to its classification as a syllable-timed language, with each syllable receiving equal timing or length during speech, as seen in the examples above.

Here are examples illustrating the characteristics of syllable timing in Igbo language:

1. "nne" (mother)
In this word, each syllable "nn" and "e" receives roughly equal time or duration during speech. There's a consistent rhythm maintained between the two syllables, regardless of the fact that the first syllable contains two consonants and the second contains one vowel.

2. "nwa" (child)
Similarly, in the word "nwa," each syllable "nw" and "a" is pronounced with consistent timing, showcasing the syllable-timed characteristic of Igbo language.

3. "mmadụ" (person)
The word "mmadụ" exhibits syllable timing, as each syllable "mm," "a," and "dụ" receives approximately equal duration during speech, maintaining a consistent rhythm.

4. "ụmụ" (children)
In the plural form of "child," each syllable "ụ," "m," and "ụ" is pronounced with roughly equal timing, demonstrating the syllable-timed nature of Igbo language.

5. "mmanụ" (oil)
The word "agụ" follows the syllable timing pattern, where each syllable "mm" "a," and "nụ" is pronounced with consistent duration, regardless of the consonant cluster in the second syllable.

Overall, understanding the rhythmic patterns of languages provides insights into how speakers organize and structure their speech. It highlights the intricate interplay between syllables, stress, and timing in shaping the musicality and rhythm of spoken language.

9.3 Pitch Accents

Pitch accents refer to distinctive variations in pitch that are used to highlight specific words or syllables within an utterance, serving to convey lexical or pragmatic emphasis. These variations in pitch contribute to the prosodic prominence of certain elements in speech, aiding in the identification and interpretation of information structure and discourse focus.

Pitch accents essentially assist in indicating to listeners the significance or applicability of specific words or syllables in spoken language. They can highlight important details, serve as a sentence's focal point, or communicate attitudes and subtle meanings. Pitch modulation is a useful tool for speakers to highlight particular points in their speech and influence the listener's interpretation of what they are saying.

Different languages employ various pitch accent systems, each with its own set of rules and patterns. Some languages have fixed pitch accent patterns, where the placement and characteristics of pitch accents are determined by phonological or grammatical rules. In contrast, other languages have variable or lexically determined pitch accents, where the pitch pattern may vary depending on factors such as word stress, context, or speaker intent.

Pitch-Accent in Igbo Pitch accent manifests in two basic ways in Igbo (a) Lexically (b) phrasal/sentential form. The tonal phenomenon in Igbo that lends credence to the existence of pitch accent in Igbo language is the alternation of pitch, as it were, among grammatical structures.

For instance, for the declarative sentence the verb root must bear the low tone irrespective of their inherent tones. As can be seen in the future particle using the prefix 'ga'--'ga' must bear a low tone while the verb root to which it is prefixed retains its inherent tone.

In future tense:

    a. me'   gà-èmé   *'will do'*
    b. pú   gà-èpú   *'will germinate'*
    c. wè   gà-éwè   *'will take'*
    d. zà   gà-ázà   *'will sweep'*
    e. zú   gà-àzú   *'will buy'*

In past tense:

    a. Ó biàrà zúó, ríé, núó, láá.
He/she came bought, ate, drank (and) left.

    b. Yáá pùó, dàá, wùó, bàá ń'úlo.
He/she went out, fell, jumped (and) entered the house.

In the serialization of Igbo verbs there is also a fixed pitch pattern. As can be seen in the following examples; when the inherent tone on the verb root is high, its pitch is retained and followed by a high-toned suffix. On the other hand, when the inherent tone is low, it is followed by a high-toned suffix. For example:

In words:

    a. mé   mèé   *'to do'*

b. pú	pùrù	*'germinated'*
c. wè	wèré	*'take'*
d. zà	zàá	*'sweep'*
e. zụ	zùó	*'buy'*

In syllable/sentence:

a. mé	méghì	*'did not do'*
b. pú	púghì	*'did not germinate*
c. wè	wéghì	*'did not take'*
d. zá	zághì	*'did not sweep'*
e. zú	zúghì	*'did not buy'*

The above examples show that in each example the pitch makes a syllable prominent. It could be high or low, but it is predictable based on the syntactic structure of the utterance.

Pitch accents are an essential component of prosody in spoken language, facilitating the expression of meaning, emphasis, and pragmatic intent. They serve as valuable cues for listeners, helping them to interpret and comprehend spoken discourse more effectively.

5.4 Phrase Boundaries

Phrase boundaries serve as markers that delineate the boundaries between syntactic units or intonational phrases within spoken language. These boundaries indicate pauses, rhythm breaks, and shifts in discourse structure, aiding in the segmentation of continuous speech into meaningful units and facilitating comprehension and interpretation for listeners.

In essence, phrase boundaries play a pivotal role in structuring spoken discourse, helping to organize information and guide the listener's understanding of the speaker's intended message. They often coincide with prosodic cues, which are elements of speech that convey additional information beyond the literal meaning of words. Such prosodic cues include pitch resets, lengthening of final syllables, and changes in intonation contour.

In written language, phrase boundaries are typically denoted by punctuation marks such as commas, periods, and question marks. However, in spoken language, these boundaries are realized through a combination of prosodic features and contextual cues. For example, in Igbo, a rising intonation and a slight pause frequently signal the end of an intonational phrase, while a falling intonation typically marks the completion of a declarative statement.

The following are examples of phrase boundaries in Igbo language:

1. "Ọ hụrụ ụgbọ oloko." (He saw a train)
In this example, "Ọ hụrụ" (He saw) and " ụgbọ oloko" (a train) represent two distinct syntactic units, with a pause or rhythm break between them indicating a phrase boundary.

2. " Nwanyị nke ọzọ gara ahịa." (The other woman went to the market)
Here, "Nwaanyị nke ọzọ" (The other woman) and " gara ahịa" (went to the market) are separated by a pause or rhythm break, indicating the boundary between two intonational phrases.

3. " Ọ ga-alụ ezigbo nwaanyị." (He will marry a good woman)
The phrase boundary occurs between " Ọ ga-alụ" (He will marry) and "ezigbo nwaanyị" (good woman), marking the end of one syntactic unit and the beginning of another.

4. " Nri ahụ na-esi ísì ụtọ" (That food smells good)
In this example, " Nri ahụ" (That food), "na-esi" (smells) and " ísì ụtọ" (good smell) are separated by a pause or rhythm break, indicating a phrase boundary.

5. "Esi m ebe a" (I am from here)
The phrase boundary occurs between "Esi m" (I am) and "ebe a" (from here), marking the transition between two syntactic units.

6. " Ọ hụrụ nwoke ahụ." (He saw the man)
Here, "Ọ hụrụ" (He saw) and "nwoke ahụ" (the man) are separated by a pause or rhythm break, indicating a phrase boundary.

7. " Nwunye m ga-esi nri." (My wife will cook)
The phrase boundary occurs between "Nwunye m" (My wife) and "ga-esi nri" (will cook), marking the end of one syntactic unit and the beginning of another.

8. " Enweghị m ego." (I don't have money)
In this example, " Enweghị m" (I don't have) and "ego" (money) are separated by a pause or rhythm break, indicating a phrase boundary.

9. " Ọ bụ onyeisi oche obodo anyị." (He is the chairman of our community)
The phrase boundary occurs between "Ọ bụ ya bụ" (He is the); "onyeisi oche" (chairman) and " obodo anyị" (our community), marking the transition between three syntactic units.

10. " Ọ gwara m na ọ dịghị mma." (He told me that it's not good)

Here, "Ọ gwara m" (He told me) and "na ọ dịghị mma." (that it's not good) are separated by a pause or rhythm break, indicating a phrase boundary.

In each of these examples, the phrase boundaries serve to demarcate the boundaries between syntactic units or intonational phrases within spoken Igbo language, facilitating comprehension and interpretation for listeners by segmenting continuous speech into meaningful units.

By marking the junctures between syntactic units or intonational phrases, phrase boundaries help to maintain the flow and coherence of spoken discourse. They allow speakers to convey complex ideas and convey nuanced meanings while ensuring that listeners can effectively process and comprehend the information being communicated. Overall, understanding and recognizing phrase boundaries are essential skills for both speakers and listeners in navigating the dynamics of spoken communication.

Tthe components of prosody—intonation, rhythm, pitch accents, and phrase boundaries—provides valuable insights into the expressive, pragmatic, and communicative functions of speech, enriching our comprehension of spoken language structure and interpretation.

Exercise

1. What are supra-segmental phonemes, and how do they contribute to the structure and meaning of speech?
2. Explain the concept of stress in phonology and provide examples from Igbo language.
3. How does intonation affect the expression of emotions and grammatical functions in spoken language?
4. Describe the role of duration in prosody and its significance in speech perception and interpretation.
5. What are contour tones, and how do they function in tone languages like Igbo?
6. Can you explain the three tones in Igbo and their phonemic distinctions?
7. What are doubly articulated consonants, and how do they differ from other consonants?
8. Explain the concept of vowel harmony in Igbo language and provide examples.
9. How does rhythm in speech differ across stress-timed, mora-timed, and syllable-timed languages?
10. Provide examples of phrase boundaries in Igbo language and explain their significance in spoken discourse.
11. How do pitch accents help in conveying lexical or pragmatic emphasis in speech?
12. Describe the manifestations of pitch accent in Igbo language, both lexically and in phrasal form.
13. What are some of the exceptions to vowel harmony rules in Igbo language, and why do they occur?
14. Can you explain the rhythmic patterns observed in stress-timed, mora-timed, and syllable-timed languages?
15. How do speakers indicate phrase boundaries in spoken language, and why are they important for comprehension?
16. Provide examples of how intonation patterns can convey various meanings and functions in spoken language.
17. What role do pitch accents play in highlighting important details or attitudes in speech?
18. How does the rhythmic consistency of Igbo contribute to its classification as a syllable-timed language?
19. Explain the concept of compound words violating vowel harmony rules in Igbo language.
20. How do prosodic features like intonation, rhythm, pitch accents, and phrase boundaries enrich our understanding of spoken language structure and interpretation?

Chapter 10

The organ of speech

10.1 Organ of Speech (Njiakpọ Okwu)
An organ is a part of an organism that is typically self-contained and has a specific vital function. Speech organs also known as vocal organs are the various organs which are involved in the production of speech sounds. The study of speech organs helps us to determine the role of each organ in the production of speech sounds. The organs of speech can be divided into three systems:

1. The respiratory system
2. The phonatory system
3. The articulatory system

9.1.1 The respiratory system **(Ọwa Nkuume)**:
This comprises of the lungs, the muscles of the chest and the windpipe. There are three air-stream mechanisms of the respiratory system. They are: Pulmonic (Ingressive & Egressive), Glottalic (Pharyngeal) and Velaric (Oral air-stream mechanism).

10.1.1. *Pulmonic airstream* (Akpọmụda Nsinangụ): Most speech sounds are produced by pushing lung air out of the body through the mouth and sometimes also through the nose. Since lung air is used, these sounds are called pulmonic sounds; since the air is pushed out, they are called egressive.

Pulmonic ingressive describes ingressive sounds in which the airstream is created by the lungs. These are generally considered paralinguistic. They may be found as phonemes, words, and entire phrases on all continents and in genetically-unrelated languages, most frequently in sounds for agreement and back channeling.

10.1.2, *Glottalic airstream mechanism* (Akpọmụda Nsineeko) involves the movement of pharynx air by the action of the glottis. An upward movement of the closed glottis will move the air out of the mouth; a downward movement of the closed glottis will cause air to be sucked into the mouth.

10.1.3. *Velaric airstream mechanism* (Akpọmụda Nsinaakpo) involves the movement of mouth air by action of the tongue. There is a velar closure formed by raising the back of the tongue when using the velaric airstream mechanism. The movement of lung air by the respiratory muscles. Most sounds are produced with a pulmonic airstream (Akpọmụda Nsinàngù) mechanism.

10.1.2 The phonatory system:
This comprises the larynx. The larnyx is situated at the top of the wind pipe and the air from the lungs. The air from the lungs has to pass through the wind pipe and the larynx. In the larynx there is a lip-like structure called the vocal cords or vocal folds—but "folds" is a more accurate description of what they're actually like.

The larynx or voice box is the basis for all the sounds we produce. It modified the airflow to produce different frequencies of sound. By changing the shape of the vocal tract and airflow, we are able to produce all the phonemes of spoken language.

There are two basic categories of sound that can be classified in terms of the way in which the flow of air through the vocal tract is modified. Phonemes that are produced without any obstruction to the flow of air are called vowels. Phonemes that are produced with some kind of modification to the airflow are called consonants. Of course, nature is not as clear-cut as all that and we do make some sounds that are somewhere in between these two categories. These are called semivowels and are usually classified alongside consonants as they behave similar to them.

The opening between the vocal folds (when it exists) is called the **glottis**. Sounds produced with wide-open glottis are called voiceless sounds (Udaogbi), e.g: peel, ten, thin, etc. Sounds produced when the vocal cords vibrate are called voiced sounds (ụdamputa), eg: bead, judge, zoo, etc.

10.1.3 The articulatory system:
This comprises of the nose, the teeth, the tongue, the roof of the mouth and the lips. The roof of the mouth comprises the teeth-ridge, the hard palate, the soft palate and the uvula.

Since the production of consonants requires modification to the airflow, unlike vowels, an obstruction is produced by bringing some parts of the vocal tract into contact. These places of contact are known as places of articulation. There are a number of places of articulation for the lips, teeth, and tongue. Sometimes the articulators touch each other as in the case of the two lips coming together to produce [b]. At other times, two articulators come into contact as when the lower lip folds back into the upper teeth to produce [f]. The tongue can touch different parts of the vocal tract to produce a variety of consonants by touching the teeth, the alveolar ridge, hard palate or soft palate (or velum).

10.2 The Tongue (Ire):

The tongue is the most important articulator of speech. This muscle is extremely strong, as it must move food around in our mouths as we chew. The tongue is a large muscular structure that nearly fills the oral cavity. The tongue is not one large muscle as some might suppose but consists of several muscles grouped as intrinsic and extrinsic tongue muscles. The tongue is able to produce incredibly fine and complex movements, by either directing the breath stream during consonant production or elevating and lowering to form a resonance vessel for vowel sounds.

In Igbo speech sound, the tongue can be divided into the front (ihu ire); which lies underneath the hard palate when the tongue is at rest, the center (ùgbò ire); which is partly beneath the hard palate and partly beneath the soft palate; and the back (àzụ ire); which is beneath the soft palate; and the root, which is opposite the back wall of the pharynx. The tip is the extreme end of the tongue. The blade lies opposite the alveolar ridge. The front lies opposite the hard palate. And the back lies opposite the *soft palate*/velum (akpo ime).

The tongue is responsible for the production of many speech sounds since it can move very fast to different places and is also capable of assuming different shapes. The shape and the position of the tongue are crucial for the production of vowel sounds. Thus, when we describe the vowel sounds in the context of the function of the tongue, we generally consider the following criteria:

Tongue Height: this is concerned with the vertical distance between the upper surface of the tongue and the *hard palate* (akpọime). With this condition, vowels can be described as close and open.

Tongue Frontness / Backness: this is concerned with the part of the tongue between the front and the back, which is raised high. From this point of view, the vowel sounds can be classified as front vowels and back vowels. By changing the shape of the tongue we can produce vowels in which a different part of the tongue is the highest point. That means a vowel having the back of the tongue as the highest point is a back vowel, whereas the one having the front of the tongue as the highest point is called a front vowel.

For speech sound to resonate effectively, the less tongue root tension (i.e. tension in the *extrinsic* muscles of the tongue), the better. For speech you want to relax the tongue up and forward, the opposite of swallowing.

10.3 The lips (Egbugbere Ọnụ):

The lips play a role in changing the resonance of different speech sounds. Human beings are **Bilabial** (two lips)—lower lip and upper lip. A bilabial sound is produced by using both lips pressed together. By altering the shape of our lips we can form different speech sounds. For instance, for plosive sounds such as /p/ and /b/ the lips are compressed and then opened to produce a rapid, explosive release of the breath stream. Also, the lips and *teeth* (eze) can interact to produce speech sound. This is known as Labiodental (lips and teeth) articulation. A labiodental sound is produced by placing the upper teeth on the lower lip. There are two common labiodental sounds: [f] voiceless (Udaogbi) and [v] voiced.

10.4 The lungs (Ngụ):

The lungs are two elastic sacs in the chest that draw in air (mainly to oxygenate the blood). To initiate speech, they push air back up through the windpipe towards the voice box. When air from the lungs reaches the larynx (through *respiration system* (Ọwa Nkuume)), the vocal folds may be held open to allow the air to pass through or may vibrate to make a sound (phonation). The airflow from the lungs is then shaped by the articulators in the mouth and nose (articulation).

10.5 The Uvular (Àshà/Nkọlọ):

This is the small fleshy mass that hangs from the back of the velum; at the entrance to the throat. Uvular is a place of articulation where the passive articulator is the uvula. A uvular can also be a specific consonant made at that place of articulation often with the back of the tongue against or near the uvula, that is, further back in the mouth than velar consonants.

10.6 The teeth (Eze):

Human teeth are crucial in the making of speech sound. Speech sounds are complex and they are produced using our teeth, lips, tongue and vocal cords. Some sounds such as vowels are formed without using teeth or lips, but many sounds rely solely on the contact between our lips and teeth or our tongue and our teeth. Human teeth help form words by controlling airflow out of the mouth. Also, our tongue strikes our teeth or the roof of our mouth as some sounds are made.

Missing molars and premolars won't affect your speech too much, but if you have any front teeth missing, you may struggle to pronounce certain sounds. If a child has lost their front teeth, then we would expect his speech sound to 'sound a little different. In general, the loss of teeth leads to an articulation difference. Teeth are needed for a variety of sounds we use in the Igbo language, like the **"sh"** sound in **"Ịsha,"** the **"f"** in **"Ifeọma,"** the **"s"** in **"Sìrì,"** and the **"ch"** in **"Chibụeze."**

Exercise

1. What are speech organs, and why are they important in the production of speech sounds?
2. Describe the three systems involved in the production of speech sounds.
3. How does the respiratory system contribute to speech production?
4. Explain the three air-stream mechanisms of the respiratory system.
5. What distinguishes pulmonic ingressive sounds from other types of speech sounds?
6. How does the glottalic airstream mechanism function in speech production?
7. What role does the velaric airstream mechanism play in speech sounds?
8. How does the phonatory system contribute to the production of speech sounds?
9. What is the significance of the larynx in speech production?
10. Distinguish between voiceless and voiced sounds in terms of the glottis.
11. What is the articulatory system, and what does it consist of?
12. How do consonants differ from vowels in terms of airflow modification?
13. Explain the concept of places of articulation in speech production.
14. What role do the tongue, teeth, and lips play in the articulatory system?
15. How does the tongue contribute to speech production?
16. Describe the different parts of the tongue and their functions in speech.
17. What criteria are used to describe vowel sounds in terms of the tongue's position?
18. How do the lips contribute to changing the resonance of speech sounds?

Chapter 11

Place of Articulation (Ebe Mkpọpụta Ụda)

As earlier explained, the standard Igbo alphabet (I*Mkpụrụ Edemede Igbo*), otherwise known as the Abịịdịị Igbo, is made up of 36 letters, which includes only a 23-letter set of the ISO basic Latin alphabet with the exemption of C, Q, and X, which are not part of Abidịị Igbo.

The 36-letter alphabet (*Mkpụrụ Edemede* or *Abidịị*) has 28 consonants (*mgbochiume*) and 8 vowels (*ụdaume*). Igbo alphabet uses the diacritics (a dot, an overline, overscore, or overbar above) on the letter Ṅ or Ñ, and the dot below three of the eight vowels; Ị, Ọ and Ụ.

A	B	CH	D	E	F	G	GB	GH	GW	H	I	Ị
J	K	KP	KW	L	M	N	Ṅ	NW	NY	O	Ọ	P
R	S	SH	T	U	Ụ	V	W	Y	Z			

The 36-letter alphabet (*Mkpụrụ Edemede* or *Abidịị*) has the grapheme of Igbo Phoneme as shown below:

a	b	t͡ʃ	d	e	f	g	g͡b	ɣ	gʷ	ɦ	i	ɪ
d͡ʒ	k	k͡p	kʷ	l	m	n	ŋ	ŋʷ	ɲ	o	ọ	p
ɹ	s	ʃ	t	u	ụ	v	w	j	z			

As already explained, a phoneme (mkpụrụụdasụsụ) is a unit of sound that can distinguish one word from another in a particular language. It is represented by one or more grapheme. A grapheme is a letter or a number of letters that represent the sounds in our speech. So a grapheme will be the letter/ letters that represent a phoneme.

Having given a brief background, let us look at the subject of speech articulation. The location at which two speech organs approach or come together to produce a speech sound; as in the contact of the tongue and the teeth to form a dental sound; is called *the place of articulation*. It is also called point of articulation.

11.1 Structure of Place of Articulation diagram

(Ihe osise njiakpọ okwu)

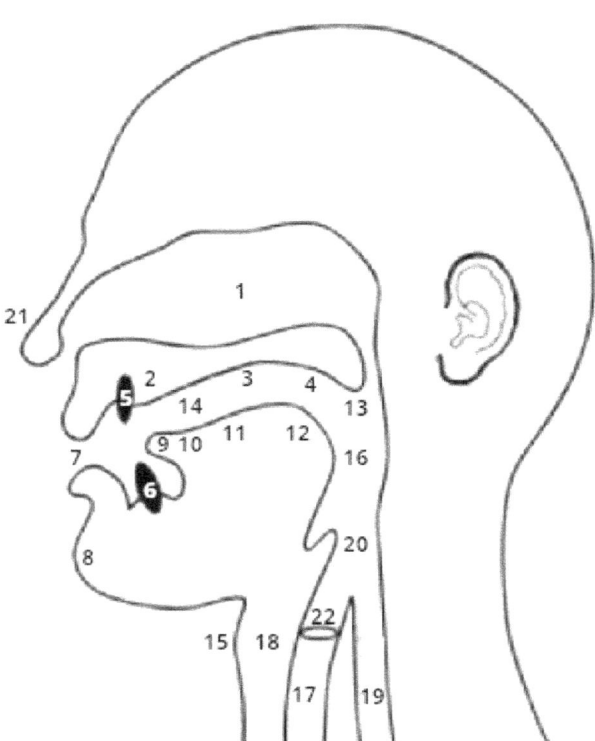

List of the parts shown (Aha na mkpọpụta ihe osise)

English   **Igbo**
1. *Nasal cavity*   Uju imi
2. *Alveolar ridge*   Anyụrụ
3. *Hard palate*   Akpo ihu

4. *Velum/soft palate* — Akpo ime
5. *Upper Teeth* — Eze elu
6. *Lower teeth* — Eze ala
7. *Lips* — Egbugbere Ọnụ
8. *Jaw* — Agba
9. *Tongue tip* — Ọnụ ire
10. *Front of tongue* — Ihu ire
11. *Blade of tongue* — Ugbo ire
12. *Back of Tongue* — Azụ ire
13. *Uvula* — Ụvụla
14. *Oral/Buccal Cavity* — Uju Ọnụ
15. *Adam's apple* — Eko akpịrị
16. *Pharynx* — Nkọlọ
    a. *Trachea/Wind pipe* — Opi akpịrị
    b. *Larynx* — Ogworo
    c. *Esophagus* — Ọwa nri
    d. *Epiglottis* — Asha
    e. *Nose* — Imi
    f. *Vocal cord* — Mkpọụda

Larynx comprises: Epiglottis, Supraglottis, Vocal cord, Glottis and Subglottis. Vocal folds are two thick flaps of muscle rather like a pair of lips. **Pharynx** is a tube which begins just above the larynx. **Soft palate/velum** allows air to pass through the nose and through the mouth. Hard palate is the roof of the mouth. **Alveolar ridge** is between the top front teeth and the hard palate. The **tongue** has the capacity to move into different places and form different shapes. The **tongue root** (Ukwu ire) is the part at the far back and bottom of the tongue, forming the front wall of the pharynx. **Nasal cavity** is a large air-filled space above and behind the nose in the middle of the face. **An oral cavity** is the part of the mouth behind the gums and teeth that is bounded above by the hard and soft palates and below by the tongue. Lips are the two soft edges at the opening to the mouth.

11.2 Place of Vowel Articulation (Ebe Mkpoputa Udaume)

Igbo language oral vowel phonemes are made up of eight vowels. The letters that make up the Igbo vowels are:

a   e   i   o   u   ị   ọ   ụ

The graphemes that made up the Igbo vowels are:

a   e   i   o   u   ị   ọ   ụ

The vowels articulation chart is a way of showing the mouth and different positions of the tongue when a vowel sound is produced. The chart below shows the grapheme of Igbo vowels.

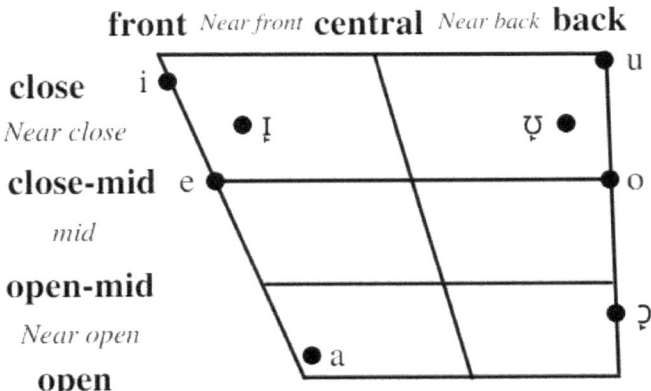

The vowels articulation transcription chart in English is shown below:

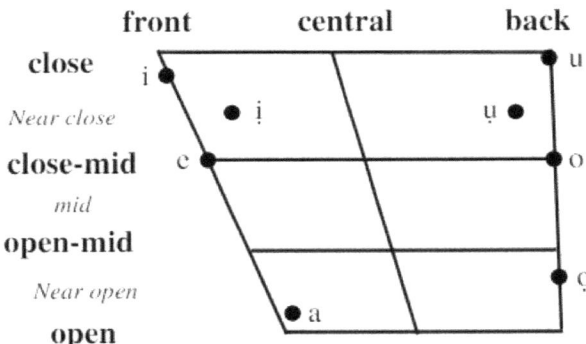

The vowels articulation transcription chart in Igbo is shown below:

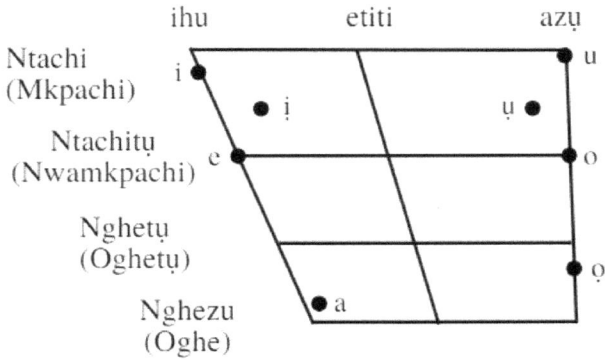

From the above vowel articulation chart, the following are the breakdown of the Igbo vowel articulation.

11.2.1 Front Vowels (Ụdaume ihu)
Front vowels located at the left-hand-side of the chart refer to vowels articulated towards the front of the mouth. To produce these vowels, the tongue rolls forward towards the front position of the mouth. This can either refer to vowels that are more front than central or, more rarely, only to fully front vowels, i.e. the ones that are articulated as far forward as possible in the mouth. For example:

Close (Ntachi/Mkpachi)	*pronounces*	/i/.
Near Close-mid (Ntachitụ/Nwamkpachi)	*pronounces*	/ị/.
Near Open (Nghetụ/Oghetụ)	*pronounces*	/e/.
Open (Nghezu/Oghe)	*pronounces*	/a/.

11.2.2 Back Vowels (Ụdaume Azụ)
Back vowels refer to vowels that are articulated as back as possible in the mouth. To produce back vowels, the tongue tends to pull back. For example:

Close (Ntachi/Mkpachi)	*pronounces*	/u/.
Close-mid (Ntachitụ/Nwamkpachi)	*pronounces*	/ụ/.
Open-mid (Nghetụ/Oghetụ)	*pronounces*	/o/.
Open (Nghezu/Oghe)	*pronounces*	/ọ/.

11.2.3 Close and Close-mid Vowels (Ụdaume Ntachi/Mkpachi na Ntachitụ/Nwamkpachi)
Close vowels are a class of vowel sounds that is produced, during articulation, when the tongue is positioned as close as possible to the roof of the mouth as it can be without creating a constriction. A constriction would produce a sound that would be classified as a consonant. The two vowels involved are: /i/ and /u/.

A close-mid vowel (also mid-close vowel, high-mid vowel, mid-high vowel or half-close vowel) is any in a class of vowel sound produced when the tongue is positioned one third of the way from a close vowel to an open vowel. The two vowels involved are: /ị/ and /ụ/.

Examples of tabular representation:

Articulation	*Front (Ihu)*	*Back (Azụ)*
Close (Ntachi/Mkpachi)	/i/	/u/
Close-mid (Ntachitụ/Nwamkpachi)	/ị/	/ụ/

11.3.4 Near Open and Open Vowels (Nghetụ (Oghetụ) na Nghezu (Oghe))

Open-mid vowel is a class of vowel sounds that is produced, during articulation, when the tongue is positioned between an open vowel (a low vowel) and a near open vowel. For example: /a/ and /ọ/. Open vowels are vowels that are more open than a mid-vowel. Examples of open vowels are:/a/ and /ọ/

Examples:

Articulation	*Front (Ihu)*	*Back (Azụ)*
Near open (Nghetụ/Oghetụ)	/e/	/o/
Open (Nghezu/Oghe)	/a/	/ọ/

11.3 Place of consonants articulation (Ebe Mkpoputa Mgbochiume).

The consonant sounds are produced with partial or total obstruction to the flow of air coming through the lungs to the mouth. In the production of the consonant sounds, the opening and close of the glottis is key. When the glottis (the opening between the vocal cords) is wide open, there is no vibration in the voice box, and this results in the production of voiceless consonant sounds (Udaogbi Mgbochiume). When the glottis is narrow (almost closed), there is a vibration in the voice box therefore the sounds being produced are voiced consonant sounds (ụdamputa Mgbochiume).

Consonants are speech sound that is characterized by an <u>articulation</u> with a closure or narrowing of the vocal tract such that a complete or partial blockage of the flow of air is produced. Consonants are usually classified according to ***place of articulation*** (the location of the stricture made in the vocal tract, such as dental, bilabial, or velar), ***the manner of articulation*** (the way in which the obstruction of the airflow is accomplished, as in stops, fricatives, approximants, trills, taps, and laterals), and ***the presence or absence of <u>voicing</u>, nasalization, <u>aspiration</u>, or other phonation.***

There are 28 letters as well as grapheme of Igbo consonants. The letter are as follows:

b	ch	d	f	g	gb	gh	gw	h	j	k
kp	kw	l	m	n	nw	ny	ṅ	p	r	s
sh	t	v	w	y	z					

The grapheme of Igbo consonants are as follows:

b	t͡ʃ	d	f	g	g͡ɓ	ɣ	gʷ	ɦ	d͡ʒ	k
k͡p	kʷ	l	m	n	ŋ	ŋʷ	ɲ	p	ɹ	s
ʃ	t	v	w	j	z					

11.4 Consonants Phoneme's chart

Manner of Articulation	VOICING	THE PLACE OF ARTICULATION							
		Bilabial	Labiodental	Alveolar	Palatoalveolar	Velar		Labial Velar	Glottal
						Plain	Labial		
STOP	Voiced	b		d		g	gʷ	gɓ	
	Voiceless	p		t		k	kʷ	kp	
AFFRICATE	Voiceless				tʃ				
	Voiced				dʒ				
FRICATIVE	Voiceless		f	s	ʃ				
	Voiced		v	z		ɣ			ɦ
GLIDE	Voiced					j		w	
NASAL	Voiced	m		n	ɲ	ŋ	ŋʷ		
RHOTIC	Voiced			ɹ					
LATERAL	Voiced			l					

11.5 Consonants Alphabet's chart

Manner of Articulation	VOICING	Bilabial	Labiodental	Alveolar	Palatoalveolar	Velar Plain	Velar Labial	Labial Velar	Glottal
STOP	Voiced	b		d		g	gw	gb	
STOP	Voiceless	p		t		k	kw	kp	
AFFRICATE	Voiceless				ch				
AFFRICATE	Voiced				j				
FRICATIVE	Voiceless		f	s	sh				
FRICATIVE	Voiced		v	z		gh			h
GLIDE	Voiced					y		w	
NASAL	Voiced	m		n	ny	ṅ	nw		
RHOTIC	Voiced			r					
LATERAL	Voiced			l					

THE PLACE OF ARTICULATION

Chaati Mkpoputa Uda Mgbochiume

Mkpuru Uda Mgbochiume

Usoro Mkpoputa Mgbochiume	Ebe Mkpoputa	Egbugbere Onu abuo	Egbugbere na Eze	Egbugbere na Akpo	Akpo ihu	Akpo ime	Anyuri na Akpo	Akpiri (Eko)
UDAIKE	Kendakpu							
	Keokporo (Kendaputa)	p b				k g	t d	
	Kemkponegbugbere	gb kp						
UDARII	Keokporo	w						
UDAYII	keegbugberenaakpo				y		r	
UDAIMI	Keokporo	m			ny	ṅ	n	
	Kemkponeegbugbere					nw		
UDALII	Keanvurunaakpo						l	
UDACHII	Kemkponaakpo				ch j			
UDASHII	Keokporo		f v		sh	gh	s z	h

Exercise

1. Explain the concept of phonemes and graphemes in the context of speech sounds.
2. Define the term "place of articulation" and its importance in speech production.
3. Provide a breakdown of the parts involved in the structure of place of articulation.
4. Describe the components of the larynx and their functions in speech production.
5. What role does the soft palate/velum play in speech articulation?
6. Explain the significance of the tongue root in articulating speech sounds.
7. How are front vowels articulated and provide examples of front vowels in Igbo.
8. Define back vowels and give examples of back vowels in Igbo.
9. Differentiate between close and close-mid vowels, providing examples for each.
10. What are near open and open vowels and provide examples from the Igbo language.
11. Explain the process of producing consonant sounds and the role of the glottis.
12. How are consonants classified in terms of place of articulation?
13. Provide examples of consonant sounds produced at different places of articulation.
14. Describe the manner of articulation and give examples of different types of consonant sounds.
15. What factors determine whether a consonant sound is voiced or voiceless?
16. How do nasalization and aspiration affect consonant sounds in speech production?
17. Explain the significance of the consonant phoneme's chart in understanding Igbo speech sounds.
18. Describe the consonant alphabet's chart and its role in representing Igbo speech sounds.

Chapter 12

Articulatory Phonetics (Amụmàmụ Mkpọpụta Ụdaasụsụ)

The 28 consonant phonemes of Igbo language are categorized into:

- 10 oral stops {/p, b, t, d, k, g, kʷ, gʷ, k͡p and g͡ɓ/}
- 5 nasal stops {/m, n, ɲ, ŋ and ŋʷ /}
- 2 affricates {/ t͡ʃ, d͡ʒ/} and
- 7 fricatives {/f, v, s, z, ʃ, ɣ and h/}
- 2 glides {/j and w/}
- 1 Approximant central rhotic {/ɹ/} and
- 1 Approximant lateral {/l/}

When there is vibration, the sounds produced are called **voiced consonant sounds (ụdampụta Mgbochiume)**. When there is no vibration, the sounds produced are called **voiceless consonant sounds (Udaogbi Mgbochiume)**.

- **The voiced consonants (ụdampụta Mgbochiume):** /n/ /m/ /l/ /j/ /ɲ/ /ŋʷ/ /ŋ/ /z/ /w/ /v/ /d͡ʒ/ /g/ /gʷ/ /g͡ɓ/ /d/ /b/ /ɦ/ /ɣ/ /ɹ/

- **The voiceless consonants (Ụdaogbi Mgbochiume):** /p/ /t/ /s/ /k/ /kʷ/ /k͡p/ /f/ /ʃ/ /t͡ʃ/

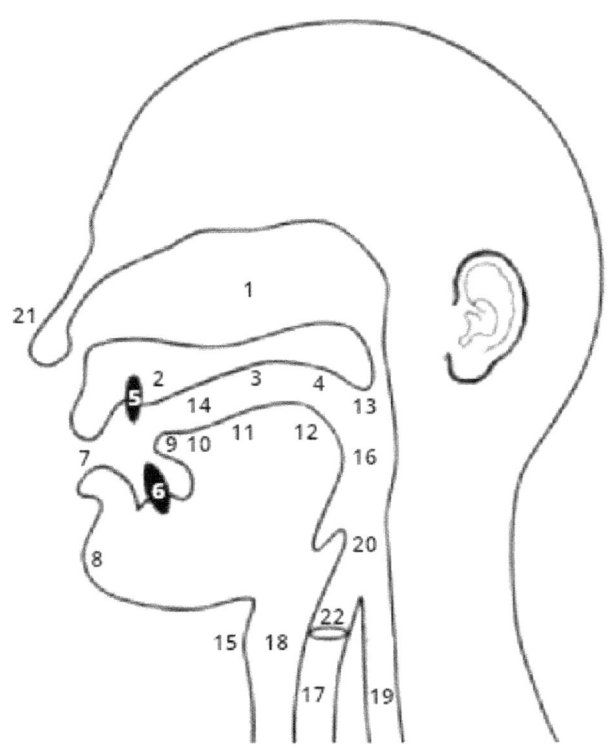

List of the parts shown (Aha na mkpọpụta ihe osise)

	English	**Igbo**
1.	*Nasal cavity*	Uju imi
2.	*Alveolar ridge*	Anyụrụ
3.	*Hard palate*	Akpo ihu
4.	*Velum/soft palate*	Akpo ime
5.	*Upper Teeth*	Eze elu
6.	*Lower teeth*	Eze ala
7.	*Lips*	Egbugbere Ọnụ
8.	*Jaw*	Agba
9.	*Tongue tip*	Ọnụ ire
10.	*Front of tongue*	Ihu ire
11.	*Blade of tongue*	Ugbo ire
12.	*Back of Tongue*	Azụ ire
13.	*Uvula*	Ụvụla
14.	*Oral/Buccal Cavity*	Uju Ọnụ
15.	*Adam's apple*	Eko akpịrị
16.	*Pharynx*	Nkọlọ

17. *Trachea/Wind pipe* — Opi akpịrị
18. *Larynx* — Ogworo
19. *Esophagus* — Ọwa nri
20. *Epiglottis* — Asha
21. *Nose* — Imi
22. *Vocal cord* — Mkpọụda

12.1 The Manner of consonant articulating:

The Manner of articulating the consonant sounds has to do with how the vocal tract (the oral cavity, nasal cavity, and pharynx) is narrowed or blocked during production. The manner of articulation is categorized into: **stops, fricatives, affricates, nasal, lateral, glide and rhotic.**

12.1.1 The stops (Ụdaike): - These are sounds produced with a total blockage of airflow or momentary blocking (occlusion) of some part of the oral cavity.

	Voiced	b	d	g	gw	gb
STOP	Voiceless (Udaogbi)	p	t	k	kw	kp

12.1.2 Fricative (Ụdashịị): - these consonant sounds are produced by bringing the mouth into position to block the passage of the airstream, but not making complete closure, so that air moving through the mouth generates audible friction.

	Voiceless (Udaogbi)	f	s	sh		
FRICATIVE	Voiced	v	Z		Gh	h

12.1.3 Affricate (Ụdachịị): - Affricates also called semiplosives are consonant sounds that begin as a stop (sound with complete obstruction of the breath stream) and concludes with a fricative (sound with incomplete closure and a sound of friction).

	Voiceless (Udaogbi)	ch
AFFRICATE	Voiced	j

12.1.4 Nasal (Ụdaimi): - Nasal, also called a nasal occlusive or nasal stop in contrast with an oral stop or nasalized consonant, is an occlusive consonant produced with a lowered velum, allowing air to escape freely through the nose. The vast majority of consonants are oral consonants.

NASAL	Voiced	m	N	ny	ṅ	Nw

12.1.5 Lateral (Ụdalịị): - lateral consonant sounds are produced by raising the tip of the tongue against the roof of the mouth so that the airstream flows past one or both sides of the tongue.

LATERAL	Voiced	L

12.1.6 Glides (Ụdayịị): Glides are speech sounds produced when the airstream is frictionless and is modified by the position of the tongue and the lips.

GLIDE	Voiced	y	w

12.1.7 Rhotic (Ụdarịị): Rhotic are consonant speech sounds produced when the front part of the tongue approaches the upper gum, or the tongue-tip is curled back towards the roof of the mouth ("retroflexion"). No or little friction can be heard, and there is no momentary closure of the vocal tract.

RHOTIC	Voiced	R

12.2 The process of speech production:

12.2.1 Bilabial sounds (Nke Egbugbere Ọnụ abụọ): Bilabial sounds involve the upper and lower lips. In the production of a bilabial sound, the lips come into contact with each other to form an effective constriction. The consonant sounds that belong to this group are:

$$m \quad b \quad kp \quad gb \quad p$$

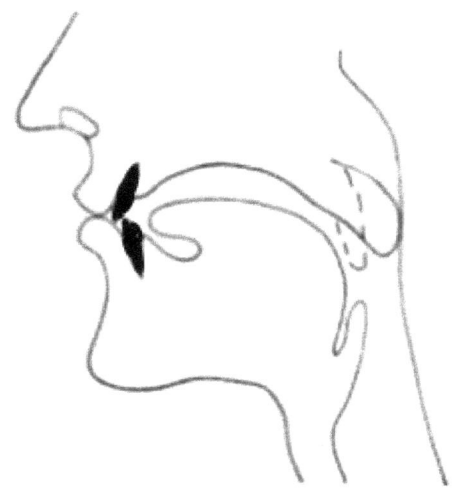

12.2.2 Labiodental sounds (Nke Egbugbere Ọnụ na Eze): Labiodental sounds involve the lower lip (labial) and upper teeth (dental) coming into contact with each other to form an effective constriction in the vocal tract. The consonant sounds that belong to this group are:

f and v

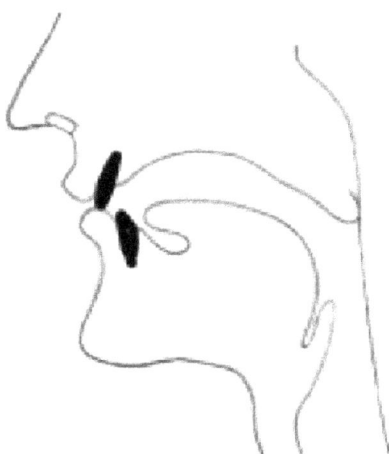

12.2.3 Alveolar (Nke Anyụrụ na Akpo): Alveolar consonants are consonant sounds that are produced with the tongue close to or touching the ridge behind the teeth on the roof of the mouth. The name comes from alveoli - the sockets of the teeth. The consonant sounds that belong to this group are:

d, t, s, z, n, r and l

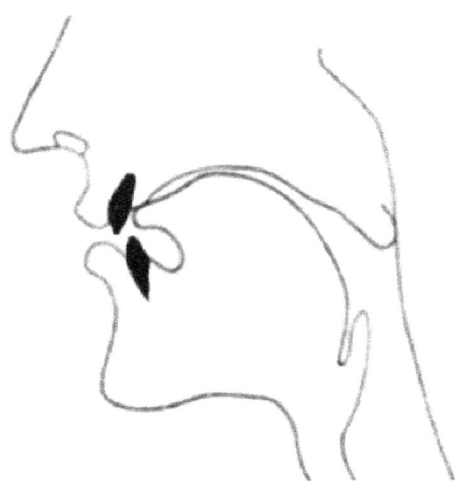

12.2.4 Palatoaveolar sound (Nke Akpo ihu na akpo ime): are consonant sounds produced by raising the blade, or front, of the tongue toward or against the hard palate just behind the alveolar ridge (the gums). The consonant sounds that belong to this group are:

    ch   j   sh   ny

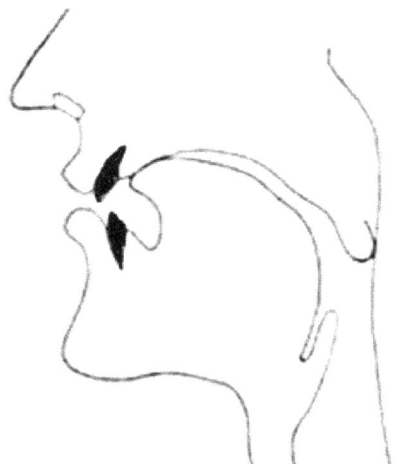

12.2.5 Velar (Egbugbere Ọnụ na Akpo): consonant that is pronounced with the back part of the tongue against the soft palate, also known as the velum, which is the back part of the roof of the mouth. The consonant sounds that belong to this group are divided into plain and labial subgroups.

    Plain: g   k   gh   y   ṅ

    Labial: gw   kw   nw

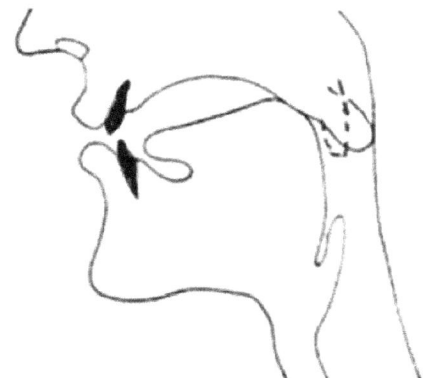

12.2.6 Labial Velar (Kemkpọnegbugbere Ọnụ): Truly doubly articulated labial-velars include the stops [k͡p, g͡b and w]. To pronounce them, one must attempt to say the velar consonants but then close their lips for the bilabial component, and then release the lips.

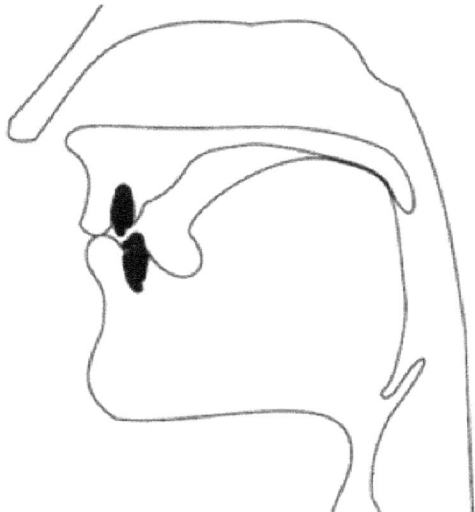

12.2.7 Glottal (Keekoapiri): Glottal sound is a sound produced when the air passes through the open space (glottis) between the vocal cords. It is the sound produced without the active use of the tongue and other part of the mouth. The consonant sound that belongs to this group is: /h/.

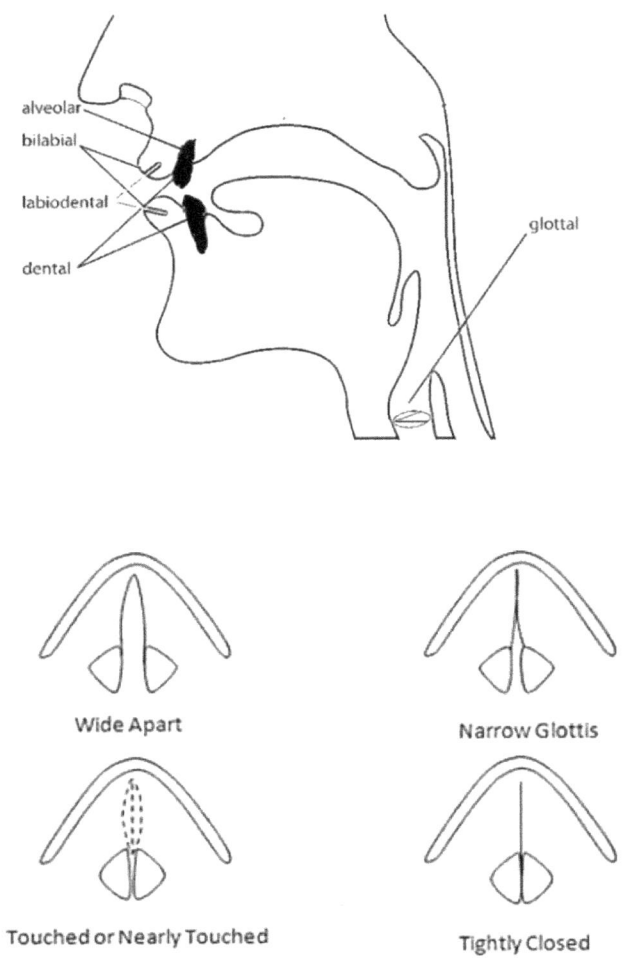

Four different states of the glottis adapted from Peter Roach.

12.3 Phonetic Transcription (Ndepụtagharị Mkpụrụụdaasụsụ Igbo)

Phonetic transcription (also known as phonetic script or phonetic notation) is the visual representation of speech sounds (or phones) by means of symbols. The most common type of phonetic transcription uses a phonetic alphabet, such as the International Phonetic Alphabet (IPA).

12.4. IPA in Igbo Phonetics

The International Phonetic Alphabet (IPA) was developed in the XIX century but is presently used for the modern language. The International Phonetic Alphabet is a system of symbols representing each sound used in the Igbo language. Linguists transcribe words in this alphabet for their research. Dictionaries use IPA to present the correct pronunciation of words. The two broad categories of International Phonetic Alphabet (IPA) are vowels and consonants.

IPA Chart and its usage

The IPA chart is a unique classification of sounds according to different aspects. There are 107 phonetic symbols and 52 diacritics in this phonemic transcription chart. Each of them represents its place in the mouth or throat. The manner in which sounds are pronounced depends on how lips, tongue, teeth and the palate work to produce them.

The IPA phonemes of Igbo language is used in transcription from Alphabet to Grapheme. The following is the representation of both with accompanying examples.

Upper case	Lower case	IPA phonemes	Examples
A	a	a	a*ka*, a*ku̞*
B	b	b	*b*ia, *b*uru
CH	ch	t͡ʃ	*ch*idi, *ch*im
D	d	d	*d*uru, *d*im
E	e	e	*e*ze, *e*de
F	f	f	*f*ere, *f*echi
G	g	g	*g*ini̞, *g*uru̞
GB	gb	g͡ɓ	*gb*ara, *gb*uru
GH	gh	ɣ	*gh*e, *gh*o̞ta
GW	gw	gʷ	*gw*a, *gw*o̞o̞
H	h	ɦ	*h*apu̞. *h*o̞ro̞
I	i	i	*i*te, *i*che
I̞	i̞	i̞	*i̞*gba, *i̞*chaka
J	j	d͡ʒ	*j*ere, *j*i
K	k	k	*k*ele, *k*ama
KP	kp	k͡p	*kp*akpando
KW	kw	kʷ	*kw*uru, *kw*ere
L	l	l	*l*ee, *l*eta
M	m	m	*m*ere, *m*ma
N	n	n	*n*na, *n*wa
Ṅ	ṅ	ŋ	a*ṅ*u̞, o̞*ṅ*u̞
NW	nw	ŋʷ	e*nw*e, o̞*nw*a
NY	ny	ɲ	*ny*e, e*ny*o
O	o	o	*o*sisi, *o*se
O̞	o̞	ɔ	*o̞*sa, *o̞*ka
P	p	p	*p*o̞o̞*p*o̞, *p*u̞ta
R	r	ɹ	*r*iri, *r*echara

129

S	s	s	*siri, sere*
SH	sh	ʃ	*ịsha, ịchafụ*
T	t	t	*teta, taa*
U	u	u	*uwe, ume*
Ụ	ụ	ʊ	*ụwa, ụkwụ*
V	v	v	*mvọ isi*
W	w	w	*weta, wwere*
Y	y	j	*ya, nyọ*
Z	z	z	*zụta, azịza*

12.5 Application of the Transcription and usage

The following examples show how Igbo words are transcribed in order to allow easy pronunciation from anyone who knows IPA symbols or graphemes without any need of assistance.

Word	*Mkpụrụokwu*	*Transceiption*
Camel	Ịnyịya ibu	/ɲɲa ibu/
Cat	Nwamba/Nwologbo	/ŋʷamba/ or /ŋʷologb͡o/
Cow/Cattle	Ehi	/eɦi/
Chick	Nwa Ọkụkọ	/ŋʷa ɔkʊkɔ/
Cock	Oke Ọkpa	/oke ɔk͡pa/
Dog	Nkịta	/nkɪta/
Donkey	Jakị	/d͡ʒaki/
Dove	nduru ala	/nduru ala/
Duck	Ọbọgwụ	/ɔbɔgʷʊ/
Female goat	Nne ewu	/nne ewu/
Fowl/Chicken	Ọkụkọ	/ɔkʊkɔ/
Goat	Ewu	/ewu/
Gold fish	Azụ ọlaedo	/azʊ ɔlaedo/
Guinea pig	Oke Bekee	/oke bekee/
Hen	Nnekwu	/nnekʷu/
Horse	Ịnyịya	/ɲɲa/
Male goat	Mkpị	/mk͡pɪ/
Parrot	Icheku	/it͡ʃeku/

Exercise

1. What are the categories into which the 28 consonant phonemes of Igbo language are divided?
2. Define voiced and voiceless consonant sounds in the context of Igbo phonetics.
3. List and explain the manner of articulation categories in consonant sounds.
4. Describe the characteristics of stops in Igbo consonant articulation.
5. What distinguishes fricatives from other types of consonant sounds in Igbo?
6. Explain how affricates are produced and provide examples from Igbo.
7. What defines nasal consonants, and which consonants belong to this category in Igbo?
8. Define lateral consonants and provide an example from the Igbo language.
9. What are glides, and how are they produced in speech articulation?
10. Describe the characteristics of rhotic consonants and provide an example from Igbo.
11. Explain the process of speech production in terms of bilabial sounds.
12. How are labiodental sounds articulated and provide examples from Igbo.
13. Define alveolar consonants and give examples from the Igbo language.
14. Describe palatoaveolar sounds and provide examples from Igbo.
15. What distinguishes velar consonants, and what are the subgroups within this category in Igbo?
16. Explain the concept of labial-velar sounds and provide examples from Igbo.
17. Describe the articulation process of glottal sounds, with an example from Igbo.
18. What is the significance of phonetic transcription in Igbo linguistics?
19. Explain the use of the International Phonetic Alphabet (IPA) in Igbo phonetics.
20. How does phonetic transcription aid in the accurate pronunciation of Igbo words?

Chapter 13
Phonological Variation and Change

13.1 Dialectal Variation

Dialectal variation refers to the variances in vocabulary, grammar, and pronunciation that speakers of a given language exhibit, which can be attributed to social, cultural, or geographic reasons. These differences occur naturally over time as populations diverge linguistically because of factors such as isolation, migration, and interaction with other languages.

Variations in vowel and consonant sounds, syllable structure, and intonation patterns among dialects are examples of phonological variances, which are one aspect of dialectal variety. For example, the overall phonetic makeup of words can be affected by dialect differences in the way vowels and consonants are articulated.

The way the vowel sound is pronounced in words like "afọ" (stomach) and "ehfọ" (stomach) is an example of how phonological variance varies among dialects. "Afọ" is frequently pronounced with unique vowel sounds in Enugu and among the Igbo people across the river, with "a" being pronounced with a "eh" sound. The diversity in vowel pronunciation between Owerri, Nkanụ, Ọnịcha, Asaba, Abakịlịkị, and other dialects is exemplified by this difference in pronunciation.

Beyond phonological differences, dialectal variation extends to lexical and grammatical aspects as well. Different dialects may use distinct vocabulary terms or have variations in grammatical structures and word order. These variations reflect the diverse linguistic practices and cultural influences present within different speech communities.

Examples of dialectal variation in Igbo language:

1. Pronunciation variations:
Pronunciation differences primarily concern the letter "a" in various Igbo dialects, where it is often articulated as "eh". In certain Igbo communities, words such as "Aka" (hand) and "anya" (eyes)

are spoken as "ehka" and "ehnya" respectively. Similarly, variations like "mvọ" and "mbọ" denote the same concept. Various phonetic elements, including vowel and consonant sounds, can diverge across dialects. For instance, the pronunciation of the vowel in "onwe m" (myself) may contrast between dialects, with the Ngwa dialect rendering it as "ogwe m".

2. Lexical Variation and Vocabulary differences:
The term "ụlọ" (house) may exhibit variation across dialects, with some dialects having it as "ụyọ" while others say "ọlọ." Likewise, the pronunciation of "Ịhụnanya" (Love) can differ between dialects, as some pronounce it as "Ịfụnanya." Similarly, "ahụ" (body) is articulated as "arụ" in certain dialects. Frequently, the consonant "h" is substituted with "f" or "r" in many instances, depending on the word's context. Furthermore, different words or expressions may be used to denote the same concept or object across dialects. For instance, "mmanwu" (masquerade) might be referred to as "ekpo" in some dialects.

3. Grammatical constructions:
Various dialects may exhibit distinct grammatical structures or arrangements of words. For instance, the expression "I am going" might be conveyed as "Ana m aga" in one dialect and "Aga ga m" in another. Similarly, the question Kedu ka I mere? ("How are you?") in some dialects like Igbere may adopt the form "Ị mere aghị?" whereas in Awknanaw it could be articulated as "Ị mere aka (ehka)?" Consequently, sentence compositions and syntactic configurations can vary among dialects, affecting the formation of questions or the expression of negation in different ways.

4. Cultural and Historic influences:
Cultural influences specific to various regions or communities within Igbo-speaking areas can also shape dialectal variations. Historical events or population migrations might have given rise to unique dialectal characteristics in different regions, thereby enriching the diversity of Igbo language variants. For instance, customs such as "Ịwa ọji" (breaking of kolanut) and festivals like "Ikeji" (yam festival), as well as traditional rites such as "Ịgba afa" (spirits consultation), can contribute to the distinctive features found in different Igbo dialects.

These examples illustrate the rich diversity of dialectal variation within the Igbo language, reflecting the cultural, historical, and geographical differences among Igbo-speaking communities. Overall, understanding dialectal variation is crucial for appreciating the richness and diversity of language usage across different regions and communities. It highlights the dynamic nature of language evolution and the nuanced ways in which language reflects social, cultural, and historical contexts.

13.2 Sociolinguistic Factors Influencing Variation

Sociolinguistic factors are fundamental influences that shape the variations observed in the pronunciation of sounds within a language community. These factors encompass a range of social dimensions, including social class, ethnicity, age, gender, and individual identity, among others. The interplay of these sociolinguistic factors contributes to the diversity of pronunciation patterns observed among speakers.

One key aspect of sociolinguistic variation is its manifestation in pronunciation differences that are associated with particular social groups or contexts. Different social groups may exhibit distinct phonological features in their speech, which can be attributed to their shared cultural practices, norms, and social experiences. For example, individuals belonging to specific social classes or ethnic communities may employ distinct pronunciation patterns that set them apart from others.

For example:

Ashebi	*Uniform dress by a group*
Ata na-agba	*Serious confusion*
Ife ajụ	*To charm and manipulate somebody*
Ịgba tọọchị	*Bribery/to give bribe*
Ịja	*Money*
Ikechi mmadụ	*To tie someone with evil power*
Ịma mmadụ (IM)	*Nepotism*
Ịsa isi	*Brainwashing*

Furthermore, sociolinguistic variation often intersects with social attitudes and perceptions regarding language use. Certain phonological features may be stigmatized or esteemed depending on their association with particular social groups. Variants associated with higher social status or prestige may be perceived as more desirable, while those linked to lower social status may be subject to prejudice or discrimination.

In order to investigate the relationship between linguistic variables and social elements in a community, sociolinguistic research is essential. Linguists study the distribution of phonological variants among various social groups and the ways in which age, gender, ethnicity, and social class affect them. Sociolinguistic studies provide light on how language reflects social identity, social structure, and power dynamics in society by examining patterns of language usage and variation.

In general, sociolinguistic elements play a crucial role in comprehending the intricacies of phonological variance among language communities. They draw attention to the dynamic relationship that exists between language and society, showing how social environment shapes linguistic practices and how those practices in turn help to form social identity and meaning.

13.3 Sound Change and Its Mechanisms

Sound change refers to the systematic modification of phonetic or phonological features within a language across time. These changes can impact individual sounds, sequences of sounds, or even entire phonological systems. They are a natural and ongoing process in language evolution, reflecting the dynamic nature of linguistic development over time.

Various factors can contribute to sound change. Phonetically, sound changes may arise due to processes such as assimilation, dissimilation, lenition, or fortition. Assimilation involves the influence of neighboring sounds on each other, leading to their becoming more similar. Dissimilation, on the other hand, involves the tendency for similar sounds to become more distinct from each other over time. Lenition refers to the gradual weakening or reduction of sounds, while fortition involves their strengthening or reinforcement.

For example,

English	*Igbo (Normal)*	*Assimilation*
Boss/Leader	Onye + isi	onyiisi
Health	Ahụ + ike	Ahiike
Peacemaker/seeker	Ọchọ + udo	Ọchuudo
Strong hand	Aka + ike	akiike
Welldone	jisi + ike	jiisike

Furthermore, sociolinguistic variables influence how sound changes. The interaction of speakers of other languages, known as language contact, can result in the borrowing of sounds or sound patterns. Additionally, speakers may accept or reject characteristics based on their social standing or identity, which can have an impact on sound modifications due to the prestige attached to particular dialects or speech types.

Sound changes can spread throughout language communities via processes like lexical diffusion, where changes propagate gradually through the lexicon, or analogical leveling, where irregular forms are reshaped to conform to regular patterns. These processes contribute to the gradual transformation of pronunciation patterns over time.

For example,

Compounnd word	*Merged*	*Pronunciation*

Nwa + eke	nweeke	nweke
Oke + anu	okaanu	okanu
Ada + obi	adoobi	adobi
Uso + ekwu	useekwu	usekwu
Ego + ọkụ	Egọọkụ	Egọkụ
Ome + ire	Omiire	Omire

One well-known example of sound change is the Great Vowel Shift, which occurred during the transition from Middle English to Modern English. This significant phonological shift involved widespread changes to the vowel system, resulting in alterations to the pronunciation of many words. The Great Vowel Shift illustrates how sound changes can have far-reaching effects on the phonological structure of a language, ultimately shaping its evolution and development across generations.

13.4 Historical Phonology

Historical phonology is a specialized field within linguistics that focuses on the study and reconstruction of phonological changes that occur in languages over time. It delves into the historical evolution of phonological systems, aiming to uncover patterns of change and trace the development of sounds across different stages of a language's history.

Historical phonologists employ various methods and techniques to investigate phonological changes. They analyze written records, comparative data from related languages, and linguistic reconstructions to reconstruct ancestral forms of languages and track the trajectory of phonological evolution.

One key method used in historical phonology is the comparative method, which involves comparing the phonological systems of related languages to identify common features and patterns of change. By examining similarities and differences across languages, historical phonologists can infer shared ancestral forms and reconstruct phonological features that have undergone change over time.

A different method used in historical phonology is internal reconstruction, which examines phonological changes inside a single language. In order to reconstruct earlier phases of a language and comprehend the mechanisms underlying phonological evolution, linguists study patterns of change within historical records of the language.

The study of word origins and evolution, or etymology, is equally important to historical phonology. Linguists are able to obtain information regarding phonological alterations and language contact phenomena by tracking the evolution of words and their phonetic forms across languages.

Through the study of phonological changes in languages over centuries and millennia, historical phonology provides valuable insights into the processes of language evolution and the relationships between languages. It helps linguists understand how languages change over time, adapt to new environments, and interact with other languages, ultimately contributing to our understanding of human language and its development.

In order to comprehend language dynamics and the processes behind linguistic variety and evolution, one must have a solid understanding of phonological variation and change. The intricate interactions between linguistic, social, and historical elements that have shaped language systems over time are reflected in phonological variation and change.

Exercise

1. What is dialectal variation, and what are its primary manifestations within a language?
2. How do variations in vowel and consonant sounds contribute to dialectal differences?
3. Provide examples of phonological variation in the pronunciation of specific words across different Igbo dialects.
4. How does dialectal variation extend beyond phonological differences to include lexical and grammatical aspects?
5. Explain the significance of cultural and historical influences in shaping dialectal variation.
6. What are sociolinguistic factors, and how do they influence phonological variation among speakers?
7. Give examples of phonological features associated with specific social groups or contexts.
8. How do sociolinguistic attitudes and perceptions impact the evaluation of phonological variants?
9. Describe the mechanisms involved in sound change within a language over time.
10. What phonetic processes contribute to sound changes and provide examples of each.
11. How does language contact influence sound change, and what role do sociolinguistic variables play in this process?
12. Explain lexical diffusion and analogical leveling as processes of sound change.
13. Define historical phonology and its primary objectives within the field of linguistics.
14. What methods do historical phonologists use to investigate phonological changes in languages over time?
15. How does internal reconstruction contribute to our understanding of phonological evolution within a single language?

Part Three:

Morphology of Igbo Linguistic (Amụmàmụ Mkpụrụasụsụ nke Mmụta Asụsụ Igbo)

Chapter 14

The nature of Igbo Morpheme

14.1 Definition of Morphology

Morphology (Amụmàmụ Ọdịdị nke Mkpụrụasụsụ Igbo) is the study of words, how they are formed, and their relationship to other words in the same language. It analyzes the structure of words and parts of words such as stems, root words, prefixes, and suffixes. It looks at the internal structure of words and the laws that control how morphemes, the smallest meaningful units of language, combine to generate complex words. The study of morphological processes including compounding, derivation, and inflection as well as the examination of morphological patterns and guidelines in various languages are all included in the field of morphology. Morphology explores the morphological characteristics of words to offer insights on the structure and inventiveness of language at the word formation level.

14.2 Morpheme

Morpheme (mkpụrụasụsụ) is the smallest linguistic unit that contains an element of a word that cannot be divided into smaller parts. They are a distinct grammatical unit of a language by which meaningful words are formed. A morpheme (mkpụrụasụsụ) is not a word. The difference between a morpheme (mkpụrụasụsụ) and a word is that a morpheme (mkpụrụasụsụ) sometimes does not stand alone, but a word on this definition always stands alone.

Examples of morpheme (mkpụrụasụsụ) within Igbo words:

Word	Morpheme (mkpụrụasụsụ)	No. of Morpheme
Bịara	[bị] + [a] + [ra]	3 - (atọ)
Cheta	[che] + [ta]	2 - (abụọ)
Chọpụtara	[chọ] + [pụ] + [ta] + [ra]	4 - (anọ)
Di	[di]	1 - (otu)
Dibịa	[di] + [bị] + [a]	3 - (atọ)
Ghọtakwa	[ghọ] + [ta] + [kwa]	3 - (atọ)
Ma	[m] + [a]	2 - (abụọ)

Mata	[m] + [a] + [ta]	3 - (ato)
Metutara	[m] + [e] + [tu] + [ta] + [ra]	5 - (ise)
Mgbochiume	[m] + [gbo] + [chi] + [ume]	4 - (ano)
Nkuzi	[nku] + [zi]	2 - (abuo)
Nwannem	[nwa] + [nne] + [m]	3 - (ato)
Ọmụmaatụ	[ọ] + [mụ] + [ma] + [a] + [tụ]	5 - (ise)
bụ	[bụ]	1 - (otu)
Zipụ	[zi] + [pụ]	2 - (abuọ)

14.3 Morpheme and Phoneme differences

The difference between morpheme (mkpụrụasụsụ) and phoneme (mkpụrụụdaasụsụ)

	Morpheme (mkpụrụasụsụ)	Phoneme
1.	*It is the smallest grammatical unit from which words are formed.*	*It is a unit of sound that can distinguish one word from another.*
2.	*It does have individual meaning and can stand alone when separated from words or in a sentence.*	*It does not have individual meaning. It rather has individual sound which is found within words.*

14.4 Identification of Igbo morphemes (mkpụrụasụsụ):

Since morphemes (mkpụrụasụsụ) are the smallest grammatical unit from which words are formed. It is important to understand how it differs from other linguistic features (like phonemes or words) by knowing certain conditions that qualifies some lexical units as morphemes (mkpụrụasụsụ). Here are five basic features of morphemes (mkpụrụasụsụ) that distinguish them from other linguistic elements:

a) Igbo morpheme (mkpụrụasụsụ) is a part of a word or a word that has meaning.
b) It has almost the same stable meaning in different verbal environments.
c) It cannot be divided into smaller meaningful segments without changing its meaning or rendering it meaningless.

(A). The following are examples of morphemes (mkpụrụasụsụ) that are a part of a word or a word that has meaning.

Word	*Morphemes (mkpụrụasụsụ) and Meaning*	
Bịa	[bị] *(live)* + [a]	*(impersonal pronoun)*
Cheta	[che] *(think)* + [ta]	*(past tense suffix)*

Chọpụta	[chọ] *(find)* + [pụ] *(go)* + [ta]	*(past tense suffix)*
Ghọta	[ghọ] *(get/catch)* + [ta]	*(past tense suffix)*
Metụta	[me] *(do/take action)* + [tụ]	*(about)*
Nwannem	[nwa] *(child)* + [nne] *(mother)* + [m] *(mine/me)*

(B). The following are examples of Igbo morphemes (mkpụrụasụsụ) that have almost the same stable meaning in different verbal environments.

Using the morpheme (mkpụrụasụsụ) – '*che*' meaning hold on, guard, think

Word	***Morphemes (mkpụrụasụsụ)***	**Meaning**
Cheta	[che] + [ta]	remember
Chere	[che] + [re]	wait/hold on
Chebe	[che] + [be]	protect
Echiche	[E] + [chi] + [che}	ideas

Using the morpheme (mkpụrụasụsụ) – '*me*' meaning do

Metụ	[me] + [tụ]	touch
Mebe	[me] + [be}	keep doing/going on
Meta	[me] + [ta]	do (it) well
Mechie	[me] + [chi] + [e]	close/shut
Emeka	[e] + [me] + [ka]	(has) done so well
Emeniike	[e] + [me] + [ni] [i] + [ke]	not done by force
Mebie	[me] + [bi] + [e]	ruin, (do) damage

Using the morpheme (mkpụrụasụsụ) – '*Gho*' meaning get

Ghọta	[ghọ] + [ta]	understand
Ghọrọ	[ghọ] + [rọ]	catch

(C). The following are examples that show that morphemes (mkpụrụasụsụ) cannot be divided into smaller meaningful segments without changing its meaning or rendering it meaningless.

Word	***Morphemes (mkpụrụasụsụ)***	
Bịara	[bị] + [a] + [ra]	3 - indivisible
Cheta	[che] + [ta]	2 - indivisible
Chọpụtara	[chọ] + [pụ] + [ta] + [ra]	4 - indivisible
Di	[di]	1 - indivisible
Dibịa	[di] + [bị] + [a]	3 - indivisible
Ghọtakwa	[ghọ] + [ta] + [kwa]	3 - indivisible

Ma	[m] + [a]	2 - indivisible
Mata	[m] + [a] + [ta]	3 - indivisible
Mkpụrụasụsụ	[m] + [kpụ] + [rụ] + [a] + [sụ] + [sụ]	6 - indivisible
Mgbochiume	[m] + [gbo] + [chi] + [ume]	4 - indivisible
Nkuzi	[nku] + [zi]	2 - indivisible
Nwannem	[nwa] + [nne] + [m]	3 - indivisible
Ọmụmaatụ	[ọ] + [mụ] + [ma] + [a] + [tụ]	5 - indivisible
bụ	[bụ]	1 - indivisible
Zipụ	[zi] + [pụ]	2 - indivisible

Illustrations below show that attempt to further divide Igbo morpheme (mkpụrụasụsụ) will either render that morpheme (mkpụrụasụsụ) meaningless or change its meaning to something different.

(a). Unit of Morpheme (mkpụrụasụsụ) [nwa]
Division [nw] + [a]

Result [nw] *is meaningless while [a] as a separate entity assume the position of an impersonal pronoun.*

(b). Unit of Morpheme (mkpụrụasụsụ) [nne]
Division [n] + [n] + [e]

Result *the two [n]s are meaningless while [a] as a separate entity assumes the position of an impersonal pronoun.*

(c). Unit of Morpheme (mkpụrụasụsụ) [ume]
Division [u] + [m] + [e]

Result *the two [u] are meaningless while [m] and [e] as separate entities assume the position of personal and impersonal pronoun respectively.*

14.5 Characteristics of Igbo morpheme (mkpụrụasụsụ):

(A). In Igbo sentences (ahịrịokwu), a pronoun that can stand alone can double as a morpheme (mkpụrụasụsụ) as well as a word. For example:

Sentence	Meaning	Pronoun/Morpheme
A sara efere.	Someone *did the dishes*	a
E siri nri.	Someone *cooked food*	e
Ị mere m ihe ọma.	*You did me a favor*	i

Ị bu ezigbo mmadu.	*You are a kind person*	ị
O buuru ụzọ.	*He/she took the lead*	o
Ọ mara ezigbo mma	*He/she is so beautiful*	ọ
M ga-abia.	*I will come*	m
Ada gwara ya	*Ada told him/her*	ya
Eze gwara ha.	*Eze told them.*	ha
Anyị bụ ụmụnne	*We are siblings*	anyị
Gịnị bụ aha gị?	*What is your name?*	gị
Unu amaghị Obi.	*You (people) don't know Obi*	unu.

(B). Igbo alphabet (Abidịị), that can stand alone and have stable meaning can double as a morpheme (mkpụrụasụsụ). Igbo alphabet has two divisions – vowels and consonants. Igbo vowels can double as morpheme (mkpụrụasụsụ) because they can stand alone as lexical unit and have meaning. A look at the preceding example shows that the following vowels are morphemes (mkpụrụasụsụ) as well.

a   e   i   ị   o   ọ

Six out of eight Igbo vowels qualify as morphemes (mkpụrụasụsụ) as you can see from the above examples. There are two Igbo vowels that do not qualify as morpheme (mkpụrụasụsụ) because they do not have meaning when they stand alone. They are:

u   and   ụ

Similarly, semi-vowels that are part of Igbo consonant have only one among the two (m and n) that qualifies as a morpheme (mkpụrụasụsụ). This is because while one would stand alone and still have meaning, the other does not have meaning as standalone. The semivowel that qualifies as morpheme (mkpụrụasụsụ) is:

m

The semivowel that does not qualify as a morpheme (mkpụrụasụsụ) because of lack of meaning is:

n

Exercise

1. What is morphology, and what aspects of language does it analyze?
2. Define morpheme and explain its role in forming meaningful units of language.
3. How does a morpheme differ from a word in terms of standing alone?
4. Provide examples of morphemes within Igbo words and analyze their structure.
5. Explain the difference between morpheme and phoneme.
6. What are the primary characteristics of morphemes in Igbo language?
7. How does morphology contribute to the structure and inventiveness of language at the word formation level?
8. Describe the morphological processes of compounding, derivation, and inflection.
9. Give examples of compounding, derivation, and inflection in Igbo language.
10. What are the five basic features of morphemes that distinguish them from other linguistic elements?
11. Provide examples of morphemes in Igbo that demonstrate stable meaning in different verbal environments.
12. Explain how attempts to divide certain Igbo morphemes render them meaningless or change their meaning.
13. How do pronouns in Igbo sentences function as both morphemes and words?
14. Discuss the role of Igbo alphabet in serving as morphemes and their stable meanings.
15. Which Igbo vowels qualify as morphemes, and why?
16. What is the significance of semi-vowels in Igbo consonants, and which ones qualify as morphemes?
17. How does the identification of morphemes contribute to understanding the internal structure of words in Igbo language?
18. Explain the importance of recognizing morphological patterns and guidelines in studying Igbo morphology.
19. How does morphology provide insights into the inventiveness and structure of language?
20. Discuss the relevance of Igbo morphological analysis in linguistic research and language preservation efforts.

Chapter 15

Types of Igbo Morpheme

15.1 Types of Igbo Morpheme

Types of Morphemes (Nkewasị Mkpụrụasụsụ Igbo): Morphemes (mkpụrụasụsụ) are the smallest meaningful lexical item in a language. It is the smallest meaningful and syntactical or grammatical unit of a language that cannot be divided without changing its actual meaning. There are two ways of classifying morpheme (mkpụrụasụsụ):

1. *Free Morpheme* (Mkpụrụasụsụ Nnọrọonwe)
2. *Bound Morpheme* (Mkpụrụasụsụ Ndabe/Ntado)

15.2 Free Morpheme

Free morpheme (Mkpụrụasụsụ Nnọrọonwe) is a morpheme (mkpụrụasụsụ) that has individual meaning and can be formed independently. For example: bi *(live)*, bụ *(is)*, dì *(for)*, dí *(husband)*, ma *(know)*, jì *(have)*, jí *(yam)*, etc. All of the words have individual meanings and are free morphemes (mkpụrụasụsụ). Morphemes (mkpụrụasụsụ) such as *anuri, happy, nwoke, man, papa, father, aka, hand,* among others can stand on their own as independent words. Free morpheme (mkpụrụasụsụ) in Igbo language can be either one letter of Igbo alphabet (such as a, e, i, ị, o, ọ or m) or indivisible grammatical unit (such as bi *(live)*, bụ *(is)*, dì *(for)*, dí *(husband)*, ma *(know)*, jì *(have)*, jí *(yam)*, anyị *(we)*, okwu *(word)*, ha *(they/them)*, ụmụ *(Kids/Children)*, nne *(mother)*, nna *(father)*, etc). Free morphemes (mkpụrụasụsụ) can be categorized into two sub-types. They are: Lexical morphemes (mkpụrụasụsụ) or Grammatical/functional morpheme (mkpụrụasụsụ).

Lexical morphemes: these are morphemes (mkpụrụasụsụ) that convey the major content or meaning of a message. They specify things, qualities or events spoken about. To identify a lexical morpheme (mkpụrụasụsụ), ask yourself this: "If this morpheme (mkpụrụasụsụ) was removed from the sentence, statement or message, would I not be able to understand the main message of this sentence?" If the answer is yes, then you have a lexical morpheme (mkpụrụasụsụ).

Functional morphemes: Functional morphemes also known as *grammatical morphemes* are morphemes (mkpụrụasụsụ) that do not convey the major content or meaning of a message, but rather help the message with function words. To identify a lexical morpheme, ask yourself this: "If this morpheme (mkpụrụasụsụ) was removed from the sentence, statement or message, would I still be able to understand the main message of this sentence?" If the answer is yes, then you have a functional morpheme.

15.3 Bound Morphemes

Bound Morphemes (Mkpụrụasụsụ Ndabe) are morphemes that do not have independent meanings of their own. They cannot form words without the help of free morphemes (mkpụrụasụsụ). Morphemes (mkpụrụasụsụ) like *ghi,* indicating negation, *beghi, ra,* meaning *past ga-* indicating *futurity, chara,* indicating completion, *li and ri,* indicating intensity, are always attached to free morphemes or free forms. It entails that bound morphemes depend on the formto which they are attached to derive meaning. Bound morphemes can be categorized into two sub-classes. They are: Bound roots (usually Isingwaa) and Affixes (mgbakwunye).

Bound Roots: Bound roots are those morphemes that have lexical meaning when they are included in other bound morphemes to form the content words. An example of bound roots is infinitive verb (Isingwaa).

An infinitive verb (Isingwaa) is a verb form that functions as a noun or is used with auxiliary verbs, and that names the action orstate without specifying the subject. In Igbo language, the letter "ị" and "i" plus the root verb comprise the infinitive form of verb. For example:

English	Igbo root verb	*English*	Igbo root verb
to be	ịbu/ịdị	*to bring*	iweta
to buy	ịzụta	*to call*	ịkpọ
to chew	ịta	*to come*	ịbịa
to cook	isi nri	*to cry*	ibe akwa
to dance	ịgba egwu	*to do*	ime
to drink	ịṅu	*to eat*	iri (nri)
to enter	ịbanye/ịbata	*to find/look*	ịchọ/chọta
to follow	isoro	*to forget*	ichefu
to fry	ighe	*to get*	inweta
to give	inye	*to go*	ịga
to have/own	inwe	*to hear*	ịnụ
to hold	ijide	*to know*	ịma
to laugh	ịchi (chi a)	*to learn*	ịmụta
to leave	ịhapụ	*to listen*	ige ntị

to look	ile (anya)	*to mark*	ịka (akara)
to get out	ịpụta	*to play*	igwu egwu
to pray	ikpe ekpere	*to read*	igụ
to remember	icheta	*to run*	ịgba ọsọ
to say	ikwu (okwu)	*to see*	ịhụ
to sell	ire (ahịa)	*to bathe*	ịsa ahụ
to sing	ịgụụ abụ/ ịbụụ abụ	*to sit*	ịnọdu
to sleep	ịrahụ (ura)	*to speak*	ịsụ/ikwu
to stand	iguzo/ikuli	*to stay*	ịnọ
to swallow	ilo	*to take*	iwere
to teach	ikuzi	*to tell*	ịgwa
to think	iche echiche	*to throw*	ịtu
to touch	ịmetụ	*to understand*	ighọta
to wait	ichere	*to walk*	iga ije
to wash	ịsa	*to wear*	iyi
to work	ịrụ	*to write*	ide

15.4 Affixes

Affixes are those bound morphemes that naturally attached to different types of words and are used to change the meaning or function of those words. Agglutination is a notable feature of Igbo language. The conjugation of verbs, for example, is done by adding different prefixes or suffixes to the root of the verb.

Roots and stems are the basic lexical units to which affixes can be attached to create new words. Roots are morphemes that carry the core meaning of a word and are typically morphemes to which affixes are added. Stems, on the other hand, may consist of a root alone or a combination of a root and one or more affixes. Stems are the morphological units that undergo inflectional or derivational processes to create different word forms. For example, in the word, : *metutara*, which means "has/that affected", is formed by *"metu"* (indicates present tense "touch"), (root of the verb *"me"* → do), tara (indicates past tense, in this case, "touched/affected"). Generally, most Igbo verbs come with affixes or other nominals as part of their complex e.g.

bá	-	*enter*	bátà	-	*enter into*
cha	-	*cut*	chapụ	-	*cut out*
chọ	-	*look for.*	chọta	-	*find*
gwá	–	*tell*	gwáá	-	*mix*
ma	-	*know*	maka	-	*because*
ri	-	*eat*	riri	-	*ate*

zi - *inform*   zipu - *send (a person)*

Affixes can be categorized into five sub-classes according to their position in the word and function in a phrase or sentence. They are:

a. Prefixes (Ngaaniihu)
b. Infixes (Nnoṇaetiti)
c. Suffixes (Nsonaazụ)
d. Derivational (Nsonaazụ Mgbanwe)
e. Inflectional (Nsonaazụ ntụaka)
f. Enclitic (Nsokwụnye)

14.4.1 Prefixes (ngaaniihu):

Prefixes are bound morphemes (mkpụrụasụsụ) included at the beginning of different types of words. In Igbo language prefixation is verb-based. There is no other word class that undergoes this kind of morphological process. Prefixes in Igbo are infinitive and participle markers that are attached to verb roots. They normally appear as bound morphemes (mkpụrụasụsụ) to the verb root in the following manner:

Participles	-	Òmekàngwaà
Infinitives	-	Mfinitiivu
Gerund	-	Jerọndụ
Noun agent	-	Ahaome/Omee
Noun instrument	-	Ahamme/Mmee

Examples with *Participles* (Òmekàngwaà):

Prefix (nganiihu)	**Verb root** (Isingwaa)	**New word** (Mkpụrụokwuọhụru)	**Meaning** (Ihe ọ pụtata)
a	bụ	abụ	*song*
a	da	ada	*first daughter*
a	kpa	akpa	*bag*
a	gba	agba	*jaw*
e	de	ede	*cocoyam*
e	nyo	enyo	*mirror*
e	je	eje	*go (ing)*
e	ti	eti	*beat (ing)*
a	nwụ	anwụ	*sun*

a	gwụ	agwụ	*maniac*

Examples with infinitives (Mfinitiivu):

Prefix (nganiihu)	**Verb root** (Isingwaa)	**Infinitives** (Mfinitiivu)	**Meaning** (Ihe ọ pụtata)
ị	ba	ịbá	*to enter*
ị	da	ịda	*to fall*
ị	kpa	ịkpa	*to discuss*
ị	gba	ịgba	*to play/dane*
i	de	ide	*to write*
i	nyo	enyo	*to peek*
i	ke	ike (wa)	*to divide*
ị	ma	ịmá	*to know*
i	re	irè	*to sell*
i	zu	izu	*to device*

Examples with *Gerund* (Jerọndụ):

Prefix (nganiihu)	**Verb root** (Isingwaa)	**Infinitives** (Mfinitivu)	**Gerund** (Jerondu)	**Meaning** (Ihe ọ pụtata)
o	ri	ri	oriri	*eating/feasting*
ọ	nyụ	nya	ọnyụnya	*driving*
ọ	ṅụ	ṅụ	ọṅụṅụ	*drinking*
ọ	dị	da	ọdịda	*falling*
o	di	de	odide	*writing*
ọ	gụ	gụ	ọgụgụ	*reading*
o	ri	re	orire	*selling*
ọ	mụ	mụ	ọmụmụ	*learning/bearing*
ọ	hụ	hụ	ahụhụ	*roasting*
ọ	sụ	sọ	ọsụsọ	*sweating*
o	bi	bi	obibi	*living (home)*
o	ti	ti	otiti	*beating*

Example with Noun agent (Ahaomee/Omee):

Prefix (nganiihu)	Two verb root (Isingwaa abụọ)	Noun Agent (Ahaomee/Omee)	Meaning (Ihe ọ pụtata)
o	me + e	omee	(noun) agent
o	de + e	ode	writer
o	le + e	olee	where/how many
o	me + e	omee	doer
ọ	ga + a	ọgaa	boss
ọ	gba + a	ọgbaa	shooter
ọ	kụ + ụ	ọkụụ	planter/sower
ọ	sụ + ụ	ọsụụ	speaker/cutter
ọ	ṅụ + ụ	ọṅụụ	drinker
o	je + e	ojee	traveler/goer

Example with Noun instrument (Ahammee/Mmee):

Prefix (nganiihu)	Verb root (Isingwaa)	Complement (Mmeju)	Ahamme/Mmee (Noun Instrument)	Translation (Ntụgharị)
m	gba	mmiri	mgbammiri	jug
m	pa	naka	mpanaka	hand lamp
m	kpa	isi	mkpaisi	scissors
m	gba	ama	mgbaama	revealer
n	che	ndo	nchendo	sun protector
n	ti	mkpu	nti mkpu	exclaimer
n	ku	ikuku	nku ikuku	fan
n	de	akwa	nde akwa	iron
n	tụ	oyi	ntụ oyi	air conditioner
n	gụ	ọnụ	ngụ ọnụ	counter

15.4.2 Infixes (Nnoṇaetiti):

In linguistics, an infix is an affix inserted inside a word stem. A word stem is an existing word or the core of a family of words. It contrasts with adfix, a rare term for an affix attached to the outside of a stem such as a prefix or suffix.

In morphology, an infix is a word element (a type of affix) that can be inserted within the base form of a word—rather than at its beginning or end—to create a new word or intensify meaning. The process of inserting an infix is called infixation. There are no infixes that exist in the English language.

In Igbo morphology, an infix occurs within two words of the same morphemes (mkpụrụasụsụ) or words of the same form. The two morphemes (mkpụrụsụsụ) or words that are joined together by an infix in Igbo morphological process are usually verbs, nouns or adverb.

Examples of Infixes (nnọnetiti)

Infix (nnọnetiti)	Verb/stem (Ngwaa/ okwu)	reduplication (Mmụba)	New word (Okwu ọhụ)	Translation (Ntụghari)
d	aga	aga + aga	agadaga	*hardy/robust*
r	aka	aka + aka	akaraka	*fate/destiny*
m	aṅụ	aṅụ + aṅụ	aṅụmaṅụ	*act of drinking*
r	apị	apị + apị	apịrapị	*man-made*
m	asụ	asụ + asụ	asụmasụ	*act of speaking*
m	ata	ata + ata	atamata	*act of chewing*
l	ebe	ebe + ebe	ebelebe	*horrifying/shocking*
m	echi	echi + echi	echimechi	*crowning*
m	ede	ede + ede	edemede	*writing*
m	ekwu	ekwu + ekwu	ekwumekwu	*speech making*
r	ekwu	ekwu + ekwu	ekwurekwu	*talkative*
m	eri	eri + eri	erimeri	*act of eating*
m	esi	esi + esi	esimesi	*act of cooking*
m	eti	eti + eti	etimeti	*act of shouting*
da	mba	mba + mba	mbadamba	*wide/width*
m	oko	oko + oko	ókómókó	*proudful*
m	oko	oko + oko	òkómókò	*troublemaker*
ka	ome	ome + ome	omekaome	*robber/criminal*

15.4.3 Suffixes (Nsonaazụ):

Suffixes are those bound morphemes included at the end of different types of words. They can add meaning, and usually determine the part of speech of a word. In Igbo language, morpheme and verbs can have suffix. Igbo language as a tonal language has also been described as a verb language. In the morphology of the Igbo language, Igbo suffixes make constant reference to the verb forms in the language. For example:

Suffix (nsonaazụ)	*Verb/Word* (Ngwaa/ Mkpụrụokwu)	*Affixation* (Mgbakwụnye)	*New word* (Okwu ọhụ)	*Translation* (Ntụgharị)
ra	ba	ba + ra	bara	*entered*
re	be	be + re	bere	*perched*
ra	cha	cha + ra	chara	*cut*
re	che	che + re	chere	*thought*
ra	da	da + ra	dara	*fell*
e	di	di + e	die	*endure*
ọ	kọ	kọ + ọ	kọọ	*scratch*
ọ	kpọ	kpọ + ọ	kpọọ	*call*
e	me	me + e	mee	*do*
rụ	mụ	mụ + rụ	mụrụ	*learned*
ọ	rụ	rụ + ọ	rụọ	*do (work)*
ọ	sụ	sụ + ọ	sụọ	*speak*
ra	za	za + ra	zara	*answered*
e	zi	zi + e	zie	*send/inform*
ri	zi	zi + ri	ziri	*sent/informed*

Exercise
1. What are the two main types of Igbo morphemes?
2. Provide examples of free morphemes in Igbo language?
3. How do lexical morphemes differ from functional morphemes?
4. Explain the concept of bound morphemes in Igbo morphology.
5. Provide examples of bound roots in Igbo language.
6. Describe the function of affixes in Igbo morphology.
7. What are the sub-classes of affixes according to their position and function?
8. Explain the concept of prefixes in Igbo morphology and provide examples.
9. How do infixes function in Igbo morphological processes?
10. Can you provide examples of infixation in Igbo language?
11. Describe the role of suffixes in Igbo morphology and provide examples.
12. What is the significance of suffixes in determining the part of speech of a word in Igbo?
13. How do Igbo suffixes relate to verb forms in the language?
14. Provide examples of verbs in Igbo language with attached suffixes.
15. How does the use of suffixes contribute to the meaning of Igbo words?
16. Explain the term "infinitive verb" as discussed in Chapter 15.
17. How do bound roots differ from affixes in Igbo morphology?
18. Discuss the significance of affixation in Igbo word formation.
19. Can you explain the concept of agglutination in Igbo morphology?
20. How does the morphological structure of Igbo verbs differ from that of other word classes?

Chapter 16

Morphological Process of Igbo Word
(Usoro Mkpụrụasụsụ nke Mkpụrụokwu)

Morphology is the study of morphemes and their arrangements in forming words. The morphological process is the process of changing the form and function of a word to fit a statement or idea, sometimes to the degree of changing the meaning and/or grammatical function. Morphological process in Igbo language can be divided into seven kinds: Affixation, Clipping, Compounding, Borrowing/Loanword, Reduplication, Blending, Acronyms.

In this chapter, we will focus on affixation because of how broad its content is in Igbo language and in the following chapter we will discuss the remaining six kinds of morphological process under word process and formation.

16.1 Inflectional Morphology

Inflectional morphology involves the modification of a word to indicate grammatical features such as tense, aspect, mood, number, case, or gender. Inflectional morphemes are typically suffixes that attach to a base word without changing its basic meaning or syntactic category. In English, examples of inflectional morphemes include the plural marker "-s" (e.g., "cat" → "cats"), the past tense marker "-ed" (e.g., "walk" → "walked"), and the possessive marker "'s" (e.g., "dog" → "dog's"). Inflectional morphology contributes to the grammatical structure of sentences and aids in conveying information about the relationships between words within a sentence.

Inflectional morphology also known as Inflectional suffix (Nsonaazụ Ntụaka) is especially important in Igbo language because it helps in conveying the intended meaning of any expression. It also shows the different forms of verbs that express tone and other aspects in speech using one consonant, one vowel, one semivowel and one syllable or more.

- *one consonant* - otu mgbochiume
- *one vowel* - otu ụdaume

- *one semivowel* - otu myiriụdaume
- *one syllable or more* - otu nkejiokwu maọbụ karịa

Igbo inflectional suffix results into its imperative mood of expression realized by applying the four open vowels suffix with four possible realizations in accordance to vowel harmony rule. The four open vowels are (o or ọ) and (a or e).

Suffix (nsonaazụ mgbanwe)	**Verb/Word** (Ngwaa/ Mkpụrụokwu)	**Inflected word** (Mgbakwụnye)	**Igbo sentence** (Ahịrịokwu)	**Translation** (Ntụgharị)
ọ	kụ	kụ + ọ	kụọ	*plant*
o	kwu	kwu + o	kwuo	*speak*
e	li	li + e	lie	*bury*
e	me	me + e	mee	*do*
a	mị	mị + a	mịa	*produce*
ọ	mụ	mụ + ọ	mụọ	*learn*
o	pu	pu + o	puo	*bud/shoot*
ọ	pụ	pụ + ọ	pụọ	*go out*
a	rị	rị + a	rịa	*climb*
e	ti	ti + e	tie	*beat*

Inflectional suffix that is added to the root or base of a word to indicate grammatical relationships in terms of tense, aspect or number can be used to mark tense, aspects, mood or negation. This gives variants of an already existing morpheme or word without forming new words. For example, the suffixes: (ra/re), (ro/kọ/tara).

Suffix (nsonaazụ)	**Verb/Word** (Ngwaa/ Mkpụrụokwu)	**Affixation** (Mgbakwụnye)	**New word** (Okwu ọhụ)	**Translation** (Ntụgharị)
ra	ba	ba + ra	bara	*entered*
re	be	be + re	bere	*perched/sliced*
ra	cha	cha + ra	chara	*cut/ripe*
re	che	che + re	chere	*thought*
ra	da	da + ra	dara	*fell*
tara	rụ	rụ + tara	rụtara	*did (work)*
tara	sụ	sụ + tara	sụtara	*spoke (well)*
ra	za	za + ra	zara	*answered*
ro	zo	zo + ro	zoro	*to hide*

Inflectional suffix can modify the form of the words or verbs to which they are attached, so that such words fit into the particular syntactic space in an expression. However, they do not change the recognizable meaning of the stem, morpheme, word or verb root.

16.2 Derivational morphology:

Derivational morphology involves the creation of new words by adding affixes, such as prefixes or suffixes, to existing words (roots or stems) to change their syntactic category or semantic content. Unlike inflectional morphemes, derivational morphemes often result in changes to the meaning or function of the base word. For example, the addition of the prefix "re-" to the verb "write" forms the derived verb "rewrite," indicating the action of writing again. Derivational morphology allows for the expansion of a language's vocabulary and the creation of new words to express nuanced meanings or concepts.

In Igbo language, derivational morphemes create new words from existing words, i.e. new words are derived from their use. Derivational morphemes produce entirely new lexemes, highly productive, belong to the open class system and can bring about a change in the word class or modify the meaning of the word. They may be either prefixes or suffixes.

There are two primary types of derivational affixes in Igbo language, namely:

1. *Derivational suffix* (Nsonaazụ Mgbanwe) and
2. *Extentional suffix* (Nsonaazụ Mgbatị).

Derivational Affixes **(Nsonaazụ Mgbanwe):** Derivational morphemes (mkpụrụasụsụ mgbanwe) make new words by changing their meaning or different grammatical categories. In other words, derivational suffix (Nsonazụ Mgbanwe) forms new words with a meaning and category distinct through the addition of affixes.

In order to identify a derivational morpheme (mkpụrụasụsụ mgbanwe), ask this question: "If this morpheme (mkpụrụasụsụ mgbanwe) was added, would it change the part of speech of this word?" If the answer is yes, then you have a derivational morpheme. For example:

Suffix (nsonaazụ mgbanwe)	*Verb/Word* (Ngwaa/ Mkpụrụokwu)	*Affixation* (Mgbakwụnye)	*New word* (Okwu ọhụ)	*Translation* (Ntụgharị)
a	ba	ba + a	baa	*enter*
e	be	be + e	bee	*slice*
o	bu	bu + o	buo	*carry*

ọ	bụ	bụ + ọ	bụọ	*dissect*
ọ	chọ	chọ + ọ	chọọ	*seek*
ọ	dụ	dụ + ọ	dụọ	*advise*
e	fe	fe + e	fee	*fly*
a	gba	gba + a	gbaa	*kick/shoot*
ọ	kpụ	kpụ + ọ	kpụọ	*mould/form*
o	ku	ku + o	kuo	*fetch*

Derivational morpheme can be categorized into two sub-classes. They are:
1. Class-maintaining derivational morphemes
2. Class-changing derivational morphemes

16.2.1. Class-Maintaining Derivational Morphemes: Class-maintaining derivational morphemes are usually produced in a derived form of the same class as the root, and they don't change the class of the parts of speech. Class maintaining derivational morpheme does not alter the word class but modifies its meaning, most prefixes are class maintaining. For example, if a verb class undergoes an affixation and still remains a verb, it means there is no change of class. Thus, it is a class maintaining derivation. Inflectional affixes are common.

Suffix (nsonaazụ mgbanwe)	***Verb/Word*** (Ngwaa/ Mkpụrụokwu)	***Affixation*** (Mgbakwụnye)	**New Verb** (Ngwaa ọhụ)	**Translation** (Ntụghari)
a	ba	ba + a	baa	*enter*
e	be	be + e	bee	*slice*
o	bu	bu + o	buo	*carry*
e	ke	ke + e	kee	*divide*
ọ	chọ	chọ + ọ	chọọ	*seek*
ọ	dụ	dụ + ọ	dụọ	*advise*
e	fe	fe + e	fee	*fly*
a	gba	gba + a	gbaa	*kick/shoot*
ọ	kpụ	kpụ + ọ	kpụọ	*mould/form*
e	che	che + e	chee	*think*

16.2.2. Class-Changing Derivational Morphemes: In contrast to Class-maintaining derivational morphemes, Class-changing derivational morphemes usually produce a derived form of the other class from the root. Class changing derivational morpheme does not alter the word class but modifies its meaning. For example, if a verb class undergoes an affixation and change from being a verb to noun of other part of speech after suffixation or prefixation. It means there is a change of class. Thus, it is a class changing derivation.

Infix (nnọnetiti)	**Verb** (Ngwaa)	**New word** (Okwu ọhụ)	**Translation** (Ntụghari)	**Part of Speech** (Nkejiasụsụ)
d	aga	agadaga	*hardy/robust*	adjective
m	aṅụ	aṅụmaṅụ	*alcoholism*	noun
r	apị	apịrapị	*man-made*	adjective
m	ata	atamata	*mastication*	noun
l	ebe	ebelebe	*horrifying/shocking*	adjective
m	echi	echimechi	*crowning*	adjective
m	ede	edemede	*writing*	noun
m	ekwu	ekwumekwu	*speech-making*	noun
r	ekwu	ekwurekwu	*talkative*	adjective
m	eri	erimeri	*feast/banquet*	noun

More class changing derivational morpheme examples.

prefix (nganiihu)	**Verb** (Ngwaa)	**New word** (Okwu ọhụ)	**Translation** (Ntụghari)	**Part of Speech** (Nkejiasụsụ)
ọ	zọ	ọzọ	*again*	adverb
ọ	zọ	ọzọ	*next*	preposition
ọ	jọọ	ọjọọ	*badly*	adverb
n	cha	ncha	*all*	adverb
a	la	ala	*down*	preposition
ta	ta	tata	*today*	adverb
e	chi	echi	*tomorrow*	adverb
m	ma	mma	*well*	adverb
e	lu	elu	*above*	preposition
n	so	nso	*near*	preposition

suffix (nsonaazụ)	**Verb** (Ngwaa)	**New word** (Okwu ọhụ)	**Translation** (Ntụghari)	**Part of Speech** (Nkejiasụsụ)
ka	dị	dịka	*as/like*	preposition
ka	ma	maka	*because of*	preposition

| pu | tu | tupu | *before* | preposition |
| o | ru | ruo | *umtil/to* | preposition |

16.3 Extentional Morphology

Extentional suffix (Nsonaazụ Mgbatị) The verb category is very unique in Igbo language. This is because it is characterized by extensive morphological fusions. Extensional suffixes refer to those suffixes that extend the meanings and intention of the Igbo word that they are attached to.

Suffix (nsonaazụ mgbanwe)	***Verb/Word*** (Ngwaa/ Mkpụrụokwu)	*Affixation* (Mgbakwụnye)	*New word* (Okwu ọhụ)	***Translation*** (Ntụgharị)
ghị	achọ	achọ + ghị	achọghị	*doesn't want*
la	aga	aga + la	agala	*went*
ghị	ahụ	ahụ + ghị	ahụghị	*didn't see*
la	ajụọ	ajụ + ọla	ajụọla	*has asked*
la	akọ	akọ + la	akọla	*has narrated*
ghị	ama	ama + ghị	amaghị	*doesn't know*
la	amụọ	amụ + ọla	amụọla	*has birthed*
la	bee	bee + la	beela	*has sliced*
la	die	die + la	diela	*has endured*
la	eje	eje + la	ejela	*has gone*
ghị	eso	eso + ghị	esoghị	*not following*
la	esu	esu + la	esula	*has burnt*
la	kpụọ	kpụọ + la	kpụọla	*has moulded*
la	kuru	kuru + la	kurula	*has carried*
la	kwuo	kwuo + la	kwuola	*has said*
la	machie	machie + la	machiela	*has banned*
la	merie	merie + la	merela	*has won*
la	mie	mie + la	miela	*has sank*
la	tie	tie + la	tiela	*has beaten*
la	zie	zie + la	ziela	*has sent*
la	zụrụ	zụrụ + la	zụrụla	*has bought*

16.4 Enclitic (Nsokwụnye)

An enclitic (Nsokwụnye) is a *clitic* that is phonologically joined at the end of a preceding word to form a single unit. It is a monosyllabic word or form that is treated as a suffix of the preceding word.

In Igbo language, enclitic is a suffix that refers to the meaning of a word preceding it and highlights the word by giving it more emphatic meaning. Enclitic is a morpheme that can either bbe attached to a verb or stand alone in Igbo sentence. In both cases, Igbo enclitic function remains the same i.e. it functions as an extentsion of the meaning of word highlighting on action words.

Enclitic as a spotlight morpheme that brings the verb into a center stage does not render a sentence meaningless when removed from it. Sentences in Igbo language do retain their full meaning without enclictic.

Enclitic can be found in Igbo nouns, pronouns and verbs. When a pronoun precedes an enclitic, the enclitic is written as a standalone but when it is preceded by a verb, the enclitics is attached to the end of the verb to form one word. Examples of Igbo enclitics are: cha, ga, kwa, kwanụ, kwu, nụ, nwa, ri and zi.

1. Anụ cha bụ ihe nwaànyị na-ere n'ahịa.
    Meat in particular is what that woman sells in the market

2. Eze zutara akwụkwọ ga n'ahịa Ogbete.
    Eze bought different books from Ogbete Market.

3. Onye kwa nọ ebe ahụ?
    Who is that person there?

4. Onye kwanụ mebiri ihe osise Eze?
    Who is that person that ruined Eze's painting/drawing?

5. Nri kwu ka O nyeghị Adamma.
    He/she could not even afford to give Adamma food.

6. Achoro m ka I nyere nwaànyị nụ aka.
    I want you to help this particular woman.

7. Ozi nwa erughị Udoka aka.
    That message didn't even get to Udoka.

8. O kwetara ri tupu Ọ mara ihe ọrụ ya bụ.
   He had agreed <u>to the terms</u> before knowing the job duties.

9. Onye zi gwara gi na-emechiri ahia?
   Who <u>is that person that</u> told you that the market is locked.

The above examples show that when an enclitic is preceded by a noun or pronoun, it stands alone as a separate morpheme or word. Other examples as in the above are:

	Igbo	English
a)	O kwa gi ka m na-agwa?	*Are you not the one I'm talking to?*
b)	Unu kwanụ?	*How about you (people/group)?*
c)	Mụ nwa gwara ya.	*I personally told him/her.*
d)	Mụ kwu?	*... even me?*
e)	Anyi zi.	*Every one of us (in particular)*
f)	Ha cha	*Every one of them (in particular)*
g)	Ha ga	*Every one of them included.*
h)	Ya sọ	*Him/Her in particular.*

In the following sentence examples, we will notice that when an enclitic is preceded by a verb, it is attached to the end of the verb to form one unitary word and still retain its highlighting function. The enclitics affixed to Igbo words are generally in the form of: cha, dị, dụ, fụ, ga, kọ, kwa (kwọ), kwanụ, kwu, nịị, nọọ, nụ, nwa, ra, rị, rịị, tụ, zi, etc. The most common verbal examples are found in--bịanụ, bụkwa, bụzi, eduga, jicha, jikwu, kpọcha, makwa, matakwanụ, sokwu, etc. For example:

	Igbo	*English*
a)	Bịanụ hụrụ.	*You (people) should come and see.*
b)	Ọ bụkwa nke a ka Ị chọrọ?	*Is this exactly the one you want?*
c)	O bụzi ihe ihere.	*It has become a disgrace (shameful).*
d)	M ga-eduga ha ụlọ ahịa.	*I will take them to the supermarket.*
e)	Ha jicha ụlọ akụ ụgwọ.	*They own the bank some money.*
f)	Dinta ahụ jikwu mma.	*That hunter had a machete as well.*
g)	Ọ kpọcha gi, Ị bịa hụ m.	*See me, after your (phone) call.*
h)	I makwa onye m bụ!	*You do not know exactly who I am.*
i)	Matakwanụ na Ọ bụ nkem	*Acknowledge that it belongs to me.*
j)	O sokwu agba asịrị	*He/she is one of the gossippers.*

Exercise

1. What are the seven kinds of morphological processes and how do they differ?
2. Can you explain the concept of affixation and its significance in Igbo morphology?
3. What role do inflectional morphemes play in conveying grammatical features in Igbo language?
4. How do inflectional morphemes differ from derivational morphemes in Igbo morphology?
5. Can you provide examples of inflectional morphemes used in Igbo verbs and their meanings?
6. What are derivational morphemes, and how do they contribute to word formation in Igbo?
7. Explain the distinction between class-maintaining and class-changing derivational morphemes in Igbo.
8. How do extensional suffixes affect the meaning of Igbo verbs?
9. Can you provide examples of Igbo verbs with extensional suffixes and their meanings?
10. What are enclitics, and how do they function in Igbo sentences?
11. How do enclitics differ when attached to nouns/pronouns compared to verbs in Igbo?
12. Can you explain the concept of class-changing derivational morphemes with examples?
13. How does affixation help in expanding the vocabulary of the Igbo language?
14. What are some common Igbo enclitics, and how do they affect the meaning of words?
15. How do derivational affixes contribute to the creation of new words in Igbo?
16. What are some challenges faced in the study of morphology in languages like Igbo?

Chapter 17

Allomorphs in Igbo Language

17.1 Definition of Allomorphs

In linguistics, an allomorph (Ndịiche Mkpụrụasụsụ nke Igbo) is a variant phonetic form of a morpheme, or, a unit of meaning that varies in sound and spelling without changing the meaning. The term allomorph describes the realization of phonological variations for a specific morpheme.

There are many allomorphs in Igbo language due to variant realization of particles, noun agents, noun instruments, infinitives, gerunds, past tense markers, among others. The allomorphs were necessitated due to the grammatical nature of Igbo language following vowel harmony rules besides linguistic restrictions that apply to synonymous words.

There are seven major types of allomorphs in Igbo language, they are:

Participles	-	Òmekàngwaà
Infinitives	-	Mfinitiivu
Gerund	-	Jerọndụ
Noun agent	-	Ahaome/Omee
Noun instrument	-	Ahamme/Mmee
Past tense	-	Nke ihe gara aga
Plural allomorphs	-	Nke Ụbara

17.2 Participles (Òmekàngwaà)

A participle is a nonfinite verb form that has some of the characteristics and functions of both verbs and adjectives. Certain groups of people see it as a word derived from a verb and used as an adjective, it is a verbal form of word that needs an auxiliary element to augment its meaning.

In the Igbo language, it is generated by prefixing a corresponding a/e to the verb root in accordance to vowel harmony rules of Igbo language. It is in the form of a/e + verb root = Participle.

Examples with *Participles* (Òmekàngwaà):

Prefix (nganiihu)	**Verb root** (Isingwaa)	**New word** (Mkpụrụokwuọhụru)	**Meaning** (Ihe ọ pụtata)
a	bụ	abụ	*song*
a	da	ada	*first daughter*
a	kpa	akpa	*bag*
a	gba	agba	*jaw*
e	de	ede	*cocoyam*
e	nyo	enyo	*mirror*
e	je	eje	*go (ing)*
e	ti	eti	*beat (ing)*
a	nwụ	anwụ	*sun*
a	gwụ	agwụ	*maniac*

The 'a' and 'e' of Igbo language are allomorphs because they are different in sound and their spelling is semantically the same. From the example above, you can see that both can be prefixed to the verb root to form infinitives and they are phonological variants of the morpheme. However, they cannot be used interchangeable in the linguistic environment because of Igbo vowel harmony rules.

Furthermore, the infinitive prefixes, 'a' and 'e' can be used as an indefinite pronoun, thus, another form of allomorphs in another grammatical environment. The rule applies here, in all environment where they perform the same grammatical function they cannot be used interchangeably. Examples of 'a' and 'e' as a pronoun is shown below:

Igbo language	*Meaning*
A kụrụ aka.	Someone clapped or knocked (at the door).
E kwuru okwu.	Someone spoke or said something.

17.3 Infinitives (Mfinitiivu)

The *infinitive* is a *grammar* term that refers to a basic verb form that often acts as a noun and is often preceded by the word *to*. An *infinitive* is formed from a verb but doesn't act as a verb. Therefore, one cannot add 's, es, ed, or ing' to the end because it is not a verb. Infinitives can be used as nouns, adjectives or adverbs.

In Igbo language, infinitive is realized by prefixation using the corresponding i/ị prefix in accordance with vowel harmony to any verb root. That is i/ị + verb root = infinitive. It is important to note that these two prefixes are the possible morphemes used in the realization of infinitive in Igbo language.

Examples with infinitives (Mfinitiivu):

Prefix (nganiihu)	Verb root (Isingwaa)	Infinitives (Mfinitiivu)	Meaning (Ihe ọ pụtata)
ị	ba	ịbá	to enter
ị	da	ịda	to fall
ị	kpa	ịkpa	to discuss
ị	gba	ịgba	to play/dane
i	de	ide	to write
i	nyo	enyo	to peek
i	ke	ike (wa)	to divide
ị	ma	ịmá	to know
i	re	irè	to sell
i	zu	izu	to device/steal

The 'i' and 'ị' of Igbo language are allomorphs because they are different in sound and their spelling is semantically the same. From the example above, you can see that both can be prefixed to the verb root to form infinitives and they are phonological variants of the morpheme. However, they cannot be used interchangeable in the linguistic environment because of Igbo vowel harmony rules.

Furthermore, the infinitive prefixes, 'i' and 'ị' can be used as second person singular pronoun, thus, another form of allomorphs in another grammatical environment. The rule applies here, in all environment where they perform the same grammatical function they cannot be used interchangeably. Some examples of 'i' and 'ị' as pronouns are shown below:

Igbo language   *Meaning*
I riri nri.   You ate food.
Ị ga-eri nri.   You will eat (food).

17.4 Gerund (Jerọndụ)

A *gerund* is like a blend of verbs and nouns. It looks like a verb, but it acts like a noun. In English ending in -ing. For example, the word swimming, asking looking, talking, playing, etc.

In the Igbo language, gerund is a verbal derivation realized by the prefixing of o/ọ to a reduplicated verb root. It is in the form of
O/ọ + verb root x 2 = Gerund.

Examples with *Gerund* (Jerọndụ):

Prefix (nganiihu)	**Verb root** (Isingwaa)	**Infinitives** (Mfinitivu)	**Gerund** (Jerondu)	**Meaning** (Ihe ọ pụtata)
o	ri	ri	oriri	*eating/feasting*
ọ	nyụ	nya	ọnyụnya	*driving*
ọ	ṅụ	ṅụ	ọṅụṅụ	*drinking*
ọ	dị	da	ọdịda	*falling*
o	di	de	odide	*writing*
ọ	gụ	gụ	ọgụgụ	*reading*
o	ri	re	orire	*selling*
ọ	mụ	mụ	ọmụmụ	*learning/bearing*
ọ	hụ	hụ	ahụhụ	*roasting*
ọ	sụ	sọ	ọsụsọ	*sweating*
o	bi	bi	obibi	*living (home)*
o	ti	ti	otiti	*beating*

The 'o' and 'ọ' of Igbo language are allomorphs because they are different in sound and their spelling is semantically the same. From the example above, you can see that both can be prefixed to the verb root to form infinitives and they are phonological variants of the morpheme. However, they cannot be used interchangeable in the linguistic environment because of Igbo vowel harmony rules.

Furthermore, the infinitive prefixes, 'o' and 'ọ' can be used as third person singular pronoun, thus, another form of allomorphs in another grammatical environment. The rule applies here; in all environments where they perform the same grammatical function they cannot be used interchangeably. Examples of 'o' and 'ọ' as a pronoun is shown below:

Igbo language	*Meaning*
O dere ihe.	S/he wrote something.
Ọ gara ahịa.	S/he went to the market.

17.5 Noun agent (Ahaomee/Omee)

An agent noun is a word that is derived from another word denoting an action, and that identifies an entity that does that action. For example, "driver" is an agent noun formed from the verb "drive". Most agent nouns end in either '-er' (standard) or '-or' in the English language (for words derived directly from Latin e.g. carpenter, debtor, electrician, employer, lecturer, performer, director, teacher, etc.

In the Igbo language, the agent noun is realized by the use of the prefix o/ọ to the verb root and the addition of a noun complement. o/ọ + verb root + Noun complement = Agent Noun

Example with Noun agent (Ahaomee/Omee):

Prefix (nganiihu)	*Two verb root* (Isingwaa abụọ)	*Noun Agent* (Ahaomee/Omee)	*Meaning* (Ihe ọ pụtata)
o	me + e	omee	*(noun) agent*
o	de + e	ode	*writer*
o	le + e	olee	*where/how many*
o	me + e	omee	*doer*
ọ	ga + a	ọgaa	*boss*
ọ	gba + a	ọgbaa	*shooter*
ọ	kụ + ụ	ọkụụ	*planter/sower*
ọ	sụ + ụ	ọsụụ	*speaker/cutter*
ọ	ṅụ + ụ	ọṅụụ	*drinker*
o	je + e	ojee	*traveler/goer*

17.6 Noun instrument (Ahammee/Mmee)

Instrument noun: it is the equipment a worker uses in carrying out his duty. In the Igbo language, noun instrument is obtained when an m/n are prefixed to the verb root and the addition of a noun complement. The combination is in the following form:
m/n + verb root + Noun complement = Instrument Noun

Example with Noun instrument (Ahammee/Mmee):

Prefix (nganiihu)	**Verb root** (Isingwaa)	**Complement** (Mmeju)	**Ahamme/Mmee** (Noun Instrument)	**Translation** (Ntụghari)
m	gba	mmiri	mgbammiri	*jug*
m	pa	naka	mpanaka	*hand lamp*
m	kpa	isi	mkpaisi	*scissors*

m	gba	ama	mgbaama	*revealer*
n	che	ndo	nchendo	*sun protector*
n	ti	mkpu	nti mkpu	*exclaimer*
n	ku	ikuku	nku ikuku	*fan*
n	de	akwa	nde akwa	*iron*
n	tụ	oyi	ntụ oyi	*air conditioner*
n	gụ	ọnụ	ngụ ọnụ	*counter*

17.6.1 Past tense (Nke ihe gara aga):

past tense is the verb form you use to talk about things that happened in the past. Past tense indicates that an action is in the past relative to the speaker or writer. It is the use of verb to express an event that happened that is being talked about or reported.

In English, we use the past tense morpheme "ed", which is most often used with past regular verbs, for example: "planted", or "washed". It always has the same function (of making a verb past), but is pronounced slightly differently depending on the verb it is bound to: in "washed" we get /t/ (wash/t/), and in "planted" we get /ɪd/ (plant /ɪd/).

In the Igbo language, the letter "r" combines with any of the letters of Igbo vowels to produce an expression in the past tense. For example:

Verb root	***/r/***	***Vowel***	***Past tense***	***meaning***
fọ	r	ọ	fọrọ	remained
ga	r	a	gara	went
kwu	r	u	kwuru	said
re	r	e	rere	sold
ri	r	i	riri	ate
sị	r	ị	sịrị	said
tụ	r	ụ	tụrụ	threw
zo	r	o	zoro	hid

Therefore, -ra, -re, -ri, -rị, -ro, -rọ, -ru, -rụ are allomorphs in the above examples and they denote past tense of the verb root. They follow vowel harmony rules during combination. For example, you cannot put forward the following: *forọ, *gare, *kwurụ, *reri, *rirụ, *siro, *tụra and *zori,

17.6.2 Plural (Nke Ụbara)

Plural is one of the values of the grammatical category of number. The plural of a noun typically denotes a quantity greater than the default quantity represented by that noun. Plural markers are affixes or letters added to singular nouns to make them plural. Once a plural marker is added to a singular noun, that noun becomes countable. The plural markers of English are: 's,' 'es,' 'ves' and 'ies' as in 'boy - boys', 'church - churches', 'thief - thieves' and 'lady - ladies', etc.

In the Igbo language plural markers are a form of allomorphs. The plural markers in the Igbo language are 'ndị' and 'ụmụ'. They increase the value or number of a noun element and make them to become more than one element. Like other allomorphs, they are not interchangeable in an environment. For example:

Singular	*Meaning*	*Plural*	*Meaning*
Nwa akwụkwọ	a student	ụmụ akwụkwọ	Students
Nwa nne	a sibling	ụmụ nne	Siblings
Nwa nnụnụ	a bird	ụmụ nnụnụ	birds

In the above examples, although 'ụmụ' and 'ndị' are both plural markers as well as allomorph, they cannot be interchanged in the above context due to connotational restriction. When used in the above context, it becomes an expression of mockery to the person or group in question. 'ndị akwụkwọ' can suggest derogatory or belittling comment.

The use of the "ndị" plural marker is in the right context in the following examples:

Singular	*Meaning*	*Plural*	*Meaning*
Onye nne	a mother	ndị nne	mothers
Onye nna	a father	ndị nna	fathers

'Ụmụ' and 'ndị' are allomorphs. They connote plural but their forms are different and they operate under specific and selective linguistic environment due to some restriction that applies to them contextually, connotatively or collocationally.

Exercise
1. What is the definition of an allomorph in linguistics, particularly in the context of the Igbo language?
2. How are allomorphs in the Igbo language characterized, and what factors contribute to their variation?
3. Explain the seven major types of allomorphs found in the Igbo language as outlined in Chapter 17?
4. How are participles formed in Igbo, and what role do vowel harmony rules play in their formation?
5. Provide examples of participles in Igbo, demonstrating the application of the vowel harmony rules.
6. What distinguishes infinitives in Igbo, and how are they realized through prefixation?
7. Give examples of infinitives in Igbo, illustrating the use of vowel harmony in their formation.
8. How do infinitive prefixes 'i' and 'ị' function as pronouns in Igbo, and what grammatical rule governs their usage?
9. Describe the characteristics of gerunds in Igbo and the process of their formation.
10. Offer examples of gerunds in Igbo, showcasing the prefixation and reduplication involved in their formation.
11. Explain the concept of noun agents in Igbo and how they are constructed using prefixes and noun complements.
12. Provide examples of noun agents in Igbo, demonstrating the prefixation and noun complement addition.
13. What is meant by noun instruments in Igbo, and how are they formed using prefixes and noun complements?
14. Offer examples of noun instruments in Igbo, highlighting the prefixation and noun complement addition.
15. Can you explain the concept of past tense in the Igbo language and how it is realized through consonant-vowel combination?
16. Provide examples of past tense forms in Igbo, showing how consonants combine with vowels to denote past actions.
17. Describe the role of plural markers in Igbo and the distinction between 'ndị' and 'ụmụ' as plural markers.
18. Give examples illustrating the use of 'ndị' and 'ụmụ' as plural markers in Igbo, along with their contextual implications.
19. How do 'ụmụ' and 'ndị' function as allomorphs in Igbo, and what restrictions govern their usage in different contexts?
20. Can you explain how allomorphs contribute to the richness and complexity of the Igbo language's morphological system?

Part Four:

Lexicology in Igbo Linguistics (Amụmàmụ Ụdịdị, Nghọta na Itinye Mkpụrụokwu Igbo N'ọrụ)

Chapter 18

Introduction to Lexicology
(Mmalite Amụmàmụ Nghọta Mkpụrụokwu)

18.1 Definition of Lexicology

Lexicology is the branch of linguistics that is concerned with the study of words as individual items. It deals with both formal and semantic aspects of words; and analyzes the vocabulary of a specific language. Although, it is concerned predominantly with an in-depth description of lexemes, it gives a close attention to a vocabulary in its totality, the social communicative essence of a language as a synergetic system being a study focus. Lexicology examines every feature of a word – including formation, spelling, origin, usage and definition. It also considers the relationships that exist between words.

In linguistics, the lexicon (vocabulary) of a language is composed of lexemes, which are abstract units of meaning that correspond to a set of related forms of a word. Lexicology looks at how words can be broken down as well as identifies common patterns they follow. Lexicology is associated with lexicography, which is the practice of compiling dictionaries.

As every word is a unity of semantic, phonetic and grammatical elements, the word is studied not only in lexicology, but in other branches of linguistics, too, lexicology being closely connected with general linguistics, the history of the language, phonetics, stylistics, and grammar.

18.2 Lexicology interrelation in linguistics

Lexicology (from Gr *lexis* "word" and logos "learning") is a part of linguistics dealing with the vocabulary of a language and the properties of words as the main units of the language. It also studies all kinds of semantic grouping and semantic relations: synonym, antonym, hyponymy, semantic fields, etc.

In this connection, the term vocabulary is used to denote a system formed by the sum total of all the words and word equivalents that the language possesses. The term word denotes the basic unit of a given language resulting from the association of a particular meaning with a particular group of sounds capable of a particular grammatical employment. A word therefore is at the same time a semantic, grammatical and phonological unit. So, the subject-matter of lexicology is the word, its morphemic structure, history and meaning. Vocabulary studies include such aspects of research as etymology, semasiology and onomasiology.

Etymology: The evolution of a vocabulary forms the object of historical lexicology or etymology (from Gr. *etymon* "true, real"), discussing the origin of various words, their change and development, examining the linguistic and extra-linguistic forces that modify their structure, meaning and usage.

Semasiology (from Gr. *semasia* "signification") is a branch of linguistics whose subject-matter is the study of word meaning and the classification of changes in the signification of words or forms, viewed as normal and vital factors of any linguistic development. It is the most relevant to polysemy and homonymy.

Onomasiology is the study of the principles and regularities of the signification of things / notions by lexical and lexico-phraseological means of a given language. It has its special value in studying dialects, bearing an obvious relevance to synonymity.

18.3 Lexicography

Lexicology is the science of the study of word whereas lexicography is the writing of the word in some concrete form i.e. in the form of dictionary. As we shall see later, lexicology and lexicography are very closely related, rather the latter is directly dependent on the former and may be called applied lexicology.

Lexicography, the oldest sub-discipline of linguistics, deals with the compilation of dictionaries. There are many types of dictionaries, depending mainly on which lexical units are included, and which of their properties—such as sound, spelling, grammatical features, meaning, etymology, and others—are described.

One further important objective of lexicological studies is the study of the vocabulary of a language as a system. Revising the issue, the vocabulary can be studied synchronically (at a given stage of its development), or diachronically (in the context of the processes through which it grew, developed and acquired its modern form). The opposition of the two approaches is nevertheless disputable as the vocabulary, as well as the word which is its fundamental unit, is not only what it is at this particular stage of the language development, but what it was centuries ago and has been throughout its history.

18.4 Basic Concepts: Lexeme, Word Formation, Semantics

18.4.1 Lexeme:

The term lexeme means a language's most basic unit of meaning, often also thought of as a word in its most basic form. Not all lexemes consist of just one word, though, as a combination of words are necessary to convey the intended meaning. Examples of lexemes include walk, fire station, and change of heart. Lexeme can be defined to include this and these in one lexeme, or as two. Demonstratives like this have little or no lexical meaning, which is the point of "lexemes". Run is a lexeme in runner, running, runs, ran because they have related meanings; this has no meaning at all outside a deictic context.

A lexeme is (i) a lexical abstraction that (ii) has either a meaning (ordinarily) or a grammatical function, (iii) belongs to a syntactic category (most often a lexical category), and (iv) is realized by one or more phonological forms (canonically, by morphosyntactically contrasting word forms).

The study of lexeme in relation to word form

There are three lower levels of a language – a phoneme, a morpheme, a word. A word is the smallest meaningful unit of a language that can stand on its own and is made up of small components called morphemes and even smaller elements known as phonemes, or distinguishing sounds. Being a central element of any language system, the word is a focus for the problems of phonology, lexicology, syntax, morphology, stylistics and also for a number of other language and speech sciences.

The modern approach to the word as a double-facet unit is based on distinguishing between *the external* and *the internal structures of the word*. By the *external structure* of the word we mean *its morphological structure*. For example, in the word *post-impressionists* the following morphemes can be distinguished: the prefixes *post-*, *im-*, the root *–press-*, the noun-forming suffixes *-ion*, *-ist*, and the grammatical suffix of plurality *-s*. All these morphemes constitute the external structure of the word *post-impressionists*. *The internal structure of the word*, or *its meaning*, is nowadays commonly referred to as **the word's semantic structure**. This is the main aspect of word. Words can serve the purpose of human communication solely the ue to their meanings.

To sum it up, a word is the smallest naming unit of a language with a more or less free distribution used for the purposes of human communication, materially representing a group of sounds, possessing a meaning, susceptible to grammatical employment and characterized by formal and semantic unity.

18.4.2 Word formation

Word formation, also known as morphology, is the process of creating new words through various morphological processes such as derivation, compounding, blending, clipping, and reduplication. Word formation processes involve the combination, modification, or rearrangement of morphemes to form new lexical units with distinct meanings or functions. Word formation contributes to the expansion and enrichment of a language's vocabulary, allowing speakers to express new concepts, ideas, or nuances of meaning. For example, the word "unhappiness" is formed through the derivation process by adding the prefix "un-" to the base "happy."

There are 4 basic kinds of words:

1) Orthographic words – this refers to words distinguished from each other by their spelling. Orthography is the part of language study concerned with letters and spelling. It is the art of writing words with the proper letters, according to accepted usage; correct spelling. This method of spelling, is by the use of an alphabet or other system of symbols.

2) Phonological words – distinguished from each other by their pronunciation, the phonological word or prosodic word is a constituent in the phonological hierarchy higher than the syllable and the foot but lower than intonational phrase and the phonological phrase. Phonological words may be smaller or larger than grammatical or orthographic words.

It is difficult to find single and fixed criteria, which can be used to define a unit 'phonological word' in every language. There is a range of types of criteria such that every language, which has a unit 'phonological word', uses a selection of these criteria. The criteria include segmental features, suprasegmental (prosodic) and phonological rules.

A phonological word can be realized depending on the different segmental features of a word. For example; sequence of phoneme types, vowel clusters between consecutive syllable, possible positioning of phonemes within a word, role of aspiration and nasalization and pausal phenomena etc. Vowel clusters occur in words with adjoining vowels. These vowel combinations are associated with specific sounds. For example, the "ee" spelling denotes a long "e" sound, as in "Ee." (translated as "yes" in English), the position of phonemes within a word involves the conditions in which phonemes are realized in speech.

Stress (or accent) and/ or tone assignment; prosodic (suprasegmental) features such as nasalization, retroflexion, vowel harmony. Stress or accent, in many languages proves one helpful criterion for defining a phonological word. It becomes easier to find the position of word boundaries from the location of stress in a word, but in some languages, stress placement may depend on a combination of morphological and phonological factors. In such cases, stress may not be a useful criterion for phonological word. A phonological word can be realized in terms of vowel harmony, which operates over a certain syntagmatic extent (see chapter two). Vowel harmony may constitute a necessary and sufficient condition for recognizing a phonological word but not all languages have such convenient phonetic rules, and even those that do present the occasional exceptions.

3) **Word-forms** which are grammatical variants; are the different ways a word can exist in the context of a language. Many words exist as nouns, verbs or adjectives and change when prefixes or suffixes are added. For example, in English language, the words beautify, beautiful and beautifully are the verb, adjective and adverb forms of the noun beauty, but they are not interchangeable when used in a sentence.

Here are some word forms:

Noun	*Verb*	*Adjective*	*Adverb*
Beauty	beautify	beautiful	beautifully
Beneficiary	benefit	beneficial	beneficially
Creation	create	creative	creatively
Decision	decide	decisive	decisively
Difference	differentiate	different	differently

4) Words as items of meaning, the headwords of dictionary entries, are called **lexemes**. **A lexeme** is a group of words united by the common lexical meaning but having different grammatical forms. The base forms of such words, represented either by one orthographic word or a sequence of words called **multi-word lexemes** which have to be considered as single lexemes (e.g. phrasal verbs, some compounds) may be termed **citation forms of lexemes** (sing, talk, head, etc.), from which other word forms are considered to be derived.

Any language is a system of systems consisting of two subsystems: 1) the system of words' possible lexical meanings; 2) the system of words' grammatical forms. The former is called **the semantic structure of the word**; the latter is **its paradigm** latent to every part of speech (e.g. a noun has a 4-member paradigm, an adjective – a 3-member paradigm, etc.)

As for **the main lexicological problems**, two of these have already been highlighted. The problem of word-building is associated with prevailing morphological word-structures and with the processes of coining new words. Semantics is the study of meaning. Modern approaches to this problem are characterized by two different levels of study: syntagmatic and paradigmatic.

On the **syntagmatic level**, the semantic structure of the word is analyzed in its linear relationships with neighboring words in connected speech. In other words, the semantic characteristics of the word are observed, described and studied on the basis of its typical contexts.

On the **paradigmatic level**, the word is studied in its relationships with other words in the vocabulary system. So, a word may be studied in comparison with other words of a similar meaning (e. g. *work,* n. – *labor,* n.; *to refuse*, v. – *to reject* v. – to *decline*, v.), of opposite meaning (e. g. *busy*, adj. – *idle*, adj.; *to accept*, v. – *to reject*, v.), of different stylistic characteristics (e. g. *man*, n. – *chap*, n. – *bloke*, n. — *guy*, n.). Consequently, the key problems of paradigmatic studies are synonymy, antonymy, and functional styles.

Exercise
1. What is lexicology?
2. How does lexicology differ from lexicography, and what is the relationship between the two?
3. Explain the significance of lexemes in the study of lexicology and how they contribute to understanding vocabulary.
4. Describe the interrelation between lexicology and other branches of linguistics such as phonetics, morphology, and syntax.
5. What are some common patterns and relationships that lexicology examines between words within a language?
6. Discuss the importance of etymology in historical lexicology and how it contributes to understanding word origins and development.
7. Explain the concept of semasiology and its relevance to the study of word meaning and semantic change.
8. What is onomasiology and how does it contribute to the study of lexical signification in language?
9. Describe the objectives and methods of lexicographical studies, focusing on the compilation of dictionaries.
10. How does lexicology contribute to the study of the vocabulary of a language as a system, and what are the different approaches used in such studies?
11. Define the term lexeme and explain its significance in linguistic analysis.
12. Discuss the process of word formation, including various morphological processes such as derivation and compounding.
13. What are orthographic words, and how are they distinguished from each other in terms of spelling?
14. Explain the concept of phonological words and the criteria used to define them in different languages.
15. Describe word-forms as grammatical variants and provide examples to illustrate their usage.
16. Discuss the concept of lexemes as items of meaning and their role as headwords in dictionary entries.
17. Explain the syntagmatic and paradigmatic levels of semantic analysis in lexicology.
18. What are the main lexicological problems, and how are they approached in modern linguistic studies?
19. Discuss the significance of synonymy, antonymy, and functional styles in paradigmatic studies of lexicology.
20. How does lexicology contribute to our understanding of language as a dynamic and evolving system of communication?

Chapter 19

Word Formation Processes

19.1 Word Formation Process

Word Formation Process (Usoro Mmụba Okwu Igbo) is a means by which new words are produced either by modification of existing words or by complete innovation, which in turn become a part of the language. A morpheme is the smallest element of a word or else a grammar element, whereas a word is a complete meaningful element of language.

A word is a unit of language that carries meaning and consists of one or more morphemes which are joined more or less tightly together. A word consists of a root or stem and/or more affixes. Words can be combined to create phrases, clauses, and sentences. The study of the origin and history of a word is known as word etymology, a term which comes from Latin, but has its origins in Greek as (e´tymon "originalform" + logia "study of").

In Igbo language, most formed words are usually independent of complement. However, if the new word is a noun, it would have its complements attached. Examples:

word	*meaning*	*class*	*new word*	*meaning*	*class*
ozi	(message)	noun	oga ozi	messenger	noun
ri	(eat)	verb-	o-ri nri	(eater)	noun
ti	(drum)	verb	o-ti igba	(drummer)	noun

19.2 Formal Word Formation Methods

In Igbo language, formal word formation include: Affixation, Clipping, Compounding, Borrowing/Loanword, Reduplication, Blending and Acronyms. The three informal methods are: Jests/slangs (Njakịrị/Akụkụ), Mispronounced/corrupt words (Okwu Mkpọhie) and Loan blend words (Mbiọgwa).

19.2.1. Clipping

Clipping refers to the creation of a new word by removing one or more syllables from a longer polysyllabic word. It involves shortening the word without considering its derivation. This reduction is facilitated by focusing on a single syllable, typically the one carrying the primary stress. A familiar instance in English is the formation of "cellphone" from "cellular phone." Additional examples include "ad" for "advertisement" and "phone" for "telephone."

The term clipping is also known as a clipped form, clipped word, shortening, and truncation. Words are clipped when they are in a closely restricted context which leads to dropping the redundant syllables.

There are four types of possible clipping processes, depending on which part of the word undergoes structural changes. The four types of clipping are: back-clipping, fore-clipping, mixed clipping and clipping compunds. The examples in English are:

1. Back-clipping: temperature as temp, rhinoceros as rhino, gymnasium as gym, cellular as cell, etc.
2. Fore-clipping: helicopter as copter, telephone as phone, aeroplane as plane.
3. Mixed clipping: influenza as flu, refrigerator as fridge.
4. Clipping-compounds: parachute + trooper as paratrooper.

In Igbo language, the first two types are predominant in Igbo names and other noun or noun phrase.

Examples of back-clipping in Igbo words:

Word	*Clipped form*	*Full meaning*
Amaobichukwu	Amobi	*God's heart is unsearchable*
Arụrụ ala	Aru	*evil act or abominable act*
Chibụeze	Chibu	*God is king*
Chimaramkpam	Chi'ma	*God knows my need*
Chimdinma	Chidi	*my God is good*
Chimsomaga	Chisom	*My God is with me*
Chinụalamọgụ	Chinua	*may God fight for me*
Ginikanwa	Ginika	*what is bigger than a child?*
nkemdịrịm	Nkem	*let my portion be for me*
Nwakaego	Nwa'ka	*Child surpasses money*
Obiọha	Obi	*people's dearness*
Ogechukwu	Oge	*God's time*
Uzọchukwuamaka	Ụzọchukwu	*God's way is beautiful*

Examples of fore-clipping in Igbo words:

Word	Clipped form	Full meaning
Chinọnye	Nọnye	*(may) God stays with me*
Ndụmọdụ	Ọdụ	*advice*
Nwaamaka	Amaka	*(to have) baby is beautiful*
Ọgba-aghara	Aghara	*confusion*
Onye isi	Isi	*head*
Onyebụchi	Bụchi	*who is equal to God?*
Onyekachi	Kachi	*Who is bigger than God*
Ukwuosisi	Osisi	*tree*
Umengwu	Ngwu	*weakness*

19.2.2. Compounding

Compounding is the morphological operation that puts together two free forms and gives rise to a new word. In this process, new words are formed or derived by combining stems or root morphemes. For example, in English language, if you take the free morpheme white, an adjective, and combine it with the free morpheme house, a noun, I get the new word whitehouse.

In compounding the two words or morphemes that are used to form a new word usually have equal morphological status. This process of joining together of different lexical items to form new words does not necessarily require the change of class of the words.

Compounding	New word	Translation
Di + mgba	Dimgba	*wrester*
Elu + igwe	Eluigwe	*heaven*
Isi + akwukwo	isiakwukwo	*brainy*
M + kpa + isi	Mkpaisi	*scissors*
N + kọwa + okwu	Nkọwaokwu	*dictionary*
N + ti + igba	Ntiigba	*drum stick*
Ndi + oshi	Ndioshi	*thieves*
Nwa + akwụkwọ	nwaakwụkwọ	*student/pupil*
Ọ + kọwa + okwu	Ọkọwaokwu	*lexicographer*
Ọ + kpụ + isi	Ọkpụisi	*barber*
O + ti + igba	Otiigba	*drummer*
Odee + akwukwo	odeakwụkwọ	*secretary*
Oje + mba	Ojemba	*Tourist*
Onye + nkuzi	onyenkuzi	*teacher*
Oshi + ite	Oshite	*cook*

Ụgbọ + ala	Ụgbọala	*car*
Ụgbọ + elu	Ụgbọelu	*airplane*
Ulo + akwukwo	Ụlọakwụkwọ	*school*

19.2.3. Coined Words (Okwu Apịrịapị)

Coined words are new words invented or made up through the joining of two or more existing words. Coined words are similar to word formation through compounding except for the fact that the new word may modify any part of the words for easy pronunciation and to distinguish it from phrasal expression. Coined words are formed using either the features or functions of a thing. Popular use of a coined word is what makes it an acceptable part of Igbo word.

For example:

Coined word	**Translation**	**Meaning/Usage**
Ahịa enwemenwe	*ownable market*	Stock market
Akpatịokwu okwu	*Talkative box*	Radio
Akpatịokwu	*Chattering box*	Radio
Akụ enwemenwe	*ownable Wealth*	Stock
Asambodo	*Asambodo*	Certificate
Ekwentị	*Ear Gong*	Handset
Igwe okwu okwu	*metal for speakers*	Microphone
Igwe okwu	*metal for talking*	Microphone
Mahadum	*know it all*	University
Mgboojii/mgbo odee	*Blackboard*	Blackboard
Mkpịsị odee	*writer's pen/pencil*	Pen, pencil
Nnyemeakangwaa	*Auxiliary verb*	Auxiliary verb
Ntorobịa	*young (man/woman)*	Youths
Ntụli aka	*to put up hand*	Vote
Nzere	*Defense (of project)*	Degree
Nzu odee	*writer's chalk*	Chalk
Ọba akwụkwọ	*book barn*	Library
Ọchịchị ndị agbada	*civilian rule*	civilian rule
Ọgbọ nta vootu	*voter's specified area*	Constitutency
Ogbunigwe	*kills in multitude*	Bomb
Ọkada	*loud noise (bike)*	Motocycle
Oke ọnwụnye	*earnable part/share*	Share
Okooko	*Flower*	Flower
Ihe Onyoonyo	*item for viewing*	Television
Ọrịa mmịnwụ	*shrinking illness*	HIV/AIDS

Ọrịa obilinaajaọcha	*grave destined illness*	HIV/AIDS
Ọzutaakụ	*Wealth buyer*	Stock broker
Ụgbọ okporoigwe	*metal track vehicle*	Train
Ụka ọgbaraọhụrụ	*Modern day's church*	Pentecostal church
Ụkọ akwụkwọ	*book holder/hanger*	Bookshelf
Ụzọ awaraawara	*graded/broad way*	Express road

The above listed coined words are used either to describe a feature or function thereby forming a noun that are used for system or things that are new in Igbo language. Notice that coined words can have up to six or more words in order to give full meaning and make the description easy to understand. For example:

Coined word	Translation	No. of words
Ndị ejị okwu ha eme ihe	*Stake-holders*	6
Nnweghari enwe+m+enwe	*Stock exchange*	4
Ọchịchị+onye kwuo uche ya	*Demoncracy*	5

19.2.4. Borrowed/Loan Word

Borrowing is the process by which a word from one language is adapted for use in another. Words from source language are borrowed or loaned as lexical items to another language. All languages are susceptible to borrowing for lexical expansion so as to cope with new functions and to meet up with their limited names for things they have no name for.

Also, borrowing can result from trade and commerce, especially where language association or linguistic contact among languages meet. Borrowing is perhaps the most common source of new words and should be seen as a regular morphological process of word formation in every language. Borrowed words are called loanwords.

Examples of Igbo loan words:

Loan word	**Source**	**Translation**
Adure	Yoruba	*dyed cloth from yoruba*
Agbada	Yoruba	*traditional free flowing outfit*
Agboro	Hausa	*tout*
Agidi	Yoruba	*solid cooked pap*
Ahụekere	Hausa	*goundnut*
Akamụ	Hausa	*Pap*
Akpati	Yoruba	*box*
Alafịa	Hausa	*enjoyment*

Alibo	Igala	*powdered cassava*
Ashawo	Yoruba	*Harlot*
Ashebi	Yoruba	*uniform attire in ceremony*
Asioke	Yoruba	*locally weaved cloth*
Ayo	Yoruba	*onions*
Banza	Hausa	*rubbish*
Bọl/bọọlụ	English	*Ball*
Bredi	English	*Bread*
Burukutu	Hausa	*fermented drink*
Chinchi	Hausa	*bedbug*
Dada	Yoruba	*dreadlock*
Disemba	English	*December*
Ekpeteshi	Ghana	*Rum*
Ekpo	Calabar/Ibibio	*type of masquered*
Eba	Yoruba	*Garri meal*
Faksi	English	*Fax*
Friza	English	*Freezer*
Gova	Portuguese	*Guava*
Gworo	Hausa	*type of kola*
Ichafo	Hausa	*headtie/Scarf*
Intanet	English	*Internet*
Isam	Ijaw/Efik	*periwinkle (snail)*
Jara	Hausa	*add small/extra*
Jenuwari	English	*January*
Jigida	Hausa	*type of waist bead*
Kaikai	Yoruba	*locally distilled liquor*
Kanda	Hausa	*used as meat or grilled meat*
Karọtụ	English	*Carrot*
Kashu	Portuguese	*Cashew*
Kebụlụ	English	*cable*
Koboko	Hausa	*whip*
Kọmputa	English	*computer*
Kpekele	Yoruba	*fried dried plantain*
Maimai/Elele	Yoruba	*prepared beans meal/cake*
Mangala	Hausa	*Fish (a type of fish)*
Mango	English	*Mango*
Mọi-mọi	Yoruba	*beans cake/meal*
Mọnde	English	*Monday*
Moto	English	*motor*

Mugu	onye nzuuzu	*a gullible/foolish person*
Netwọkụ	English	*network*
Njin	English	*engine*
Njinịa	English	*engineer*
Ọga	Yoruba	*master*
Ogede	Ịgala	*plantain*
Okwute	Yoruba	*stone*
Onuku/Oluku	Ịgala	*idiot/fool*
Osikapa	Hausa	*rice*
Oyooyo	Yoruba	*delicious*
Pọọpọ	English	*pawpaw*
Redio	English	*radio*
Salaka	Chad/Yoruba	*generous/free gift*
Suya	Hausa	*peppery smoked meat*
Tebulu	English	*table*
Tọọchi	English	*torch*
Tozo	Hausa	*cow's rhomboid muscles*
Trauza	English	*trouser*
Tuuzdee	English	*tuesday*
Vidio	English	*video*
Wahala	Yoruba	*trouble*
Waka	Hausa	*abuse*
Waya	English	*wire*
Wayo	Yoruba	*cheat*
Windo	English	*window*
Wuruwuru	Yoruba	*deception/cheating*
Yabasi	Hausa	*onion*

The borrowed word never remains a perfect copy of its original. It is made to fit the phonological, morphological, and syntactic patterns of its new language. For example, the Hausa pronunciation of shinkafa is very different from the Igbo pronunciation Osikapa. Likewise, the Hausa pronunciation of **albasa** is pronounce Yabasi in Igbo language. The same applies to so many other borrowed words.

19.2.5. Reduplication

Reduplication is a morphological process in which the root or stem of a word or even the whole word is repeated exactly or with a slight change. Reduplication is common in Igbo language. It is also, a word-formation process in which all or part of a word is repeated to convey some form of meaning.

Reduplication is often used to show plurality, distribution, repetition, customary activity, increase of size, addedintensity, continuance, etc. It is found in many languages of the world, however, its morphological methods vary from language to language.

In general, reduplication is a process of repeating a syllable orthe word as a whole (sometimes with a vowel change) and putting it together to form a new word. In English language words like byebye (exact reduplication), super-duper (rhyming reduplication) or chitchat, pitter-patter, zigzag, tick-tock, flipflop are examples of reduplication.

Examples of reduplication Igbo words:

Two similar Words	*Reduplicated form*	*Translation*
Aga + aga	Agaaga	*impassable*
Aja + aja	Ajaaja	sandy
Aka + aka	Akaaka	ageless/timeless
Aṅwụ + aṅwụ	Aṅwụaṅwụ	immortal/deathless
Anya + anya	Anyaanya	looker/staring
Ata + ata	Ataata	sinewy
Awa + awa	Awaawa	unbreakable
Eri + eri	Erieri	stingy
Mkpu + mkpu	mkpumkpu	shortness
Mmiri + mmiri	Mmiri mmiri	watery
Ngwa + ngwa	Ngwangwa	hurriedly
Ngwọ + ngwọ	Ngwọngwọ	pepper soup
Ọsọ + ọsọ	Ọsọsọ	hurriedly

19.2.6. Blending

Blending is a morphological process of taking two or more mrophemes or words, removing parts of each, and joining the residues together to create a new word whose form and meaning are taken from the source words. It is typically accomplished by taking only the beginning of one word and joining it to the end of the other word.

In Igbo words formation, if there are two vowels in each of those separate morphemes, one of such vowels is dropped before the new word is realized. For instance, anya + anwụ becomes anyanwụ (sunshine), a is dropped. See more examples below:

Blending	*New word*	*Translation*
anya + anwụ	anyanwụ	sunshine

chi + na + asa	chinasa	God answers
chi +na + eke	chineke	God the creator
Di + ibia	dibia	doctor
di+ ike	dike	strong
nwa + oke	nwoke	male/man
nwa + orie	nworie	child born on orie day
nwa+ afọ	nwafọ	child born on afọ day
nwa+ eke	nweke	child born on eke day
uka + amaka	ukamaka	Church/way (going) is good
uso + ekwu	usekwu	stove/tripod wood stove

19.2.7. Acronyms

Acronym is formed by joining together the initial letters (or sometimes a little larger part of other words and is pronounced as a word. It is important to note that acronyms are not the same thing as abbreviation.

Abbreviation is the shortening of existing words to create a new word, usually in a form that is informal to the originals. There are several ways this can be done. It includes making one or more syllables shorter leaving out other, as in doc for document, Dr. for doctor, app for application and prof for professor. Usually, the syllable remaining after the rest has been removed provides enough information to allow us to identify the word it is an abbreviation of, though at times this is not the case.

The difference between an acronym and an abbreviation is that abbreviation is usually formed shortening, e.g. doc, dr, prof and so on, while acronyms is formed from the letter of each word.

In some instances, the acronym is pronounced as a sequence of letter names, as in UN, US, or SUV. In other instances, such as WHO from World Health Organization and UNICEF from United Nations International Children's Emergency Fund, the acronym can be pronounced as an ordinary English word.

There are few acronyms in Igbo language. This may be because Igbo language and culture embrace comprehensive expression of message in words or they use figure of speech to populate a message which demands deep mental thought and reasoning from the listeners. Some of the common Igbo language acronyms are as follows:

Acronuym	*Full expression*	*Translation*
DGZ	dere gawazie	etcetera/and so on
ONU	Onye Nche Uka	Church warden

19.3 Informal Word Formation Methods

*19.3.1. Slang/Jests (*Njakịrị/Akụkụ*)*
Slang is often considered as very informal words and expressions that are more common in speech than writing and are typically restricted to a particular context or group of people. A set of colloquial words or phrases in a language.
Slang is very colloquial; the language and dialect tend to be specific to a particular territory and it is considered as "youth language" by many adults.

Though, certain jests and slangs are typically restricted to a particular context or group of people, it is language and culture specific and is often transmitted from one culture and language to another. With the advent of internet and mobile communications, the rate at which slangs or jests are being used and shared on social media has increased.

There are several forms of Igbo language jests and slangs but there are seven major categories that they can fall under, namely:

1. *Advisory words* (okwu ndụmọdụ)
2. *Assaultive jest/slang* (okwu mkparị)
3. *Disgraceful words* (okwu mmebọ)
4. *Flaring words* (okwu njali)
5. *Hypercritical jest/slang* (okwu akọmụọnụ)
6. *Laudatory words* (okwu otito)
7. *Side-talk* (okwu akụkụ)

Jests and slang usually start from either a location or group of people. When it starts from a location or group and becomes common in that location or among the group, it will inadvertently find its way into the society where people can choose to localize it or use it without restriction. The location or group of people could be students, traders, construction workers, young men and women, musicians, media or journalists, broadcasters, and so on.

When a jest or slang is formed and used for the first time, it is usually the people around at the time that would have full understanding of the meaning and it is through them that the meaning and intention is conveyed to other people that would hear the jest or slang later. Hence, when it becomes common to everyone; it would then become a new word. If it is not considered as a derogatory or hate phrase, many people would start using it.

19.3.2. Situational/Advisory words (okwu ọnọdụ/ndụmọdụ)

These are words that are used to describe a thing, a situation, condition of thing, behavior, and lifestyle. They may come in the form of advisory or coded situational expressions. Some of the jests/slang may come in the form of a noun, phrase, clause, figure of speech, and so on. For example:

Igbo word	***English translation***
Aghọtaghị ije	*Unable to understand what is going on.*
Anịkịrịja	*An old bicycle that makes a lot of noise.*
Bọchaa	*Escape/Get out immediately.*
Bredị	*Money*
Gbachaa m	*Give me money or find something for me.*
Ịghọta ije	*Able to understand what is going on.*
Ịnya mmadụ	*to trick somebody.*
Na-ekwe oyooyo	*Affirmation/acclamation for looking good.*
Oko	*An old person*
Okongwu	*An old person*
Owu ịsa mmadụ	*Serious lack of money*
Owu ite	*bankrupt/poverty-stricken*
Paakuul	*Cool down/relax.*
Sụlịa	*To play football well.*
Ụwa mgbede	*prosperity towards the end of one's life.*
Wụsa ọwara	*to ask someone calm down or relax*

19.3.3. Assaultive jest/slang (okwu mkparị)

These are words that show gross indignity, an instance of insolent or contemptuous word or speech that is used to describe an action, behavior and lifestyle. Some of the jests/slang may come in the form of noun, phrase, clause, figure of speech, and so on. For example:

Igbo word	***English translation***
Akụla	*Madness*
Atịmgbo/atịlarị	*A deaf person*
Mugu	*A novice or person who is not sociable.*
Mumu	*Foolishness*
Okpo	*A foolish person/A stupid person*
Onye mgbu	*A foolish/stupid person*
Onye owo	*A loser*
Ọnyụpa	*Slow/sluguish movement*

19.3.4. Disgraceful words (okwu mmebọ):
These are words that bring a deserving loss of reputation or respect as the result of a dishonorable action. It is a shameful, dishonorable, and disreputable expression that tells that someone has been exposed for his or her shameful act. Some of the jests/slang may come in the form of noun, phrase, clause, figure of speech, and so on. For example:

Igbo word	**English translation**
Gbara ọgwụ gị nwụọ	*Mind your business.*
Ịgba buutu	*to ignore somebody.*
Ịkụpụ ntị	*to ignore.*
Ilita mmadụ	*to avoid somebody politely.*
Itebọ/imebọ mmadụ	*to disgrace somebody*
Ịwụ n'ala	*to humiliate somebody.*
O chogo gị	*You have missed something*

19.3.5. Flaring words (okwu njali)
These are words that bring a deserving motivation or flares up someone's reputation or flashy name. It is a boastful and exaggerated expression that tells about someone's status, a magnified status or exaggerated action. Some of the jests/slang may come in the form of noun, phrase, clause, figure of speech, and so on. For example:

Igbo word	**English translation**
Akpụrụka	*Well-built/strong (though not original)*
Awara awara	*Fast running vehicle.*
Gbaraagba	*A huge person*
Ịkpa ọwa	*to drive a motocycle/vehicle meticulously.*
Kụsuo/pịasuo	*to provoke/ ginger somebody to act.*
Obere nsị	*A stout-hearted person*
Onye ọwa	*A person who drives meticulously.*
Waa waa wa	*Wreckless driving.*

19.3.6. Hypercritical jest/slang (okwu akọmụọnụ):
These are words that are excessively and unreasonably critical of someone's behavior, (sometimes of small faults). It may not come as a result of unnecessary fault finding but a different choice of words that describes someone's inadequacy, immaturity or intentional misbehaviour. Some of the jests/slang may come in the form a noun, phrase, clause, figure of speech and so on. For example:

Igbo word   **English translation**

Anịnị	*A thief/Robber*
Ipara	*Attempt to pay less for more value (product)*
Ịparaala/ịparaana	*Stingy buyer*
JJC	*Newcomer/Fresher*
Mpịrịmpị	*A staunch bargainer*
Nzama	*Cheating with profit*
Ogbu oge (abbr. "oo")	*Someone who wastes precious time*
Ọta mgbe	*Someone who wastes his precious time*

19.3.7. *Laudatory words* (okwu otito):

These are words that express praise; extolling someone or something. It is a eulogistic or commendatory expression that can be used to describe the specialty or uniqueness of a thing or someone. It may come in the form of flattery words or sincere words of admiration of someone action, personality or beauty. Some of the jests/slang may come in the form of noun, phrase, clause, figure of speech and so on. For example:

Igbo word	**English translation**
Ajịbọ	*elegant or sophisticated lady*
Aka nchawa	*good luck*
Akwa nwa	*A pretty woman/lady/baby*
Asụkaramụ	*Richness/wealth*
Bebi ị dị okee	*A pretty lady who dressed very beautifully.*
Ebe anọ	*Current trend*
Ị chara ife ị ga-acha	*You are looking good*
I nwerọ polo	*You don't have any problem.*
Ị towara ntị	*very beautiful/dressing very beautiful*
Ichi okere	*to show off.*
Igbu ozu	*Richness/wealth*
Iji ija	*Richness*
Iji nkụ	*Richness*
Ịma ihe arụrụ	*Understanding the current trend.*
Ịnọ mma	*Being good for somebody.*
Ịnọ n'ofe	*Being in a better condition/state.*
Ịsụ pụtụ pụtụ n'ofe	*successful person/ enjoying better life.*
Iwete ọkụ	*A giver/being generous or active sexually.*
Nkwọbi	*Sliced meat/fish mixed with vegetables.*
Odeku	*Stout beer*
Ọkpa ọkụ	*Fine and smooth leg*
Pọọpọ nwa	*Pretty girl or lady with glowy skin*

Santana	*Pounded cassava.*
Sherikoko	*Beautiful young lady/girl*
Tamtam	*Perfect/something that is very fine.*
Yoriyori	*Something beautiful/sweet/good*

19.3.8. *Characteristic word* (okwu nke agwa):

These are words that are used to describe a thing, a situation, condition of thing, behavior, and lifestyle in a manner that only people that know what it means would understand. They may also be descriptive expressions of a specialty of a thing. It is not limited to natural things but includes magical and diabolical slangs. Some of the jests/slang may come in the form of noun, phrase, clause, figure of speech, and so on. For example:

Igbo word	***English translation***
Adịgboroja	*Fake or old-fashioned*
Akpịrịko	*A price gouger/ trickster*
Akwunakwuna	*Harlotry*
Ashebi	*Uniform dress by a group*
Ata na-agba	*Serious confusion*
Ife ajụ	*to charm and manipulate somebody.*
Ịgba tọọchị	*Bribery/to give bribe.*
Ịja	*Money*
Ikechi mmadụ	*to tie someone with evil power.*
Ịma mmadụ (IM)	*Nepotism*
Ịsa isi	*Brainwashing*
Nchọchọ	*Money*
Ndị eke	*Police officers.*
Odeshi	*protective charm*
Okerieọnwụọ	*poison/deadly substance or product*
Ọkịrịka	*Fairly used clothes/secondhand clothes*
Ọkụ enu/ọkụelu	*Prostitute*
Ọtapịapịa	*Poisonous/deadly substance*
Ọtụmọkpọ	*undefendable and dependable charm*
Tokumbo	*Fairly used vehicles or wares*

19.3.9. *Mispronounced/Corrupt Words* (Okwu Mkpọhie):

This is another way of word formation in Igbo language. Mispronounced Words/Corrupt Words (Okwu Mkpọhie) are usually foreign words that are pronounced incorrectly. Although, they may be categorized under borrowed/loan words, however, because many rightful Igbo words were set aside in an attempt to stay according to the source that might fall under this new category.

Igbo self-westernization has a big role in this. Their effort to either anglicize or francization themselves (especially the young generation) is making some Igbo names for things disappear. Anglicization refers to the process by which a place or person becomes influenced by English culture or British culture, or a process of cultural and/or linguistic change in which something non-English becomes English. Likewise, Francization and other languages that are being copied in exchange for what Igbo names objects and things bear.

It is important to note that names of things that do not exist in Igbo lexeme but were borrowed qualify for Igbo dictionary standard words entries, but corrupt words may not be considered especially when there is an Igbo name for the thing which foreign name has been acquired for.

The following are examples of Mispronounced Words/Corrupt Words (Okwu Mkpọhie):

Words	*Place of Origin*	*Source word*
Abada	English	*Haberdashery*
Afụ	English	*Half penny*
Aloo	English	*Hello*
Barangidi	English	*Blanket*
Bọkwụ	French	*Beacoup*
Brezi	English	*Brassier*
Dọbụrụbaa	English	*Double barrel*
Gadarum	English	*Guard room*
Ịchafụ	French	*Le chifon*
Karafish	English	*Crayfish*
Kọtụma	English	*Court (man) messenger*
Mbụrọda	English	*Umbrella*
Nkachiifu	English	*Handkerchief*
Ofesi	English	*Overseas*
Oloko	English	*Locomotive*
Oroma	Portuguese	*Orange*
Potoki	English	*Portuguese*
Sajiin	English	*Sergent*
Shimi	English	*Chemise (an under wear)*
Sọfịa	English	*Surveyor*
Tapoolu	English	*Tarpauline*

19.3.10. *Loan Blend* (Mbiọgwa)

Loan blend are words formed by joining and blending Igbo words with a foreign word often for descriptive purpose. This sometime may come from young people who have learned a foreign word for a thing that has Igbo name and who want to show that they know what both side calls an object or to specify what they mean if they cannot lay hold of any Igbo expression that would replace their foreign knowledge. For example:

Loan blend words	**Translation/meaning.**
Efere *plastik*	Plastic plate
Ite *aluminọm*	Aluminum pot
Ite *pọọtụ*	Metal pot
Ngazị/ngaji *plastik*	Plastic spoon
Oche *plastik*	Plastic chair
Ọkụ *eletrik*	Electric light
Tekinụzụ	Technology
Ụzọ moto	Tarred Road

In the above examples, the italicized words beside Igbo words are the loan foreign words that were blended with Igbo words. Many people have come to accept the usage of this blend, although in formal standard writing they are rarely used.

Informal words formed from jest/slnags, loan words or loan blend can have a negative impact on original Igbo words. It can facilitate the disappearance of lexeme that have existed for years. There are many Igbo words that were used in the past five decades that are today going down the road of extinction. For example:

	Igbo word	**Translation**
1.	ákpàtà/àlụbálá	measles
2.	Égbúgbú	tattoo
3.	éjù	earthenware
4.	ekpenta	leprosy
5.	ékú	wooden spoon
6.	ékwú	kitchen
7.	m kpílíté	a small wooden mortar
8.	mbụrụ	stick (that is aimed and thrown at a tree top)
9.	mkpà	scissors
10.	mkpú	room
11.	mkpúkè	woman's bedroom/house
12.	mpanaka	lantern
13.	ǹchìchè	yaw disease

14.	ńgigā	basket hanging (over kitchen's stove)
15.	óché ékwu	kitchen stool
16.	ògbòdù	the uninitiated (into the masquerade cult)
17.	ókpēsị	symbol of divinity
18.	ọkpọgā	a type of chair
19.	ọkù	clay bowl
20.	òkwú-álụsi	shrine
21.	ọtáńjélé	local eye pencil
22.	òtòlò	diarrhea
23.	ufie	a reddish powder for beautification
24.	ùgànị	famine
25.	ùkó	shelf/counter
26.	ùri	make up for women.

Exercise

1. What is a morpheme, and how does it relate to word formation?
2. Explain the concept of word etymology and its significance.
3. How are new words typically formed in the Igbo language?
4. Describe the process of clipping in word formation and provide examples from Igbo words.
5. What are the four types of clipping processes, and how do they differ?
6. Give examples of back-clipping and fore-clipping in Igbo words.
7. What is compounding in word formation, and how does it work?
8. Provide examples of compound words formed in Igbo.
9. How are coined words different from compounded words?
10. Give examples of coined words in Igbo and explain their formation.
11. What is borrowing in word formation, and why do languages borrow words?
12. Provide examples of loanwords borrowed into Igbo from other languages.
13. What is reduplication, and how is it used in word formation?
14. Give examples of reduplicated Igbo words and explain their meanings.
15. Explain the concept of blending in word formation and give examples from Igbo.
16. What are acronyms, and how are they formed in language?
17. Provide examples of Igbo language acronyms and their meanings.
18. Describe the different categories of slang and jests in the Igbo language.
19. Give examples of assaultive jests and disgraceful words in Igbo slang.
20. How do characteristic words differ from other forms of slang, and provide examples from Igbo culture?

Chapter 20

Semantic Relations

Words in a language may semantically relate or differ from another, hence meaning relation. Meaning relation is considered using more than one word. When two or more words are considered in terms of their similarities and differences, meaning relation is employed to determine where they fall into. Synonym is a meaning relationship between two or more words that have different sounds and spellings but have similar or exact meaning.

20.1 Synonyms (Myìrì mkpụrụokwū):
A synonym is a word or morpheme (mkpụrụasụsụ) that means exactly or nearly the same as another word or morpheme (mkpụrụasụsụ) in the same language but often with different implications and associations. For example, in the English language, the words begin, start, commence, and initiate is synonymous.

Two or more words sharing the same semantic similarities are synonyms. Synonymous words are often times interchangeable in communicative effects. Although not in all contexts as we would see in the following description. The use of synonyms can help one avoid repetition and spice up expression.

Words have a certain uniqueness that another that is supposedly alike may not have. As a result, certain Igbo synonyms word cannot always be used exactly the same way in a sentence. This gave rise to two forms of synonyms, namely:

- Absolute synonyms and
- Partial synonyms

201.1. Absolute Synonyms
Absolute synonyms are also known as exact, true, total, complete synonyms is a term used to describe two words have all meaning components in common and regarded as complete synonyms. When a word shares the majority of its meaning components with other words and shares exactly

the same communicative effect in every context in which they are used, such two words are classified as absolute synonymous.

Also, absolute synonymous words are interchangeable and can be used in similar environments all the time without a change in meaning. Some of the common English examples for absolute synonyms are: everybody/everyone, anybody/anyone, somebody/someone, frequently/often, rarely/seldom and so on. When all the contextual relations of two words are identical, they are considered as absolute synonymous words. For example:

Total synonyms	*Translation*
àchàrà/ọtọsí	*bamboo*
ákílū/ágbílū/ùgórò	*bitter kola*
ákụkụ/ágà	*side*
àkùpe/ǹkùfe/ǹkụcha	*hand fan*
ànyásị/ùchíchì/ùjíshì	*night*
ébírí/Ọgbọ	*age-mate*
éfè/óhérē	*chance*
égwú/úrí	*song*
éríri/ékwéré/ụdọ	*rope*
gírígírí/ńgálíngá	*slim/thin*
gùzó/kwụrụ	*stand*
ìbèríbè/ńzúzú	*stupidity/silliness*
kịrịkịrị/írighírí	*tiny*
kítàà/ùgbúà/ǹnwéé	*now*
ḿbá/òóló	*no*
mgbèdè/ùhúrúchì	*evening*
mkpà/ǹchà	*scissors*
nááni/sọọsọ	*only*
ǹkàtà/èkètè	*basket*
ǹkịtị/ụkpọrọ	*nothingness*
ọgụ/òtí	*hoe*
ògúgù/ípā	*palm frond*
ọmụ (nkwụ)/ọkpúkpà	*newly sprout palm frond*
ònwéghì/òméhè	*nothing*
ọsọọsọ/ńgwáńgwá	*quickly/hurriedly*
ótù/òfú/ńnáā	*one*
ụbàrá/mmánụ	*many/plural/numerous*
ùbé ḿgbā/ùbé òkpòkó	*black pear*
úbì/úgbō	*farmland*

ùwé/èfè/mweyì   *cloth*

20.1.2. Partial Synonyms

Partial synonyms, also known as synonyms are words very similar to another but not identical in contextual application usage because of their incongruent meaning and inexactness in their associative meaning. These words often have the same communicative effect in some contexts but not in all contexts.

Also, partial synonyms can refer to words that are identical in meaning but fail to meet the condition of all-round application as in the case of absolute synonymy. These words have the same reference but are not encompassing in all aspects of associative meaning.

An example of partial synonyms in English language is vacant and empty. Whereas one can say, *vacant room* or *empty room*; it is incompatible to use them as in *vacant job* and *empty job*. Another example is *"work"* and *"job"*. One can say, *"I work in an office"* but cannot say *"I job in an office"*. The above two examples are partial synonyms in English language.

Partial synonyms	*Translation*
àzụ ụlọ/Òwèrè	*backyard*
búté/bútá/pátá	*carry/lift to*
ékwú ígwè/òshí ìtè/ákwụkwà	*tripod stove stand.*
ghúò/síè	*cook*
kú/gbú (mmiri)	*fetch (water)*
kwá/dụ	*sew*
sú/sá (ákwà)	*wash cloth*
té/hịọ/fịá	*rub*

Partial synonyms result from three types of restrictions that exist in Igbo language. Contextual, collocational, and connotative restrictions exist in Igbo words and are revealed when pairs of synonyms are placed in certain sentence or contexts of expression.

20.2 Restrictions in Igbo Synonyms

There are three ways in which Igbo synonyms can be restricted in usage and they are as follows:

- Collocational restriction
- Connotative restriction and
- Contextual domain restriction

Before taking a look at each of the restrictions mentioned above, let us have a look at the overview of Standard Igbo synonyms based on common meanings as follows:

Synonyms	Meaning	Synonyms	Meaning
Ábàlị/Ùchíchì	Night	Ábụ̀/Ùkwé	Poem/Song
Àgbụ̀rụ̀/Ébó	Tribe	Ághá/Ọ̀gụ̀	War
Àmàmíhé/Àkọ	Wisdom	Àtùmàtù/Ámùmà	Idea/Plan
Bé/Ụ̀lọ	House/home	Dúm/Níílē	All
Ényì/Ọyị	Friend	Èzí/Mbárá	Compound
Óyìbó/Bèkéè	English	Ńsọpụ̀rụ̀/Ùgwù	Respect
Ìbèríbè/Ńzúzù	Foolish	Ìgbé/Ákpàtị	Box
Íké/Úmé	Strength	Ìnyòm/Nwáànyị	Woman
Ísí-mkpē/Àjàdù	Widow	Òmùmé/Àgwà	Character
Ìzìzì/Mbụ	First	Jé/Gá	Go
Jédébé/Kwụsị	End	Mbídó/Mmàlíté	Beginning
Mkpọtụ/Ụ̀zù	Noise	Mméē/Ọ̀bàrà	Blood
Mméhìè/Njọ	Sin	Mpàkó/Ńgàlá	Pride
Ngá/Mkpóóró	Prison	Ngáná/Úmé-ngwụ	Lazy
Ógè/Mgbè	When/Time	Ónyé ndū/Ónyé ísī	Leader
Ọchị/Ámụ	Laughter	Ọgbákọ́/Ńzùkọ	Meeting
Ọgbọ/Ébírí	Peer	Ọmikō/Èbérè	Mercy
Ọsọ ọsọ/Ńgwá ńgwá	Quickly	Sịrị/Kwùrù (Sị/kwú)	Said
Úbì/Úgbō	Farm	Ụ̀bịàm/Ógbènyè	Poverty
Ùgègbè/Ènyò	Mirror	Ùghá/Àsị	Lie
Ùhúrúchī/Mgbèdè	Evening	Úsà/Ázịzá	Answer
Ùwé/Ákwà	Cloth/dress	Ụjọ̄/Égwù	Fear
Ụkwụ/Ọkpà	Leg	Èbùmnúchè/Èbùmnóbì	Intention

20.2.1 Collocational restriction

Collocational restriction is a linguistic term that is used to refer to the fact that in certain two-word phrases or expressions, the meaning of an individual word is restricted to that particular phrase or expression. Collocation is the tendency of words to co-occur with each other. It is a function of the relationship that words have together which makes them stay together in certain expression. Words that are strongly attached together often restrict a member of a synonymous pair from co-occurring with lexical phrases. For example, in English language, the adjective dry can only mean 'not sweet' in combination with the noun wine.

In Igbo language, the rule of specific selection of words operates within the innate linguistic knowledge of a speaker and allows him or her to match not only sounds and meanings in their message but place relational co-occurring words with each other. When selectional rule is observed in an expression, other synonymous member(s) will be collocationally restricted. Selectional restrictions are the semantic restrictions that a word imposes on an environment in which it occurs that restrict the use of another synonymous member.

The following are examples of collocational restriction in Igbo language.

Synonyms:	Àmàmíhé/Àkọ	
Meaning:	Wisdom	
1st instance:	***Akọ* na uche**	*(permitted)*
Translation:	*Wisdom*	
2nd instance:	***Amamihe* na uche**	*(restricted)*
Translation:	*Wisdom and mind*	
Synonyms:	Dúm/niile	
Meaning:	All	
1st instance:	**Ndị *niile* bịara ebe a ụnyaahụ**	*(permitted)*
Translation:	*Everyone that came here yesterday.*	
2nd instance:	**Ndị *dum* bịara ebe a ụnyaahụ**	*(restricted)*
Translation:	*Everyone(s) (pl) that came here yesterday.*	
Synonyms:	Èbùmúchè/Èbùmóbì	
Meaning:	Intention	
1st instance:	***Èbùmúchè* edemede.**	*(permitted)*
Translation:	*Objective of study*	
2nd instance:	***Èbùmóbì* edemede.**	*(restricted)*
Translation:	*intention of writing (different usage)*	
Synonyms:	Èzí/Mbárá	
Meaning:	Compound (residential/home)	
1st instance:	***Ezi* na ụlọ/Ezinụlọ**	*(permitted)*
Translation:	*Family*	
2nd instance:	***Mbara* na ụlọ**	*(restricted)*
Translation:	*Compound and house (different meaning)*	
Synonyms:	Ìgbé/Ákpàtị	
Meaning:	Box	
1st instance:	***Igbe* mma**	*(permitted)*
Translation:	*Epitome of Beauty*	
2nd instance:	***Akpatị* mma**	*(restricted)*

Translation: *(Storage) box for beauty*

Synonyms: Íké/Úmé
Meaning: Strength
1st instance: **Ike ọkpụkpụ (aka)** *(permitted)*
Translation: *Physical strength*
2nd instance: **Ume ọkpụkpụ (aka)** *(restricted)*
Translation: *personal effort*

Synonyms: Ìnyòm/Nwaáànyị
Meaning: Woman
1st instance 1: **"Ndị inyom** *(permitted)*
Translation: *Women*
2nd instance: Ụmụ inyom *(restricted /lacks concordance)*
3rd instance: **Ndị nwaanyị** *(restricted/lacks concordance)*
4th instance: Ụmụ nwaanyị *(permitted))*
Translation: *Women*

Synonyms: Jé/Gá
Meaning: Go
1st instance: **Njé Njé/Njém** *(permitted)*
Translation: *Travel/Journey*
2nd instance: **Ngá ngá/Ngám** *(restricted)*
Translation: *Ngángá as a compound word means "boasting."*

Synonyms: Mbídó/Mmàlíté
Meaning: Beginning
1st instance: **Isi mbido** *(permitted)*
Translation: *Beginning*
2nd instance: **Isi mmalite** *(restricted)*
Translation: *head of beginning*

Synonyms: Mkpọtụ/Ụ̀zụ̀
Meaning: Noise
1st instance: **Ụzụ akwa** *(permitted)*
Translation: *Wailing*
2nd instance: **Mkpọtụ akwa** *(restricted)*
Translation: *Noise of cry*

Synonyms:	Mméē/Òbàrà	
Meaning:	blood	
1st instance:	**Ahụ na ọ***bara* **Kraịst**	*(permitted)*
Translation:	*flesh and blood of Christ*	
2nd instance:	**Ahụ na** *mmee* **Kraịst**	*(restricted /no concordance)*

Synonyms:	Ngá/Mkpọrọ	
Meaning:	Prison	
1st instance:	***Nga* mkpụrụ ọka**	*(permitted)*
Translation:	*Life-time imprisonment*	
2nd instance:	***Mkpọrọ* mkpụrụ ọka**	*(restricted /no concordance)*

Synonyms:	Ńjédébé/Ńkwụsị/Mmechi	
Meaning:	End	
1st instance:	**Isi** *njedebe*	*(permitted)*
Translation:	*The end*	
2nd instance:	**Isi** *nkwụsị*/***mmechi***	*(restricted /no concordance)*

Synonyms:	Ónyé ndŭ/ Ónyé Ísī	
Meaning:	Leader	
1st instance:	***Onye isi* oche**	*(permitted)*
Translation:	*Chairman*	
2nd instance:	***Onye ndu* oche**	*(restricted /no concordance)*

Synonyms:	Ónyìbó/Bèkéè	
Meaning:	English/Foreign	
1st instance:	**Ala** *Bekee*	*(permitted)*
Translation:	*Foreign country*	
2nd instance:	**Ala** *Oyibo*	*(restricted /no concordance)*

Synonyms:	Ọchị/Ámụ	
Meaning:	Laughter	
1st instance:	**Ọchị eze**	*(permitted)*
Translation:	*Deceptive smile*	
2nd instance:	***Amụ* eze**	*(restricted /no concordance)*

Synonyms:	Ọgụ/Ághá/Mgbá
Meaning:	Fight/Struggle/War

1st instance:	**Ọgụ na mgba**	*(permitted)*
Translation:	*Difficulty/up hilled*	
2nd instance:	***Agha* na mgba**	*(restricted /no concordance)*
Translation:	*War and Fight*	

Synonyms:	Ùwé/Ákwà	
Meaning:	Cloth	
1st instance:	***Uwe* mwụda**	*(permitted)*
Translation:	*Long loose gown*	
2nd instance:	***Akwa* mwụda**	*(restricted /no concordance)*
3rd instance:	Obi/ukwu *akwa*	*(permitted)*
Translation:	*Wrapper/Lappa/Pagne*	
4th instance:	**Obi/ukwu *uwe***	*(restricted /no concordance)*

Synonyms:	Ụjọ/Égwù	
Meaning:	Fear	
1st instance:	**Onye *ụjọ* ọgwụ**	*(permitted)*
Translation:	*A pharmacophobia/trypanophobia*	
2nd instance:	**Onye *egwu* ọgwụ**	*(restricted /no concordance)*

Synonyms:	Ụkwụ/Ọkpà	
Meaning:	Leg	
1st instance:	**Ndị *ọkpa* atụrụ**	*(permitted)*
Translation:	*Saboteurs*	
2nd instance:	**Ndị *ụkwụ* atụrụ**	*(restricted /no concordance)*

20.2.2 Connotative restriction

Connotation and Denotation are two principal methods of describing the meanings of words. Connotation refers to the wide array of positive and negative associations that most words naturally carry with them, whereas denotation is the precise, literal definition of a word that might be found in a dictionary.

Connotative meaning is an idea or quality that a word makes you think about besides its meaning. The *connotative meaning* of a word includes the feelings that people may connect with that word. A word may have negative/positive connotations for different people. For example, in English the word "fat" has negative connotations for many people because of its associative meaning to obesity. The word "childlike" has the connotation of innocence because of its associative meaning to children's innocence.

In Igbo language, the rule of specific selection of words in line with their connotative meaning operates within the innate linguistic knowledge of a speaker who would consider the intention of the message and make use of meaningful matching words that would not confuse the receiver.

The following are examples of connotative restriction in Igbo language would show you how a synonymous pair can produce different meaning in the same sentence or expression.

Synonyms:	Ághá/Ọgù
Meaning:	War/fight
1st instance:	**Eze na Emeka lụrụ ọgụ.**
Translation:	*Obi and Obinna fought each other.*
2nd instance:	**Eze na Emeka lụrụ agha.**
Translation:	*Obi and Obinna fought the war.*
Synonyms:	Átùmàtù/Ámùmà
Meaning:	Idea
1st instance:	**Anyị nwere amụma dị iche iche.**
Translation:	*We have different programs.*
2nd instance:	**Anyị nwere atụmatụ dị iche iche.**
Translation:	*We have different ideas.*
Synonyms:	Ázịzá/ Ụsà
Meaning:	Answer
1st instance:	**Kedụ ihe bụ azịza gị?**
Translation:	*What is your answer?*
2nd instance:	**Kedụ ihe bụ ụsa gị?**
Translation:	*What is your response?*
Synonyms:	Mpàkó/Ńgàlá
Meaning:	Pride
1st instance:	**Onye ngala**
Translation:	*A glamorous person.*
2nd instance:	**Onye mpako**
Translation:	*A prideful individual/ An arrogant person.*
Synonyms:	Ńsọpùrù/Ùgwù
Meaning:	Respect
1st instance:	**Obinna enweghị nsọpụrụ.**
Translation:	*Obinna has no respect.*

2nd instance:	**Obinna enweghị ugwu.**
Translation:	*Obinna has no good reputation.*
Synonyms:	Ọmìíkō/Èbérè
Meaning:	Mercy
1st instance:	**Onye (obi) ebere**
Translation:	*A merciful person.*
2nd instance:	**Onye omiiko**
Translation:	*A compassionate person.*
Synonyms:	Úbì/Úgbó
Meaning:	Farm
1st instance:	**Ejere m n'ugbo m.**
Translation:	*I went to my farm (land, fish pond, piggery, etc.).*
2nd instance:	**Ejere m n'ubi m.**
Translation:	*I went to my farmland.*
Synonyms:	Ụkwụ̀/Ọkpà
Meaning:	Leg
1st instance:	**Ada nwere ụkwụ ogologo.**
Translation:	*Ada cuts corners.*
2ns instance:	**Ada nwere ọkpa ogologo.**
Translation:	*Ada has long legs (physical).*

20.2.3 Contextual domain restriction

Synonyms, in Igbo language, are context sensitive as a result of the general idea or concept of usage combined with all other characteristics or particulars of the Igbo language lexemes. Contextually restricted synonyms are a condition in which a pair of lexemes is not able to substitute each other in all contexts. Context is a term used to describe words and sentence that surround any part of a written or spoken communication and that helps to determine its meaning. Words that are synonym lexemes are interchangeable with each other within contexts; they would be used as alternative in communication without any restriction.

A substitution test would reveal if a pair of synonyms are interchangeable in all contexts or not. When there is, at least, one context where a pair cannot be used interchangeably and give the same meaning, then one can draw a logical conclusion that they are not absolute synonyms. For example, ákwà/ùwé.

The general knowledge of an average Igbo native speaker views ákwà as to include any form of cloth material, and ùwé as being a specific term for "dress." And with other examples as shown below, one can understand that there are contexts where members of a synonymous pair are appropriate while in other contexts, they are not. When synonymous lexemes cannot substitute one another in all contexts based on the intuition of the native speaker, a speaker would conceptualize meanings within contexts and intuitively select the contextually appropriate member of a pair in a particular context of his or her message.

The result of this is that the uses of synonyms are based on how the Igbo native speakers conceive meanings in various contexts of written or spoken communication. When synonyms are used within the contexts of any communication, it is easier to determine the differences between them and to classify them as either absolute or partial synonyms. For example:

Synonyms:	Ábàlị/Ùchíchì
Meaning:	Night
1st instance:	**Abalị dị egwu** *(compatible context)*
Translation:	*Thief/Robber (idiomatic or metaphoric expression)*
2nd instance:	**Uchichi dị egwu** *(incompatible context)*

Synonyms:	Ábụ/Ùkwé
Meaning:	Poem/Song
1st instance:	**Ugonna na-abụ abụ.** *(Compatible context)*
Translation:	*Ugonna is singing.*
2nd instance:	**Ugonna na-abụ ukwe.** *(Incompatible context)*

The present continuous tense *"na-abụ"* does not go with ukwe. To get the same meaning one would have to use a present continuous tense *"na-ekwe"* to get the same meaning, e.g. *Ọ na-ekwe ukwe.* He/she is singing.

Synonyms:	Ághá/Ọgụ
Meaning:	War
1st instance:	**Obi busoro m agha.** *(Compatible context)*
Translation:	*Obi fought me.*
2nd instance:	**Obi busoro m ọgụ.** *(Compatible context)*

Synonyms:	Bé/Ụlọ
Meaning:	House/home
1st instance:	**Ada nọ n'ụlọ.** *(Compatible context)*
Translation:	*Ada is at home.*

2nd instance:	**Ada nọ na be.** *(Incompatible context)*
Synonyms:	Dúm/Níilē
Meaning:	All
1st instance:	**Ndị niile bịara ahịa …** *(Compatible context)*
Translation:	*All that came to the market …*
2nd instance:	**Ndị dum bịara ahịa . . .** *(Incompatible context)*
Synonyms:	Ényì/Ọyị
Meaning:	Friend
1st instance:	**Ada na nwata akwụkwọ kọleji na-ayị ọyị.** *(Compatible context)*
Translation:	*Ada is befriending a college student.*
2nd instance:	**Ada na nwata akwụkwọ kọleji na-ayị enyi.** *(Incompatible context)*
Synonyms:	Ìbèríbè/Ńzúzù
Meaning:	Foolish
1st instance:	**Uchenna dara iberibe.** *(Compatible context)*
Translation:	*Uchenna is foolish.*
2nd instance:	**Ọ dara nzuzu.** *(Incompatible context)*
Synonyms:	Íké/Úmé
Meaning:	Strength
1st instance:	**Ike ya gwụrụ m.** *(Compatible context)*
Translation:	*I'm tired of him/her.*
2nd instance:	**Ume ya gwụrụ m.** *(Incompatible context)*
3rd instance:	**Ike dị n'okwu ahụ.** *(Compatible context)*
Translation:	*There is power in those words.*
4th instance:	**Ume dị n'okwu ahụ.** *(Incompatible context)*
5th instance:	**Ọ bụghị site n'ike.** *(Compatible context)*
Translation:	*It's not by strength/might.*
6th instance:	**Ọ bụghị site n'ume.** *(Incompatible context)*
Synonyms:	Ísí mkpē/Àjàdù
Meaning:	Widow
1st instance:	**Mgbeorie bụ ajadu.** *(Compatible context)*
Translation:	*Mgbeorie is a widow*
2nd instance:	**Mgbeorie bụ isi mkpe.** *(Incompatible context)*
Synonyms:	Ìzìzì/Mbụ

Meaning:	First
1st instance:	**Na mbụ na mbụ̀...** *(Compatible context)*
Translation:	*First and foremost*
2nd instance:	**N'izizi n'izizi...** *(Incompatible context)*

Synonyms:	Mkpọtụ/Ụ̀zụ̀
Meaning:	Noise
1st instance:	**Ụmụ akwụkwọ tụrụ ụzụ mgbe mgbịrịgba kụrụ.** *(Compatible context)*
Translation:	*students made noise when the bell rang.*
2nd instance:	**Ụmụ akwụkwọ tụrụ mkpọtụ mgbe mgbịrịgba kụrụ.** *(Incompatible context)*

Synonyms:	Mméē/Ọ̀bàrà
Meaning:	Blood
1st instance:	**Ọbara anaghị atụ asị.** *(Compatible context)*
Translation:	*Blood does not lie.*
2nd instance:	**Mmee anaghị atụ asị.** *(Incompatible context)*
3rd instance:	**Amaka na Emeka bụ otu ọbara.** *(Compatible context)*
Translation:	*Amaka and Emeka are blood relations/ related by blood.*

Synonyms:	Mpàkó/Ńgàlá
Meaning:	Pride
1st instance:	**Tinye ngala n'egwu a.** *(Compatible context)*
Translation:	*Add glamour to the dance steps.*
2nd instance:	**Tinye mpako n'egwu a.** *(Incompatible context)*

Synonyms:	Njọ/Mméhiè
Meaning:	Sin
1st instance:	**Ọ bụrụ na mmehie adịghị, mgbaghara agaghị adị.** *(Compatible context)*
Translation:	*To err is human and to forgive is divine*
2nd instance:	**Ọ bụrụ na njọ adịghị, mgbaghara agaghị adị.** *(Incompatible context)*

Synonyms:	Óge/Mgbè
Meaning:	Time/When
1st instance:	**Ada na-egbu oge.** *(Compatible context)*
Translation:	*Ada is wasting time.*

2ⁿᵈ instance:	**Ada na-egbu mgbe.** *(Incompatible context)*
Synonyms:	Ọgbákọ/Ńzụkọ
Meaning:	Meeting
1ˢᵗ instance:	**Ezinụlọ Okeke ga-àkụ nzụkọ n'afọ ọzọ.** *(Compatible context)*
Translation:	*Okeke family will host next year's meeting.*
2ⁿᵈ instance:	**Ezinụlọ Okeke ga-àkụ ọgbakọ n'ọnwa ọzọ.** *(Incompatible context)*
Synonyms:	Sịrị/Kwùrù (Sị/kwú)
Meaning:	Said
1ˢᵗ instance:	**Ụkọchukwu sịrị anyị bịa.** *(Compatible context)*
Translation:	*The priest/pastor said that we should come.*
2ⁿᵈ instance:	**Ụkọchukwu kwuru anyị bịa.** *(Incompatible context)*
Synonyms:	Ụ̀bịàm/Ógbènyè
Meaning:	Poverty
1ˢᵗ instance:	**Ikenna bụ nwa ogbenye.** *(Compatible context)*
Translation:	*Ikenna is poor.*
2ⁿᵈ instance:	**Ikenna bụ nwa ụbịam.** *(Incompatible context)*
Synonyms:	Ùhúrúchī/Mgbèdè
Meaning:	Evening
1ˢᵗ instance:	**Ụwa mgbede ka mma.** *(Compatible context)*
Translation:	*Life at old age is better.*
2ⁿᵈ instance:	**Ụwa uhuruchi ka mma.** *(Incompatible context)*
Synonyms:	Ùwé/Ákwà
Meaning:	Cloth
1ˢᵗ instance:	**Kpuchie nwa ahụ akwa.** *(Compatible context)*
Translation:	*cover that baby with a cloth.*
2ⁿᵈ instance:	**Kpuchie nwa ahụ uwe.** *(Incompatible context)*
3ʳᵈ instance:	**Ndị otu ya kpuru/tụrụ ya akwa.** *(Compatible context)*
Translation:	*Members of his group decorated/honoured him/her with a cloth (es)*
4ᵗʰ instance:	**Ndị otu ya kpuru/tụrụ ya uwe.** *(Incompatible context)*
5ᵗʰ instance:	**Nne Ugomma ma akwa n'obi.** *(Compatible context)*
Translation:	*Ugomma's mom tied a wrapper over her chest.*
6ᵗʰ instance:	**Ada ma uwe n'obi.** *(Incompatible context)*
7ᵗʰ instance:	**Benye m akwa.** *(Compatible context)*

Translation:	*Sell clothing (material) to me.*
8th instance:	**Benye m uwe ọcha.** *(Incompatible context)*
Synonyms:	Ụghá/Àsị
Meaning:	Lie
1st instance:	**Ọ tụrụ asị.** *(Compatible context)*
Translation:	*He/she lied*
2nd instance:	**Ọ tụrụ ụgha.** *(Incompatible context)*

20.3 Antonnyms (Okwu Mmegide)

An *antonym* is a semantic term for a word that has an opposite meaning to another word. It is a lexical term of relation that pivots on opposite in meaning of lexical items. Learning common Igbo antonyms sharpens your sense of Igbo language and expands your vocabulary.

Antonyms in the Igbo language can be grouped into:
1. Gradable
2. Complementary
3. Converse
4. Multiple taxonomies

20.3.1. Gradable antonyms:

Graded (or gradable) antonyms are word pairs whose meanings are opposite and which lie on a continuous spectrum. In English language, they are typically pairs of adjectives that can be qualified by adverbs like very, extremely, etc. So, for example, we can say the tuition fees were expensive or were cheap.

However, as expensive, and cheap are gradable antonyms, we can also qualify how expensive or cheap using adverbs like very, extremely, etc. Further examples of gradable antonyms are bland/delicious, bright/dull, delicious/disgusting, friendly/unfriendly, hot/cold, interesting/boring, large/small, modern/old-fashioned, wet/dry and so on.

In Igbo language, similar to English, gradable canbe tested with the addition of 'ezigbo' or 'tụ' or 'tụrụ' (which are measuring indicators) or by finding their intermediate words. The third line of each set is the application of the mid-interval words or scaling indicators, for instance:

Antonyms:	nnukwu/obere
Meaning:	big/small
1st instance:	Ofe Adanne kunyere m dị*tụ* obere.

Translation:	The soup that Adanne served me is quite small.
2nd instance:	Ofe Adanne kunyere m bu*tụrụ* ibu.
Translation:	The soup that Adanne served me is slightly big

Antonyms:	mma/njọ
Meaning:	beautiful/ugly
1st instance:	**Adaeze mara *ezigbo* mma**
Translation:	*Adaeze is very beautiful*
2nd instance:	**Adaeze ma*tụrụ* mma**
Translation:	*Adaeze is slightly beautiful*

Antonyms:	ogologo/mkpụmkpụ
Meaning:	tall/short
1st instance:	**Emeka toro *ezigbo* ogologo**
Translation:	*Emeka is very tall*
2nd instance:	**Emeka to*tụrụ* ogologo**
Translation:	*Emeka is slightly tall*

Antonyms:	ọcha/oji
Meaning:	fair/black
1st instance:	**Nwamaka dị*tụ* ọcha/oji.**
Translation:	*She is slightly fair/dark.*
2nd instance:	**Nwamaka dị *ezigbo* ọcha/oji**
Translation:	*She is very fair/dark*

Antonyms:	nwata/okenye
Meaning:	young/old
1st instance:	**Okeke emeela *ezigbo* okenye.**
Translation:	*Okeke is very old.*
2nd instance:	**Okeke eme*tụ*la okenye.**
Translation:	*Okeke is slightly old.*

Antonyms:	warawara /obosara
Meaning:	narrow/wide
1st instance:	**Okporo ụzọ Aba dị *ezigbo* warawara**
Translation:	*The road to Aba is very narrow*
2nd instance:	**Okporo ụzọ Aba dị*tụ* warawara**
Translation:	*The road to Aba is slightly narrow*

Antonyms:	Ogbenye/ ọgaranya
Meaning:	Poor-rich
1st instance:	**Nwankwo nwere *ezigbo* ego**
Translation:	*Nwankwo is very rich*
2nd instance:	**Nwankwo nwe*tụrụ* ego**
Translation:	*Nwankwo is slightly rich*

Antonyms:	nso/anya
Meaning:	near/far
1st instance:	**Ụlọ akwụkwọ anyị dị *ezigbo* nso.**
Translation:	*Our school location is very near.*
2nd instance:	**Ụlọ akwụkwọ anyị dị*tụ* nso.**
Translation:	*Our school location is slightly near.*

Antonyms:	uju/ụkọ
Meaning:	plenty/lack
1st instance:	**Ọ nọ n'*ezigbo* uju ego.**
Translation:	*He is in the season of (very) plenty of money.*
2nd instance:	**Ọ nọ n'*ezigbo* ụkọ ego.**
Translation:	*He is in the season of (extreme) lack of money.*

Antonyms:	iwe/aṅụrị
meaning:	angry/happy
1st instance:	**Mmeri ahụ nyere ya *ezigbo* aṅụrị.**
Translation:	*That victory made him/her very happy.*
2nd instance:	**Mmeri ahụ we*tụrụ* ya iwe.**
Translation:	*That victory made him/her very angry.*

Antonyms:	ọsọọsọ/nwayọ-nwayọ
Meaning:	fast/slow
1st instance:	**Obinna na-eje*tụ* nwayọ-nwayọ karịa Uchenna.**
Translation:	*Obinna walks slightly slower than Uchenna.*
2nd instance:	**Obinna na-eje*tụ* ọsọọsọ karịa Uchenna.**
Translation:	*Obinna walks slightly faster than Uchenna.*

Antonyms:	ihụnaanya/akpọmasị
Meaning:	love/hate
1st instance:	**Ekene were *ezigbo* ihụnaanya n'ebe Adanna nọ.**
Translation:	*Ekene greatly loves Adanna.*

2nd instance:	**Ekene were *ezigbo* akpọmasị n'ebe Adanna nọ.**
Translation:	*Ekene greatly hates Adanna.*

Antonyms:	ilo/enyi
Meaning:	enemy/friend
1st instance:	**Ngwere na Agwọ bụ *ezigbo* ndị ilo**
Translation:	*Lizard and Snake are arch enemies.*
2nd instance:	**Ngwere na Agwọ bụ *ezigbo* ndị enyi**
Translation:	*Lizard and Snake are very good friends.*

Antonyms:	ọkụ/oyi
Meaning:	hot/cold
1st instance:	**Mmiri ahụ dịtụ ọkụ (ṅara ṅara).**
Translation:	*The water is slightly hot (lukewarm).*
2nd instance:	**Mmiri ahụ dịtụ oyi (ṅara ṅara).**
Translation:	*The water is slightly cold (lukewarm).*

Antonyms:	isi/ ọdụ
Meaning:	head/tail
1st instance:	**Okwu ahụ enweghị isi nke o ji enwe ọdụ.**
Translation:	*Those words have neither head nor tail.*
2nd instance:	**Okwu ahụ nwere *ezigbo* isi.**
Translation:	*Those words are very important.*

Antonyms:	mbido/njedewe
Meaning:	beginning/end
1st instance:	Ọ bịara na mbido emume ahụ.
Translation:	He came at the beginning of the ceremony.
2nd instance:	Ọ bịara na njedebe emume ahụ.
Translation:	He came at the end of the ceremony.

All the examples above are scalable, that is, they have intermediate measurable values thus gradable.

20.3.2. Complementary antonyms:

Complementary antonyms also known as non- gradable (or binary) antonyms are word pairs whose meanings are opposite and do not lie on a continuous spectrum (push, pull). In English language, complementary antonyms are pairs of words that are opposite in meaning, cannot be graded and are mutually exclusive. That means, they can exist independently of each other and there is no intermeadiate place inbetween. Examples of complementary opposites are: alive/dead, black/white, boy/girl, exit/entrance, lift/drop, push/pull, right/wrong, silence/noise, treat/punishment, yes/no, and so on.

In Igbo language, similar to English, complementary antonyms do not have any measuring indicators or intermediate words. They are absolute antonyms. The presence of one means automatic absence of the other. They are also complementary to each other, for instance:

Antonyms	Meaning	Antonyms	Meaning
Ee/mba	*yes/no*	iheọma/iheọjọọ	*right/wrong*
ihiụra/ịmụanya	*asleep/alive*	nbuli/nbuda	*lift/drop*
nkịtịị/ụzụ	*silence/noise*	nwoke/nwaanyị	*man/woman*
ojii/ọcha	*black/white*	oke/nwunye	*male/female*
ọnwụ/ndụ	*dead/alive*	ọpụpụ/mbata	*exit/entrance.*

20.3.3. Converse/Reverse antonyms:
Converse (and reverse opposite) antonyms are word pairs where opposite makes sense only in the context of the relationship between the two meanings (teacher, pupil).

In English language, converse antonyms are pairs of opposites where one cannot exist without the other. For example, to have a patient, you must be a doctor. Therefore, doctor and patient are complementary antonyms. Further examples of complementary antonyms are: above/below, defence/prosecution, doctor/patient, husband/wife, night/day, parent/child, plug/socket, policeman/criminal, teacher/student and so on.

In Igbo language, similar to English, converse antonyms describe a relation between two entities fromalternate viewpoints. They are converse terms in the sensethat when one is applied, the other automatically assumes the opposite side. It is also used to describe a relationship between antonyms in terms of movement or direction, where one term describes movement in onedirection, the other in the opposite direction. Examples of Igbo converse antonyms are as follows:

Antonyms:	Onyenkuzi/nwaakwụkwọ
Meaning:	Teacher/student
1ˢᵗ instance:	**Ọlụchi bụ Onyenkuzi anyị.**
Translation:	*Ọlụchi is our teacher.* (Conversely, We're Ọlụchi's students)

Antonyms:	nne/nwa
Meaning:	mother/child
Instance:	**Mgbeorie bụ nne Onyeka.**

Translation:	*Mgbeorie is Onyeka's mother.*
	(Conversely, Onyeka is Mgbeorie's child)
Antonyms:	okwuu/ọnụụ
Meaning:	speaker/hearer
Instance:	**Akụchi bụ okwuu na mmemme anyị.**
Translation:	*Akụchi is the speaker in our program.*
	(Conversely, we're Akụchi's hearer/audience)
Antonyms:	ọgụegwu/ọgbaegwu
Meaning:	singer/dancer
Instance:	Ada bụ Ọgụegwu; anyị bụ ọgbaegwu.
Translation:	Ada is the singer, and we are the dancer.
Antonyms:	di/nwunye
Meaning:	husband/wife
Instance:	**Emeka bụ di Ọlụchi**
Translation:	*Emeka is Ọlụchi's husband.* (conversely Ọlụchi is Emeka's wife)
Antonyms:	Mgbago/mgbada
Meaning:	North/south
Instance:	**Kalụ is from the southern part of their country,**
Translation:	*Kalụ si n'akụkụ mgbada obodo ha.*
	(conversely Kalụ is not from the north)
Antonyms:	akanri/akaekpe
Meaning:	Right-hand/left-hand
Instance:	**Emeka na-eme akaekpe.**
Translation:	*Emeka is left-handed.* (conversely, Emeka is not right-handed)
Antonyms:	ọdịda anyanwu/ọwụwa anyanwu
Meaning:	west/east
Instance:	**Ndị Igbo si na ọwụwa anyanwu.**
Translation:	*The Igbo are from the east.*
	(Conversely, The Igbo are not from the west)
Antonyms:	Bịa/gaa
Meaning:	Come/go

Instance:	**Eze ga-abịa ebe a.**
Translation:	*Eze will come here.* (Inversely, Eze will not go there)
Antonyms:	Gaa/lọọ
Meaning:	Go/return
Instance:	**Ada ga-aga ahịa.**
Translation:	*Ada will go to the market.*
	(Inversely. Ada has not return from the market)
Antonyms:	Ime/mpụta
Meaning:	In/out
Instance:	**Uche nọ n'ime ụlọ**
Translation:	*Uche is in the house.* (Inversely, Uche is not out of the house)
Antonyms:	Gbago/gbada
Meaning:	Up/down
Instance:	**Obi si ya gbago elu ụlọ.**
Translation:	*Obi told him/her to go up the stair of the house.*
	(Inversely, Obi did not ask them to come down)
Antonyms:	nye/nara
Meaning:	Give/Receive (take)
Instance:	**Nye ya ego.**
Translation:	*Give him/her money.*
	(inversely, Do not recieve money from him/her)
Antonyms:	Ihu/azụ
Meaning:	Front/back
Instance:	**Gaa n'iru oche.**
Meaning:	*Go to the front seat.* (Inversely, don't go to the back seat)
Antonyms:	binye/biri
Meaning:	lend/borrow
Instance:	**Binye ya ego.**
Translation:	*Lend him/her some money.* (Inversely, do not borrow from him/her)

20.4 Hyponymy

Hyponymy is a semantic relationship in which the meaning of one word (the hyponym) is buried beneath the meaning of another (the hypernym). Hyponyms are particular cases or illustrations of a larger category that the hypernym represents. As an illustration, the hyponyms "rose," "tulip," and "daisy" belong to the hypernym "flower." Lexical objects can be categorized and classified according to their semantic qualities by means of hyponymy, which represents an ordered set of ideas.

Here are examples of hyponymy:

1. Mkpụrụ osisi *(Fruit)* - Mkpụrụ vaịn *(Grape)*, Oroma *(Orange)*, Unere *(Banana)*.
2. Anụmanụ *(Animal)* - Nkịta *(Dog)*, Nwamba *(Cat)*, Ịnyịnya *(Horse)*, Ọdụm *(Lion)*.
3. Agba *(Color)* - Mme mme/ọbara ọbara *(Red)*, Anụnụ anụnụ *(Blue)*.
4. Akwa/Uwe *(Clothing)* - Uwe elu *(Shirt)*, Uwe ogologo ọkpa *(Pants)*, Uwe mwụda *(Dress)*
5. Ihe ọṅụṅụ *(Beverage)* - Kọfị *(Coffee)*, Tii *(Tea)*, Soda *(Soda)*
6. Ọdịdị *(Shape)* - Okirikili *(Circle)*, Nhataọnụanọ *(Square)*, Ọnụ-atọ *(Triangle)*.
7. Ọrụ aka *(Profession)* - Dọkịta *(Doctor)*, Onye nkuzi *(Teacher)*, Onye ọrụ ugbo *(Farmer)*.
8. Ngwá ọrụ *(Tool)* - Ahuru *(Iron Slag)*, Ányá óshí *(Pry/crowbar)*, Íhúamá *(Anvil)*.
9. Nri *(Food)* - Osikapa *(Rice)*, Ofe *(Soup)*, Akamụ *(Pap)*, Akara *(Beans-cake)*.
10. Nnụnụ *(Bird)* - Nza *(Sparrow)*, Ugo *(Eagle)*, Nduru *(Dove)*. Chekeleke *(Egret)*.
11. Ụmụ ahụhụ *(Insect)* - Ijere *(Ant)*, Aṅụ *(Bee)*, Ilokolo Ibuba *(Butterfly)*,
12. Ihu Igwe *(Weather)* - *Mmiri ozuzo (Rain)*, Ibuba oyi *(Snow)*, Anwụọchịchz *(Sunshine)*.

In each case, the hyponyms represent specific examples or instances of the broader category represented by the hypernym.

20.5 Homonymy

Homonymy refers to the relationship between words that are spelled or pronounced the same but have different meanings. Homonyms can be classified into homographs, which have the same spelling but different meanings (e.g., "bat" as in the flying mammal and "bat" as in the sports equipment), and homophones, which have the same pronunciation but different meanings and may or may not have the same spelling (e.g., "two," "to," and "too"). Homonymy can lead to ambiguity in language comprehension and requires contextual cues for disambiguation.

Here are examples of homonyms:
1. Agwa (Behavior – *person's character*) and Agwa (Beans – *a type of food*)
2. Agba (Color – *the hue or shade of something*) and Agba (Jaw – *a part of human body*)
3. Ọkụ (*result from flow electrical power*) and Ọkụ (*having high degree of heat*).

4. Mma (good – *very satisfactory, enjoyable*) and Mma (beauty – *an attractive quality*).
5. Ugo (*Eagle*) and Ugo (*eminence*)
6. Ugwu (*respect*) and Ugwu (*dignity*)
7. Uri (*Poem*) and Uri (*native facial or skin Cosmetic*)
8. Ime (*to be pregnant*) and Ine (*to be in or inside*)
9. Ihu (face – *part of the body*) and Ihu (*front or ahead*)
10. Iyi (stream – *a small narrow river*) Iyi (*to swear*)
11. Akwara (*Veins and Artery*) and Akwara (*Roots*)
12. Ilu (*Proverbs*) and Ilu (*bitter taste*)

Homonyms are words that have the same spelling or pronunciation but different meanings.

20.6 Polysemy

Polysemy is the phenomenon whereby a single word or lexeme has multiple related meanings that are connected through shared semantic features. Polysemous meanings are typically related metaphorically, metonymically, or analogically, reflecting conceptual extensions from a central or core meaning. Polysemy allows for semantic richness and flexibility in language use, enabling words to express a range of related concepts within a coherent semantic network. For example, the word "bank" can refer to the side of a river, a financial institution, or a place where money is kept, all connected through the central idea of storage or accumulation.

Here are examples of polysemy:

1. Ihu (face – *part of the body*) and Ihu (front or ahead)
2. Ime *(to be pregnant)* and Ine *(to be in or inside)*
3. Mma (good – *very satisfactory, enjoyable*) and Mma (beauty – *an attractive quality*).
4. Ọkụ (*result from flow electrical power*) and Ọkụ (*having high degree of heat*).
5. Ugwu (*respect*) and Ugwu *(dignity)*
6. Ọnụ (*mouth*) and Ọnụ (*entry point or hole opening*)
7. Anya (*eyes*) and Anya (*far distance*).
8. Akị (*Kernel/Nut*) and Akị (*stiffened or not easy to break*)
9. Egwu (*music/song*) and Egwu (*dance to music*).
10. Ndụdụ (*fork – material used for taking up*) and Ndụdụ (*needle – piercing material*).

Polysemy refers to words or phrases that have multiple related meanings. These meanings are often connected through a common underlying concept or association.

Understanding these semantic relations provides insights into the organization and structure of lexical meanings in language, facilitating effective communication and interpretation of linguistic expressions. Semantic relations play a crucial role in lexical semantics, lexical acquisition, and language processing, shaping the ways in which words are used and understood in diverse linguistic contexts.

20.7 Multiple Taxonomies

Multiple taxonomies are groups or fields of words such as days of the week, months of the year, etc., that comprise a fixed system. As such, they are distinct from the pairs of opposites described above as they feature three or more items in the system. Further examples in English language include:

- fail/pass/merit/distinction,
- Mon-Tue-Wed-Thu-Fri-Sat-Sun,
- north/south/east/west,
- solid/liquid/gas,
- spades/hearts/diamonds/clubs,
- spring/summer/autumn/winter, and so on.

In Igbo language, multiple taxonomies refer to the classification of items that belong to one group. Market days are the most common taxonomy. It comprises: Eke, Orie, Afọ, Nkwọ. These four market days can only have an individual day each. That is, Eke market day can never be Orie, Afọ or Nkwọ on the same day. It means that the presence of one means the absence of others. Some groups of multiple taxonomies are closed systems that is no new member can be added to it. Igbo's market days is a typical example.

Birds: ọkụkụ (*fowl*), ọkwa, ọgazị (*guinea fowl*), ichoku(*parrot*), nza, obu, ikwikwii (*owl*), ọkịrị, torotoro (*turkey*) etc.

Colours: edoedo (*yellow*), akwụkwọndụ-akwụkwọndụ (*green*), ọbaraọbara/uhieuhie (*red*), urukpuurukpu (*blue*), ajaaja/ ncharanchara (*brown*), oji (*black*), ọcha (*white*), awọawọ (*grey*), etc.

Vegetables: onugbu (*bitter-leaf*), ugu (*pumpkin*), nchaanwụ(*scent-leaf*), akwụkwọaṅara (*garden-egg leaf*), etc.

The three sets of antonyms above when one item in the group is active the rest are inactive. A woman who buys chicken/fowls did not buy guinea fowl or any other bird in the taxonomy. A shoe that is red in colour cannot be black at the same time. A soup that was prepared with scent-leaf, was not cooked with bitter-leaf unless there were a mixture of vegetables in the soup.

Exercise

1. What is the difference between absolute synonyms and partial synonyms?
2. Can you provide an example of a pair of Igbo words that exhibit collocational restriction?
3. Explain the concept of connotative restriction in the context of Igbo synonyms.
4. How does contextual domain restriction affect the interchangeable usage of synonymous pairs in Igbo language?
5. Provide an example of a pair of Igbo words that demonstrate contextual domain restriction.
6. What is the difference between gradable and complementary antonyms in Igbo language?
7. How can you determine gradable antonyms in Igbo using scaling indicators?
8. Give examples of complementary antonyms in Igbo that do not have measuring indicators.
9. Explain the concept of converse antonyms in Igbo language with examples.
10. Provide examples of hyponyms in Igbo language and explain how they relate to hypernyms.
11. What is the semantic relationship between hyponyms and hypernyms?
12. Can you distinguish between homographs and homophones? Give examples in Igbo language.
13. How does homonymy contribute to ambiguity in language comprehension?
14. Give examples of Igbo words that are homonyms and explain their different meanings.
15. How do homonyms impact communication in Igbo language?
16. What is polysemy and how does it contribute to the semantic richness of language?
17. Can you provide examples of polysemy in Igbo language and explain how they are connected through shared semantic features?
18. How does understanding polysemy aid in language comprehension and interpretation of linguistic expressions?
19. Explain the concept of multiple taxonomies and provide examples from Igbo language.
20. How do multiple taxonomies function as closed systems in Igbo culture, using examples such as market days and classifications of birds or colors?

Chapter 21

Lexical Category of Word

The lexical category, also known as part of speech (Nkejiasụsụ Igbo), refers to the classification of words based on their syntactic and semantic properties within a language. It categorizes words into distinct groups according to their grammatical functions, usage patterns, and meanings in sentences. Common lexical categories include nouns, verbs, adjectives, adverbs, pronouns, prepositions, conjunctions, and interjections. Understanding the lexical category of a word is essential for analyzing its role in a sentence and determining its grammatical and semantic characteristics. There are eight categories that words are placed into based on what they mean and how they are used in a sentence.

21.1 Mkpoaha/ Aha (Noun)
A noun is a name of a person, place, thing or an idea.
Examples

English	Igbo	English	Igbo
Classroom	Klaasị	Train	Ụgbọ oloko
Food	nri	Dog	Nkịta
Forest	Ọhịa	Table	Okpokoro
Joy	Ọṅụ		

21.1.1. *Proper Noun (Ahaaka)*: A proper noun is the name given to something to make it more specific. It identifies a particular person, place, or thing (e.g., Nnamdi, Chidi, Awka, Ikwerre, Brian, California). Proper nouns differ from common nouns because common nouns are the words for something in general.

21.1.2. *Common Noun (Ahaizugbe)*: refers to people, places, or things in general e.g. abụ (song), ọṅụ (joy), okorobia (boy), nkịta (dog), obodo (city), ụbọchị (day). Common nouns are written with a capital letter only when they start a sentence.

21.1.3. *Collective Noun (Ahaigwe)*: refers to a set or group of people, places, animals, or things e.g. Ezinụlọ (family), akwụkwọ (books), igwe (multitude).

21.1.4. *Compound Noun (Ahaukwu)*: compound nouns are words for people, animals, places, things or ideas, made up of two or more words, e.g. umu-akwụkwọ (students), umuaka (children), ụlọ-akwụkwọ (school), ndi-ọrụ (workers), etc.

21.1.5. *Abstract Noun (Ahauche/Ahaechereche)*: this refers to ideas, qualities, conditions and things that do not exist physically e.g. ọṅụ (joy), enyi (friendship), ihunanya (love).

21.1.6. *Concrete Noun:* refers to people and things that exist physically e.g. mmadụ (person), ụwa (planet), osisi (tree), enwe (monkey).

21.1.7. *Countable Nouns (Aha-agutaraonu)*: countable nouns are nouns that can be counted individually; you can put a number before it as a quantity, e.g. Ụgbọ-ala abụọ (two cars), Nkịta anọ (four dogs), Ụmụnne atọ (three brothers), etc.

21.1.8. *Uncountable Nouns (Aha-Agutaonu)*: uncountable nouns refer to things that can't be individually counted, and don't take an indefinite article (a or an) in front of them e.g. ego (money), akụ (wealth), mmiri (water), egwu(music), ịhụnanya (love), etc.

Note that money is uncountable but ego-igwe (coin) or ego akwụkwọ (bank notes) are countable. Water is uncountable but glass of water is countable.

21.2 Nnochiaha (Pronoun)

Igbo pronouns, unlike other language, are not gendered as a result the same pronouns are used for male, female and inanimate beings. There are four singular pronouns (i, ị, o, and ọ) and two impersonal pronouns (a and e).

Every Igbo pronoun stands alone in a sentence. They do not join to verb or noun except they are in prefixed form, as in the case of first person singular and third person plural. The following are examples of standalone and prefixed forms of Igbo pronouns:

First person singular   Igbo
    I went to the market.   Ejere m ahia.
    I asked a question.   Ajụrụ m ajụjụ.

2nd person singular   Igbo
    You made my day.   Ị mere taa ụbọchịọma nye m.

You are kind.	Ị bụ ezigbo mmadụ.

3rd person singular   Igbo
She is so beautiful	ọ maka/ ọ mara ezigbo mma
He is handsome	ọ maka/ ọ mara ezigbo mma
It is so beautiful	ọ mara ezigbo mma

3rd person plural   Igbo
They did the dishes	Asara efere.
They cooked food	Esiri nri

The following are various types of pronouns.

21.2.1. Subject Pronoun (Nnochiaha) is a word that takes place of a noun in a sentence. It functions as and acts as a substitute for a noun or nouns. Examples: I, you, it, they, we, he, she.

21.2.2. Personal Pronoun (Nnochionye): this type of pronoun refers to the speaker or the person spoken to, or to a person or things whose identity is clear, usually because they have already been mentioned. For example:

Subject

English	*Igbo*	*Plural*	*Igbo*
I/me	*m, mụ*	We	*anyị*
You	*Ị, gị*	You	*unu*
He/she/it	*o*	They	*ha*
He/she/it	*ọ*	They	*ha*
He/she/it	ya	They	*ha*

Object

Me	*m/mụ*	Us	*anyi*
You	*gị*	You	*unu*
Him/her/it	*ya*	them	*ha*

21.2.3. *Impersonal pronoun (Nnochimpesin)*: Also known as impersonal pronoun, impersonal pronoun is used in a sentence to show non-specific beings, objects, or places. This can be used to represent countable noun or uncountable nouns, e.g. it (a, e). The two impersonal pronouns in Igbo language are a and e.

21.2.4. *Possessive Pronoun (Nnochinke)*: This type of pronoun is used in a sentence to show that something belongs to someone, e.g. my, our, your, his, her, its, and theirs. There exists an independent form of each of the above possessive pronouns and they are: mine, ours, yours, his, hers, its, and theirs. For example:

English	Igbo	English	Igbo
mine	nke m	*Yours*	nke gị
His	nke ya	*Her*	nke ya
Our/ours	nke anyị	*Their/theirs*	nke ha

21.2.5. *Demonstrative Pronoun (Nnochingosi)*: This type of pronoun is used in a sentence to point out specific things. There are only four demonstrative pronouns, and they are: this, that, these and those. Examples in Igbo language are as follows:

English	Igbo	English	Igbo
This	ihe a	That	ihe ahụ
These	ihe ndị a	Those	ihe dị ahụ

21.2.6. *Reflexive pronoun (Nnochionwe/Nnochinkowa)*: This type of pronoun is used in a sentence to refer to subject of the sentence. It is preceded by adverb, adjective, pronoun, or noun to which it refers, so long as that antecedent is located within the same clause. They end with the suffix 'self' (onwe); e.g. myself, yourself, himself, herself, oneself, itself, ourselves, yourselves, and themselves.

Examples:

English	**Igbo**	English	Igbo
Myself	onwe/ Munwà	*Yourself*	onwe gi/ Ginwà
Himself	onwe ya	*Herself*	onwe ya
Oneself	onwe ya	*Itself*	onwe ya
Ourselves	onwe anyi/ Anyịnwà	*Yourselves*	onwe unu
Themselves	onwe ha		

21.2.7. *Emphatic Pronoun (Nnochionweonye)*: This type of pronoun is used in a sentence to explain the action done by a noun without anyone's help. Examples of emphatic pronouns are the same form as reflexive pronouns. However, the difference between emphatic pronouns and reflexive pronoun is that reflexive pronoun acts as direct or indirect object in a sentence while emphatic pronouns are essentially unnecessary.

For example:

1. I went to the hospital myself. (Reflexive pronoun)

E jere m ụlọ-ọgwụna nke onwe m.

2. The doctor himself treated me. (Emphatic pronoun)
   Dọkịta na onwe ya lekọtara anya.

The word "myself" in the first sentence serves to reinforce that it was the subject (i.e. the president) that performed the action. Please note that emphatic pronouns can be removed from a sentence and the meaning of the sentence would still remain intact.

21.3 Verbs (Ngwaa)

21.3.1. *Infinitive Verbs (Isingwaa)*: This is a verb form that functions as a noun or is used with auxiliary verbs, and that names the action or state without specifying the subject. In Igbo language, the letter "ị" and "I" plus the root verb comprise the infinitive form of verb.

Examples:

Verb root	English	Verb root	English
ịbu/ịdị	to be	ịzụta	to buy.
ịta	to chew	isi nri	to cook.
ịgba egwu	to dance	iṅu	to drink.
ịbanye/ịbata	to enter	isoro	to follow.
ịchọ/chọta	to find/look	ichefu	to forget.
ighe	to fry	inweta	to get.
inye	to give	inwe	to have/own.
ijide	to hold	ịchi (chi a)	to laugh.
ịhapụ	to leave	ile (anya)	to look.
ịpụta	to get out	ikpe ekpere	to pray.
icheta	to remember	inweta	to get.
ịga	to go	ịnụ	to hear.
ịma	to know	ịmụta	to learn.
ige ntị	to listen	ịka (akara)	to mark.
ịgụ	to read	ịgba ọsọ	to run.
ịhụ	to see	ire (ahịa)	to sell.
ịgụ	to sing	ịbụọ abụ	to sing.
ịpụ	to sit	ịrahụ (ura)	to sleep.
ịsụ	to speak	iguzo/ikuli	to stand.
ịnọ	to stay	ilo	to swallow.
ikuzi	to teach	iche echiche	to think.

ịmetụ	*to touch*	ịghọta	*to understand.*
ichere	*to wait*	ịga ije	*to walk.*
ịsa	*to wash*	ịyi	*to wear.*
ịrụ	*to work*	ide	*to write.*

21.3.2. *Linking Verbs (njiko ngwaa)*: This type of verb that connects a noun or a pronoun with a word that identifies or describes it; e.g. is, am, are, etc.

Examples:

English	*Igbo*
is	bụ
am	bụ
are	bụ

21.3.3. *Auxiliary Verbs (Enyemaka ngwaa)*: This is a verb that changes or helps another verb, e.g. am, is, are, was, were, be, been, will, has, have, had, do, does, did. In Igbo language, auxiliary verbs often complement verb form to express an action in simple, continuous or future tense. When an auxiliary verb is complementing a simple participle, the auxiliary verb is joined to the complement with a hyphen. This is especially the case when the infinitive accompanying starts with a vowel. The hyphen is used to differentiate/separate the auxillary verb which is a form of prefix of the simple participle from main verb.

For example:

Igbo	*English*
1. Ben gà-enweta ụgbọ ala.	*Ben will catch the bus.*
2. Eze nà-àbia ebe a.	*Eze is coming here.*
3. Ngọzị ga-àbịa	*Ngọzị will come.*
4. Ọ ga-àbịa	*He/She will come.*
5. Eze na-abịa	*Eze is coming.*
6. Ọ na-abịa	*He/She is coming.*

However, when the auxiliary verb takes on the suffix of negation, it is written separately from the complement without a hyphen and as a one word with the suffix.

For example:

Igbo	*English*
1. Ngọzị agaghị àbịa	*Ngọzị will not come.*

2. Ọ gaghị àbịa — *He/She will not come.*
3. Eze anaghị abịa — *Eze is not coming.*
4. Ọ naghị abịa — *He/She is not coming.*

21.4 Conjunction (Njikọ)

Conjunction: A conjunction is a word that joins words or groups of words in a sentence together, e.g. and, but, yet, because, so,

Igbo	English	Igbo	English
kama	*instead of*	mgbe ahụ	*then*
rue	*until*	tupu	*before*
maka	*as, so*	otu	*as, that*
mana/kama	*but, if, that, whether*	na	*and, that*
ka mgbe	*since*	ka	*so that, that*
n'ihi	*because*	ma ọ bụ	*or*
ọzọkwa	*moreover*		

Examples:

Igbo	English
1. Achọrọ m Ji kama Garri	*I want Yam instead of Garri.*
2. Eri kwala nri, tupu m gawa.	*Do not eat until I go.*
3. Maka na ọ dịmma, ka m jirị rie ya	*As this is good, I enjoyed it.*
4. Ọ dị mma otu osi buru izu ụka.	*It is good, as it is the weekend.*
5. Ihe a mara mma mana ọdị oke ọnụ	*This is good, but expensive.*
6. Mụ na gị na-eje ahịa	*You and I are going to shop.*

21.5 Adjective (Nkowaha)

An adjective is a word that describes or gives more information about a noun or pronoun. It tells you what kind, how many, or which one. The following are examples of adjectives:

Igbo	English	Igbo	English
ala	*low*	ọsịsọ	*fast*
chakoo	*empty*	elu	*high*
iwe	*angry*	ihere	*shy*
nsọ	*holy/sacred*	anya	*far*
obi ụtọ/aṅụrị	*happy*	obi ọjọọ	*sad*
ọcha	*bright*	ọcha	*clean*
ocha	*light*	oji	*dark*

ogologo	*long*	ntakịrị	*short*
ohu/ohuru	*new*	ochie	*old*
ọjọọ	*ugly*	ọjọọ	*bad*
ọkụ	*hot*	oyi	*cold*
ọma/mma	*beautiful*	ọma	*good*
siri ike	*hard*	dara ọnụ	*expensive*
ukwu	*big*	nta	*small*
ụtọ	*sweet*	ilu	*bitter*

21.5.1 Demonstrative adjectives

Demonstrative adjective are used to modify a noun so that we know which specific person, place, or thing is mentioned. Examples of demonstrative adjectives in Igbo language are: ahụ (that). Nke a (this), ndị ahụ (those), ndị a (these). In Igbo language, demonstrative adjectives follow the noun they are modifying.

For example:

Igbo	*English*
Nye m kalama ahụ	*Give me that bottle.*
Achọrọ m akwụkwọ ndị ahụ	*I want those books.*
Ọ chọrọ izute ya ụbọchị ahụ	*He wanted to meet her that day.*
Mango ndị a na-ere ure	*These mangoes are rotting.*
Apụghị ichefu ihe ahụ mere	*I can't forget that incident.*
Ụmụ ntakịrị ndị ahụ were iwe	*Those children were angry.*
Mkpịsị odide ahụ bụ nke m	*This pen belongs to me.*
Ụlọ ahụ nwere ụlọ-ahịa	*That building has a shop.*

21.5.2. Attributive Adjectives:

Attributive adjectives are adjectives that directly modify or describe nouns and are typically placed before or after the noun they modify in Igbo language. They provide additional information about the noun, such as its qualities, characteristics, or attributes. For example, in the phrase okooko osisi mara mma *(beautiful flowers)*, " mara mma *(beautiful)*" is an attributive adjective modifying the noun "okooko *(flowers)*."

Here are more examples of attributive adjectives:

1. Osisi toro ogologo — *tall tree*
2. Nri tọrọ ụtọ — *delicious food*
3. Ụlọ ochie — *old house*
4. Akwụkwọ ọhụrụ — *New book*

5. Big Dog   *nnukwu nkịta*

In each example, the attributive adjective directly modifies the following noun, providing additional information about its qualities or characteristics.

21.5.3. Predicative Adjectives:

Predicative adjectives are adjectives that come after linking verbs (e.g., bụ *(is/be)*, dị ka *(seem)*, ịbụ *(become)*) and describe the subject of the sentence. Unlike attributive adjectives, which directly modify nouns, predicative adjectives predicate something about the subject. For example, in the sentence "Okooko osisi ahụ mara mma *(The flowers are beautiful)*," "mara mma *(beautiful)*" is a predicative adjective describing the subject "flowers."

Here are more examples of predicative adjectives:

1. Ihu igwe dị urukpuru.   *The weather is cloudy.*
2. O dịka obi adị ya ụtọ.   *She seems happy.*
3. Mmiri ahụ dị oyi.   *The water feels cold.*
4. Ihe nkiri ahụ dị ụtọ.   *The movie was entertaining.*
5. Olu ya na-ada ụda obi siri ike.   *His voice sounds confident.*
6. Ime ụlọ ahụ dị ọcha.   *The room looks tidy.*

In each example, the predicative adjective comes after a linking verb (such as "bụ *(is)*," "dị ka *(seems)*," "dị ka *(feels)*," etc.) and describes the subject of the sentence.

21.5.4. Comparative Adjectives:

Comparative adjectives are used to compare two or more things and indicate a higher or lower degree of a quality. They are often formed by adding "Ka *(-er/more)*" to the adjective. Examples of comparative adjectives:

Adjective	**Comparative**
Tall (*ogologo*)	taller (*ka ogologo*)
Fat (*ibu*)	fatter (*ka ibu*)
Big (*nnukwu*)	bigger (*ka nnukwu*)
Simple (*mfe*)	simpler (*ka mfe*)
Good (*mma*)	better (*ka mma*)
Bad (*njọ*)	worse (*ka njọ*)
Much (*ukwuu*)	more (*ka*)
Little (*obere*)	less (*ka pee mpe*)

Sad (*nwute*)   sadder (*ka ewute*)

Comparative adjectives are used to compare two things and indicate a higher or lower degree of a quality. They are often formed by adding "ka *(-er/more)*" to the adjective.

21.5.5. Superlative Adjectives:

Superlative adjectives are used to compare three or more things and indicate the highest or lowest degree of a quality. They are often formed by adding "kacha/kasị/kachasị *(-est/most)*" to the adjective. Examples of superlative adjectives:

Adjective	Superlative
Bad (*njọ*)	worst (*kasị njọ*)
Big (*nnukwu*)	biggest (*kacha nnukwu*)
Fat (*ibu*)	fattest (*kachasi ibu*)
Good (*mma*)	best (*kacha mma*)
Little (*obere*)	least (*kacha pee mpe*)
Much (*ukwuu*)	most (*kasị*)
Sad (*nwute*)	saddest (*kacha ewute*)
Simple (*mfe*)	simplest (*kasi mfe*)
Tall (*ogologo*)	tallest (*kasi ogologo*)

Superlative adjectives are used to compare three or more things and indicate the highest or lowest degree of a quality. They are often formed by adding "kacha/kasị/kachasị *(-est/most)*" to the adjective.

21.5.6. Coordinate Adjectives:

Coordinate adjectives are two or more adjectives that independently modify the same noun and can be separated by a comma or "nke/ma *(and)*." They contribute equally to the description of the noun. For example, in the phrase " nwoke toro ogologo, dị ojii, mara mma *(a tall, dark, and handsome man)*," " ogologo *(tall)*," "ojii *(dark)*," and " mara mma *(handsome)*" are coordinate adjectives modifying the noun " nwoke *(man)*."

1. Ofe di mmiri mmiri, na-atọ ụtọ.   *A creamy, delicious soup*
2. Osisi Iroko toro ogologo, siri ike.   *A tall, sturdy Iroko tree*
3. Ụbọchị mara mma, anwụ na-acha.   *A beautiful, sunny day*
4. Ihe mkpuchi mara mma, dị mma.   *A cozy, comfortable blanket*
5. Ịnyịnya igwe ochie nke nchara.   *An old, rusty bicycle*
6. Nnukwu enyo nke ịchọ mma.   *A large, ornate mirror*

7. Ekwentị mara mma, nke ọgbara ọhụrụ.   *A sleek, modern smartphone*
8. Obodo dị ndụ ma na-ekwo ekwo.   *A lively, bustling city*

Coordinate adjectives are two or more adjectives that independently modify the same noun and can be separated by a comma or "nke/ma *(and)*." They contribute equally to the description of the noun.

21.5.7. Appositive Adjectives:

Appositive adjectives are adjectives that rename or identify a noun or pronoun and provide additional information about it. They are often separated from the noun by commas. For example, in the phrase " Emeka, onye na-eme ihe nkiri a ma ama, bịarutere *(Emeka, the famous actor, arrived),*" " ama ama *(famous)*" is an appositive adjective providing more information about "Emeka."

Here are examples of appositive adjectives:

Obi, onye na-eme ihe nkiri a ma ama, rutere n'isi ụtụtụ.
Obi, the famous actor, arrived early.

Ụlọ oriri na ọñụñụ ahụ, bụ ebe a ma ama n'obodo ahụ, jupụtara na mmadụ.
The restaurant, a popular spot in town, was crowded.

Nkịta m, onye enyi na-eguzosi ike n'ihe, na-eso m aga ebe niile.
My dog, a loyal companion, followed me everywhere.

Obodo ahụ, bụ obodo ukwu na-ekwo ekwo, ehitụbeghị ụra.
The city, a bustling metropolis, never slept.

Enyi m, onye ọkachamara na-isi nri, kwadebere nri dị ụtọ.
My friend, an expert chef, prepared a delicious meal.

Ụlọ ihe ngosi nka, ebe nhumaama ngosi akụkọ ihe mere eme, nwere ihe ndị dị oke ọnụ ahịa.
The museum, a historical landmark, housed priceless artifacts.

In each example, the appositive adjective provides additional information about the noun by renaming or identifying it. It often appears after the noun and is separated by commas.

21.6 Adverb (Nkwuwa)

An adverb is a word that describes a verb, adjective, or another adverb by giving more information about how or when something happens. It tells how, when, where, or to what extent, e.g. loudly, slowlqy, quickly, finally, always, tomorrow.

	Igbo	English
1.	Ọ na-agụ egwu n'olu dara ụda	*She sings loudly.*
2.	Ọ gbara ọsọ ngwa ngwa	*He/she ran quickly.*
3.	Ọ kwuru okwu n'olu dị jụụ	*He/she spoke softly.*
4.	Eze kwara ụkwara n'olu dara ụda	*Eze coughed loudly.*
5.	Ọ na-afụ Ọja nke oma.	*He plays the flute beautifully.*
6.	Ha riri achịcha bekee n'anyaukwu	*They ate the cake greedily.*

21.6.1 Interrogative adverb

Interrogative adverb are used to ask a question. In Igbo, a question can only be initiated by either an interrogative or a personal pronoun. Following interrogatives are commonly used:

Igbo	*English*	*Igbo*	*English*
Kedụ	*how, when, where, which?*	ebee	*where, which place?*
olee	*how much, how many?*	onye	*Who?*
gịnị/ọ gịnị?	*What?*	kedụ?	*How?*
maka gịnị?	*Why?*	ma ncha	*Never*
tara akpụ	*Rarely*	mgbe ụfọdụ	*Sometimes*
mgbe niīle	*Usually*	mgbe niīle	*Always*
nkeọma	*Very*		

21.6.2. Adverbs of Manner:

Adverbs of manners describe how an action is performed or the way in which something happens. They often answer the question "how?"

Here are the adverbs of manner used in sentences:

1. O ji **nlezianya** hazie okooko osisi ndị dị na ite ahụ.
   *She **carefully** arranged the flowers in the vase.*

2. Mbe ahụ ji **nwayọọ nwayọọ** gafee okporo ụzọ.
   *The turtle moved **slowly** across the road.*

3. Ụmụntakịrị na-achị ọchị n'**olu dara ụda** maka ihe ọchị ahụ.

*The children laughed **loudly** at the funny joke.*

4. O bere ákwá nke **mwute** mgbe ọ nụrụ akụkọ ọjọọ ahụ.
   *He cried **sadly** when he heard the bad news.*

21.6.3. Adverbs of Place:

Adverbs of place indicate the location or position of an action or event. They answer the question "where?" Examples include here, there, everywhere, nowhere, and upstairs. For example, in the sentence " Nwamba na-arahụ ụra n'elu ụlọ *(The cat is sleeping upstairs)*," the adverb " elu ulo *(upstairs)*" indicates the location of the cat's sleep.

Here are the sentences with the adverbs of place:

1. O ji **umemmapụ** elegharịa anya ichọ igodo ya furu efu.
   *She looked **around** anxiously for her lost keys.*

2. Nwamba ahụ maliri **elu** makwasi n'elu ụlọ.
   *The cat jumped **up** onto the roof.*

3. Ha nọdụrụ **ala** na tebụl (Agada/Nkwago/Ndokwasa/Okpokoro) iri nri abalị.
   *They sat **down** at the table to have dinner.*

4. Ụmụaka na-egwuri egwu n'**èzí**/iro n'ogige ahụ.
   *The children played **outside** in the garden.*

5. Nnụnụ ndị ahụ fefere n'**elu** nke igwe.
   *The birds flew **overhead** in the sky.*

6. Ọ zoro n'**okpuru** ihe ndina mgbe a na-egwu egwuregwu nzuzo.
   *He hid **underneath** the bed during the game of hide-and-seek.*

7. Ụgbọ mmiri ahụ **gafere** oke osimiri ahụ gaa n'ala ndị dị anya.
   *The ship sailed **across** the ocean to distant lands.*

8. Osa rigoro **elu** osisi ka o rute mkpụrụ aki ahụ.
   *The squirrel climbed **up** the tree to reach the nuts.*

9. E liri akụ ahụ n'**ime** ala n'ime ọgba/ọnụala ahụ.
   *The treasure was buried **deep** underground in the cave.*

21.6.4. Adverbs of Time:

Adverbs of time indicate when an action occurs or the frequency of its occurrence. They answer the questions " mgbe ole *(when)*?" or "ugboro ole *(how often)*?" Examples include ugbua *(now)*, emechaa *(later)*, ụnyahụ *(yesterday)*, kwa ụbọchị *(daily)*, and kwa afọ *(annually)*. For instance, in the sentence " Anyị ga-ezute echi *(We will meet tomorrow)*," the adverb "echi *(tomorrow)*" indicates the time of the meeting.

Here are more examples of adverbs of time in sentences.

1. Ọ ga-abata **echi** maka nzukọ ahụ.
   *She will arrive **tomorrow** for the meeting.*

2. Anyị zutere **unyaahu** maka kọfị.
   *We met **yesterday** for coffee.*

3. Ọ na-eteta ụra n**'isi** ụtụtụ ọ bụla imega ahụ́.
   *He wakes up **early** every morning to exercise.*

4. Ha ga-apụ **ngwa ngwa** maka ezumike ha.
   *They will leave **soon** for their vacation.*

5. Ụlọ ahịa ahụ na-emepe **kwa ubọchi** na elekere iteolu nke ụtụtụ.
   *The store opens **daily** at 9 AM.*

6. Ha lụrụ **kemgbe** afọ 2010.
   *They have been married **since** 2010.*

7. Ọ na-ezube ịga **mba ọzọ/ofesi** n'afọ ọzọ.
   *She plans to travel **abroad** next year.*

21.6.5. Adverbs of Frequency:

Adverbs of frequency indicate how often an action occurs. They answer the question "ugboro ole *(how often)*?" Examples include mgbe niile *(always)*, ọtụtụ mgbe *(often)*, adịkarịghị *(rarely)*, mgbe ụfọdụ *(sometimes)*, and agaghị eme *(never)*. For example, in the sentence "She always arrives early," the adverb "always" indicates the frequency of her early arrivals.

Here are examples of adverbs of frequency used in sentences.

1. Ọ na-abịa **mgbe niile** n'isi ụtụtụ. (Ọ na-abịakarị n'isi ụtụtụ).
   *She **always** arrives early for work.*

2. Ọ na-aga **ọtụtụ mgbe** ịgba ọsọ n'ogige ịgba ọsọ.
   *He **often** goes jogging in the park.*

3. Anyị na-aga **mgbe ụfọdụ** ileta nne na nna anyị ochie na ngwụcha izu.
   *We **sometimes** visit our grandparents on weekends.*

4. Ụgbọ oloko na-abịa **mgbe dum** n'oge. (Ụgbọ oloko na-abịakarị n'oge).
   *The train **usually** arrives on time.*

5. Ha na-aga ebe ihe nkiri **mgbe ụfọdụ** maka ntụrụndụ.
   *They **occasionally** go to the movies for entertainment.*

21.6.6. Adverbs of Purpose:

Adverbs of purpose indicate the reason or intention behind an action. They answer the question "why?" Examples include ya mere *(therefore, consequently, thus, and so)*. For instance, in the sentence " Ọ gụrụsiri akwụkwọ ike ka ọ gafee ule ahụ *(She studied hard to pass the exam)*," the adverb "ike *(hard)*" indicates the purpose of her studying.

Here are more examples of adverbs of purpose used in sentences.

1. O kwuru okwu n'**ụzọ doro anya** iji hụ na onye ọ bụla ghọtara ya.
   *He spoke **clearly** to ensure everyone understood him.*

2. Ha jiri **nlezianya** chekwaa ego maka ezumike ha.
   *They saved money **carefully** for their vacation.*

3. Ọ rụsiri ọrụ **ike** iji mezuo ebumnuche ya.
   *He worked **diligently** to achieve his goals.*

4. Ha na-eme njem n'**mkpachapụ anya** ka ha ghara inwe ihe mberede ọ bụla.
   *They traveled **safely** to avoid any accidents.*

5. O siri nri nke **na-atọ ụtọ** iji masị ndị ọbịa ya.
   *She cooked **deliciously** to impress her guests.*

6. O gere ntị **nke ọma** ka ọ ghọta ntụziaka ahụ.

*He listened **attentively** to understand the instructions.*

7. Ha kwakọbara **nke ọma** iji kwado ihe niile dị n'akpa ahụ.
   *They packed **efficiently** to fit everything in the suitcase.*

8. O kwuru okwu **dị nro** ka ọ ghara inye nwa ahụ na-ehi ụra nsogbu.
   *She spoke **softly** to not disturb the sleeping baby.*

21.6.7. Adverbs of Degree:

Adverbs of degree modify adjectives, verbs, or other adverbs to indicate the extent or degree of something. They answer the question "to what extent?" Examples include nke ukwuu *(very/extremely)*, nnọọ *(quite)*, kama *(rather)*, and kwa *(too)*. For example, in the sentence " O nwere ọgụgụ isi nke ukwuu *(She is very intelligent)*," the adverb "nke ukwuu *(very)*" modifies the adjective " ọgụgụ isi *(intelligent)*" to indicate a high degree of intelligence.

Here are more examples of adverbs of degree used in sentences.

1. Obi tọrọ ya **ezigbo** ụtọ ịhụ enyi ya ochie.
   *She was **very** happy to see her old friend.*

2. Ihe nkiri ahụ na-atọ ụtọ **nke ukwuu**.
   *The movie was **extremely** entertaining.*

3. Ike agwụrụ ya **nke ukwuu** ịpụ apụ n'abalị a.
   *She is **too** tired to go out tonight.*

4. Ọ fọrọ **nke nta** ka ọ rụchaa ọrụ ya.
   *He is **almost** finished with his work.*

5. Ha nwere nnọọ obi ụtọ banyere akụkọ ahụ.
   *They are **absolutely** thrilled about the news.*

21.6.8. Conjunctive Adverbs:

Conjunctive adverbs connect clauses or sentences and show the relationship between ideas. They can indicate time, cause and effect, contrast, or other relationships. Examples include mana/otú ọ dị *(however)*, ya mere *(therefore)*, ka ọ dị ugbu a *(meanwhile)*, ka o sina dị *(nevertheless)*, and ọzọkwa *(furthermore)*. For instance, in the sentence " Ọ gụrụ akwụkwọ nke ọma; ya mere, ọ gafere ule ahụ *(He studied hard; therefore, he passed the exam)*," the conjunctive adverb "ya mere *(therefore)*" shows the cause-and-effect relationship between studying hard and passing the exam.

Here are more examples of conjunctive adverbs used in sentences.

1. Ọ gụrụ akwụkwọ nke ọma maka ule; **otú o dị**, ọ emechaghị nke ọma.
   *She studied hard for the exam; **however**, she still didn't perform well.*

2. Ọ chọrọ ịga oriri; otu **o sila dị**, o kpebiri ịnọrọ n'ụlọ mụọ akwụkwọ.
   *He wanted to go to the party; **nevertheless**, he decided to stay home and study.*

3. Ha mere atụmatụ ịpụ n'isi ụtụtụ; **kama**, ha mechara nọrọ n'apụghị n'oge.
   *They planned to leave early; **instead**, they ended up staying late.*

4. Ọ tufula igodo ya; **ka ọ dị ugbu a**, ọ gbazitere nke onye ya na ya bi.
   *She had lost her keys; **meanwhile**, she borrowed her roommate's spare.*

5. O ji nlezianya mụọ akwụkwọ maka ule; **n'ihi ya**, o nwetara akara ugo mmụta mbụ.
   *She studied diligently for the test; **as a result**, she got an A grade.*

9. Focusing Adverbs:
Focusing adverbs emphasize a particular part of a sentence or draw attention to a specific aspect. They include words like naanị *(merely/solely/only)*, dị nnọọ *(just)*, and ọbụna *(even)*. For example, in the sentence " Naanị akwụkwọ nri ka ọ na-eri *(She only eats vegetables)*," the focusing adverb "naanị *(only)*" emphasizes that she eats exclusively vegetables.

Certainly! Here are 10 examples of focusing adverbs used in sentences, with the focusing adverbs highlighted in bold:

1. Ọ chọrọ iri **naanị** ofe egwusi maka nri abalị.
   *She **only** wanted to eat egwusi soup for dinner.*

2. Ọ rịọrọ **kpọmkwem** maka oche dị na mbo nke ụgbọelu ahụ.
   *He **specifically** asked for a window seat on the plane.*

3. Ọ na-elekwasị anya **nkekacha mkpa** n'ihe ọmụmụ ya n'ime izu.
   *She **primarily** focuses on her studies during the week.*

4. Ọ na-amasị ya **karịsịa** ịkpọ piano n'oge ezumike ya.
   *He **particularly** enjoys playing the piano in his free time.*

5. Ha na-eji **naani** ụgbọ njem ọha aga ọrụ.
   *They **solely** use public transportation to commute to work.*

6. Ọ **kacha** amasị ya iri nri enweghị anụ.
   *He **chiefly** prefers to eat vegetarian meals.*

These different types of adverbs serve various functions in sentences by providing additional information about the manner, place, time, frequency, purpose, degree, connection, or focus of an action or event.

21.7 Preposition (Mbuuzo)

Preposition: A preposition is a word that describes a relationship between a noun or pronoun and another word in a sentence, e.g. at, on, in, across, besides, during, for, of, to, with, throughout etc. It goes before a noun or pronoun to specify a place, position or time. In Igbo, there is only one preposition "na". When preceding a vowel, it drops its vowel sound and letter and takes on the tone of noun that follows it. It is written as n'.

Examples:

Igbo	English	Igbo	English
na	and	n'okpuru	under
tupu	before	n'ikpeazụ	after
n'ime	inside	n'ihe/n'ilo	outside
na	with	mana	but
maka	for	si	from
je	to	ime	in

Examples:

ọ dị n'elu akwa ndina.	*it is on top of the bed.*
ọ dị n'okpuru akwa ndina.	*it is under the bed.*
ọ dị n'ime akpati	*it is inside the box.*
ọ dị n' akụkụ akwa ndina.	*it is beside the bed.*
ọ nọ n'ụlọ.	*he/she n is in the house.*
ọ dị n'elu aja.	*it is on sand.*

In combination with a noun, it can specify the location of the preposition in more detail:

Noun	**Mkpoaha**	**Preposition**	**Mbuuzo**
top	elu	*in, at, on*	na (common)

top	elu	*up*	n'enu
underside	okpuru	*under, below*	n'okpuru
interior	ime	*inside*	n'ime
edge	ọnụnụ	*on top of*	n'onunu
beside	n'akụkụ		

21.8 Interjection (Ntimkpu)

An interjection is a word or phrase that expresses a strong feeling or an emotion, e.g. Hurrah, Yippee! Wow! Oh, no! Ouch, Oops, Aha, Eww, etc. Interjections are divided into six types namely, greeting, joy, surprise, approval, attention and sorrow.

21.8.1. Interjections for Greeting (Ntimkpu nke ekele):
This type of interjection is used in a sentence to indicate the emotion of warmth to a person or group of people during meeting with them. Examples:

English	Igbo
Hello!	Ndeewo!
Hello Igbo people	Igbo Kweenu! Yee

21.8.2. Interjections for joy (Ntimkpu nke ọnụ):
This type of interjection is used in a sentence to indicate immediate joy and happiness when a happy occasion occurs.

Examples:

English	Igbo
Wow!	Ewo!
Good!	Ezigbo!
Hurrah!	Ịjị ya!

21.8.3. Interjections for Attention (Ntimkpu nke akpọmoku):
This type of interjection is used in a sentence to draw attention of someone to something.

Examples:

English	Igbo
Look!	Lee anya!
Behold!	Lee!
Listen!	Ge Ntị!

Shh!	Shh!

21.8.4. Interjections for approval (Ntimkpu nke nnabata):
This type of interjection is used in a sentence to express a strong sense of approval or agreement for something that has happened or something that someone did.

Examples:

English	Igbo
Well done!	Daalụ!
Brilliant	Akonuche!
Bravo!	Agụ/Dike!
Wait!	Chelu!
Sure!	Isee!

21.8.5. Interjections for surprise (Ntimkpu nke mberede):
This type of interjection is used in a sentence to express a strong sense of surprise about something that happened or something that someone did.

Examples:

English	Igbo
What!	Gini!
Oh!	Ewo!
Ah!	Ah Ah!

21.8.6. Interjections for sorrow Ntimkpu nke iriuju):
This type of interjection is used in a sentence to express the emotion of sadness or disappointment about something that happened.

Examples:

English	*Igbo*
Alas!	Ewo!
Oops!	Ha yie!
Ouch!	Ha yie!
Ah!	Ah ah!

Exercise

1. What is the lexical category of a word, and why is it important in language analysis?
2. Can you differentiate between proper nouns and common nouns, providing examples in both English and Igbo?
3. Explain the concept of collective nouns and provide examples from both English and Igbo languages.
4. How are compound nouns formed, and what role do they play in linguistic expression?
5. Discuss the difference between abstract nouns and concrete nouns, giving examples from Igbo language.
6. What distinguishes countable nouns from uncountable nouns, and how are they used in sentences?
7. Describe the different types of pronouns in Igbo language and their functions in sentences.
8. How do Igbo pronouns differ from those in other languages, particularly in terms of gender?
9. Explain the various forms of verbs in Igbo, including infinitive verbs, linking verbs, and auxiliary verbs, with examples.
10. How do auxiliary verbs complement main verbs in Igbo sentences, and what role do they play in expressing tense and mood?
11. What is the Igbo word for "because," and how is it used in a sentence?
12. Explain the difference between attributive adjectives and predicative adjectives in Igbo with examples.
13. Provide three examples of Igbo adverbs of place and explain their usage in sentences.
14. How are superlative adjectives formed in Igbo, and provide an example sentence using a superlative adjective.
15. What is the function of conjunctive adverbs in Igbo, and provide an example sentence using a conjunctive adverb.
16. Give an example of a coordinating conjunction in Igbo and explain its role in connecting clauses.
17. Describe the function of interjections for sorrow in Igbo, and provide an example sentence using such an interjection.
18. How are adverbs of frequency used in Igbo sentences? Provide two example sentences.
19. Explain the role of prepositions in Igbo sentences and provide an example sentence demonstrating the use of a preposition.
20. Give an example of an interjection used for greeting in Igbo and explain its significance in communication.

About the Author

Elisha O. Ogbonna hails from Enugu in Igbo land, where Igbo is his mother tongue. His journey with the Igbo language began at the age of nine when he started on reading Igbo books and the Akwụkwọ Nsọ, aiming to assist his late parents who were unable to read or write in Igbo. This early exposure to language sparked his passion for teaching and translating English expressions into Igbo, a skill he honed throughout his high school years. Elisha's dedication and diligence is reflected in his outstanding performance in Igbo language in the West Africa Examination during his secondary education.

As he progressed through his academic journey, Elisha actively engaged in translation and interpretation work, contributing his expertise in both traditional and religious contexts. Even during his time as a teacher, he took on the responsibility of instructing adult learners in the intricacies of the Igbo language. His enthusiasm for sharing his knowledge led him to establish a platform dedicated to aiding those interested in learning Igbo.

Looking ahead, Elisha is excited about his forthcoming book tailored for advanced learners, signaling his commitment to advancing the proficiency of Igbo language enthusiasts. With his wealth of experience and unwavering dedication, Elisha remains a beacon of support and guidance for anyone embarking on their journey to master the rich and vibrant Igbo language.

Other Books

Comprehensive Igbo Language: *A Contemporary Guide for Beginners And Intermediate Learners*

Comprehensive Igbo Language provides thorough and effective ways to learn and master the skills you need for Igbo communication, reading, and writing. Unlike every other Igbo language book, it contains a guide to pronunciation and a detailed explanation of pitch accent marking and syllable formation. Syllables are often considered the phonological "building blocks" of words. This book helps you in-depth guide on a unit of pronunciation and the formation of the whole or a part of a word.

It has a solid grounding in grammar basics and a progressive approach to learning Igbo in the manner in, which people naturally acquire language. You will be introduced to the most essential structures that will help you communicate in the Igbo language almost immediately, It uncovers the most common concepts that govern verbs and sentences used in everyday communication.

The comprehensive Igbo Language presents a unique and easy structure to master essential, grammar, verbs, and vocabulary. It contains words and names used for family, friends, people, plants, animals, foods, time, colors, days, nature, occupation, and so on. It also has exercises to help you test what you've learned and measure your progress.

Advanced Igbo Language: *A Simplified Guide to Igbo Orthography, Phonology, Morphology and Lexicology*

This straightforward and comprehensive book deals with encamping features of Igbo linguistics in a manner that is new, exciting, and revealing to both speakers and learners.

It is a well-organized and systematic material that started from the foundational principles of language study. This excellent book presents Igbo orthography, phonemes: phonemic analysis: phonetic transcription: place of articulation: prefixes: prosody: segmental phoneme: morphemes: class-changing: class-maintaining: word formation, lexeme, synonyms, antonyms, ambiguities, and solution to ambiguities in Igbo language.

This book should form a useful textbook for high and tertiary institutions: and private establishments where Igbo language is learned and taught.

Standard Igbo Language: *A Complete Guide to Learning and Speaking Igbo Language*

"Standard Igbo Language" is an expanded edition of "Comprehensive Igbo Language." It is comprehensive guide designed to empower learners to master the intricacies of standard Igbo language. It unlocks a deeper understanding of Igbo grammar. Starting with an exploration of the Igbo alphabet and pronunciation, readers are introduced to the foundational elements of the language, including vowels, consonants, and tonal accents. Through engaging exercises and practical examples, learners develop a strong foundation in Igbo phonetics and orthography.

The book takes readers on a journey through the essential components of the Igbo language. As readers progress through the chapters, they delve into a diverse array of topics, from common verb phrases and simple conversation to parts of speech, tenses, and punctuation. Each chapter offers insights into the nuances of Igbo grammar and syntax, accompanied by interactive exercises to reinforce learning.

Beyond language proficiency, "Standard Igbo Language" offers a holistic view of Igbo culture, with chapters dedicated to numerals, shapes, colors, nature, animals, and social institutions. Readers gain a deeper appreciation for the word usage and richness, as they explore the vocabulary and concepts that shape everyday life in Igbo society.

With its comprehensive and practical approach, "Standard Igbo Language" serves as an indispensable resource for learners of all levels, from beginners to advanced speakers. Whether you're seeking to reconnect with your Igbo heritage or embark on a journey of language learning, this book is your guide to mastering the language and embracing the vibrant spirit of Igbo culture.

Igbo Linguistics: *An Expanded Guide To Igbo Orthography, Phonology, Morphology & Lexicology*

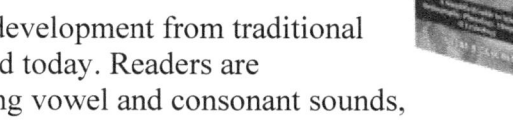

"Igbo Linguistics: An Expanded Guide to Igbo Orthography, Phonology, Morphology, and Lexicology" offers a comprehensive exploration of the linguistic landscape of the Igbo language in an extensive form, providing readers with a deep understanding of its structure, sound system, word formation, and vocabulary.

The book starts with Igbo Orthography, tracing its development from traditional systems like Nsibidi to the standardized writing used today. Readers are introduced to the diverse Igbo orthography, including vowel and consonant sounds, spelling rules, and punctuation conventions.

It continued with Phonology and Phonetics, examining the sounds of Igbo and their articulation. From the classification of phonemes to the structure of syllables and the mechanics of speech production, readers explore the fundamental elements of Igbo phonology. Practical exercises reinforce learning, allowing readers to refine their pronunciation and phonetic transcription skills.

Further, the exploration extends to the Morphology of Igbo Linguistics, unraveling the structure and formation of words in the language. Readers delve into the nature of morphemes, the types of morphological processes, and the intricacies of word formation. In Lexicology, it examines the semantic relationships and lexical categories of words.

"Igbo Linguistics" serves as an indispensable resource for students, educators, and enthusiasts seeking to deepen their understanding of Igbo language. Through its accessible approach and comprehensive coverage, the book equips readers with the knowledge and skills to engage meaningfully with the linguistic heritage of the Igbo people. Whether you're a beginner embarking on your language learning journey or an advanced learner seeking to refine your skills, "Igbo Linguistics" is your guide to mastering the intricacies of this vibrant and dynamic language.
Through detailed explanations and exercises, learners gain proficiency in reading and writing Igbo with accuracy and fluency.

Igbo Syntax: *The Structure And Rules That Govern Igbo Phrases And Well-Formed Sentences*

Igbo Syntax is a comprehensive guide that delves into the intricate workings of Igbo grammar, offering readers a deep understanding of how phrases and sentences are constructed in the language. From the foundational concepts of syntax to the advanced principles of transformational grammar, each chapter of the book provides a thorough exploration of the key elements that shape Igbo linguistic structure.

The beginning chapters introduce to readers the basic units of Igbo syntax, including words and clitics, laying the groundwork for a comprehensive understanding of the language's grammatical framework. It then proceeded with exploring word order typology and syntactic categories, gaining insight into the different types of word groups and the hierarchical structure of Igbo sentences. Through practical exercises, learners develop proficiency in identifying and analyzing the syntactic components of Igbo language.

The middle chapters focus on the lexicon and phrasal categories, examining the diverse range of noun phrases, adjective phrases, and prepositional phrases found in Igbo discourse. Readers learn how these phrasal categories contribute to the overall structure and meaning of sentences. Toward the end, readers delve into Igbo phrase structure rules, transformational grammar, and grammatical functions, gaining insight into the underlying principles that govern sentence formation and communication in Igbo.

Igbo Semantics: *A Comprehensive Exploration Of Simple And Complex Meanings In Igbo Language*

"Igbo Semantics" delves deep into the intricate world of meaning within the Igbo language, offering readers a comprehensive exploration of semantic structures and relationships. From the nuances of word meanings to the complexities of sentence interpretation, this book provides a thorough understanding of how meaning is conveyed and understood in Igbo communication.

Readers will embark on a journey through the semantic landscape of Igbo, uncovering the rich tapestry of meanings embedded within its vocabulary. Through detailed analyses and insightful explanations, the book examines the various semantic domains present in Igbo, including lexical semantics, compositional semantics, and discourse semantics.

Drawing on linguistic theory and empirical research, "Igbo Semantics" explores key topics such as semantic ambiguity, lexical relations, and semantic roles. Readers will gain valuable insights into how meaning is constructed through the interaction of words, phrases, and discourse contexts in Igbo language use.

Whether you are a student, researcher, or language enthusiast, "Igbo Semantics" offers a valuable resource for deepening your understanding of the intricacies of meaning in Igbo communication. With its accessible approach and comprehensive coverage, this book is an essential companion for anyone interested in exploring the fascinating world of Igbo semantics.

Index

A

Abịdịị 29
Acoustic phonetics 76
Acronyms 159, 187, 195
Adjective 237; *Demonstrative Adjectives* 238
Adverb 242; *Interrogative Adverbs* 242
Affixes 150, 151, 152, 161
Agglutination 151
allomorph 169, 175
Alphabet: Igbo Alphabet 38
Alveolar ridge 110, 111, 122
Antonnyms 219
Articulatory Phonetics 76
Auditory phonetics 77
away 70

B

bed 52, 92, 248
Bilabial 92, 106, 124
Blending 159, 187, 194
Bound Morphemes 150

C

Chroneme 80
Class-Changing 162
Class-Maintaining 162
Clipping 159, 187, 188
Coined Words 190
Compounding 95, 159, 187, 189
Conjunction 237
Consonant: Elision 57
consonants 14, 20, 33, 39, 40, 46, 57, 58, 59, 61, 62, 63, 64, 75, 76, 77, 78, 81, 91, 92, 93, 104, 106, 109, 114, 121, 124, 125, 127, 128, 147
Consonants: letters 55
Contour tone 91
cook 52, 92
Corrupt Words 200, 201

D

Derivational morphemes 161
diacritical marks 15, 36, 51, 58
Diacritics 51, 58
Diagraphs 14, 40
Diphthong 44

E

Enclitic 152, 165
Epiglottis 111, 123
Esophagus 111, 123
Etymology 180
Extentional suffix 161, 164

F

Fire 70
Free morpheme 149
fry 38
Functional morphemes 150

G

Gerund 152, 153, 169, 171, 172
Glottalic airstream 104
grapheme 20, 77, 78, 109, 110, 112, 114

H

Hard palate 110, 111, 122
Heavy Vowel 39
Hello 249
hot 238
house 46, 248

I

Infinitives 152, 153, 169, 170, 171, 172
Infixes 152, 154, 155
Inflectional suffixes 159

Interjection 249; Approval 250; Attention 249; Greeting 249; joy 249; surprise 250
Intonation 89
Isuama Igbo Studies 29

J

jests 196, 197, 198, 199, 200

L

labiodental 106
Larynx 111, 123
Lexeme 181
Lexical morphemes 149
Lexicology 1, 177, 179, 180
Light Vowel 39
Loan Blend 202
Loan Word 191
love 68, 232
lungs 77, 103, 104, 106, 114

M

Mazi Ọnwụ committee 37
Minimal pairs 78
Mispronounced Words 200, 201
Monophthong 43, 44, 45
Morpheme 143, 144, 146, 149
Morphology 1, 141, 143, 159
Multiple Taxonomies 228

N

Nasal cavity 110, 111, 122
new 14, 16, 238
Noun 231; *Abstract Noun* 232; *Collective Noun* 232; *Common Noun* 231; *Compound Noun* 232; *Concrete Noun* 232; *Countable Noun* 232; *Proper Noun* 231; *Uncountable Noun* 232
Noun agent 152, 154, 169, 173
Noun instrument 152, 154, 169, 173
Nsibidi 27, 28, 29
nterjection: sorrow 250

O

Onomasiology 180
organ of speech 103
Orthography 1, 17, 22, 27, 33, 34, 36, 37, 182

P

Participles 152, 169, 170
Past tense 169, 174
Pharynx 111, 122
Phoneme 77, 79, 81, 93, 109, 115, 144
Phonemes 75, 76, 81, 89, 104
Phonetic transcription 128
Phonetics 73, 75, 76, 77, 121, 128
Phonology 1, 73, 75
place of articulation 77, 106, 110, 114
Place of Articulation 109, 110
Plural 169, 175, 233
police 70
Prefixes 152
Preposition 248
Pronoun 232; *Demonstrative Pronoun* 234; *Emphatic Pronoun* 234; *Impersonal Pronoun* 233; Personal Pronoun 233; *Possessive Pronoun* 233; Subject Pronoun 233
prosody 89
Prosody 75
Pulmonic airstream 103
punctuation: apostrophe 68; colon 68; comma 67; ellipsis 70; exclamation 69; full stop 67; hyphen 69; parentheses 69; question marks 68; quotaation marks 69; semi-colon 68; slash 70
Punctuation 67

R

Reduplication 159, 187, 193, 194
remember 55

S

Segmental phoneme 81
Semasiology 180
Slang 196
soft palate 104, 105, 111, 122, 126
spelling rules 61
Stress 89, 182
Suffixes 152, 155
Supra-segmental phonemes 89
Synonyms 205, 207, 208, 209, 210, 211, 212, 213, 214, 215, 216, 217, 218, 219

T

The SPILC 35
The Union Igbo Studies 32
Tonal: Accent Marks 51, 58
Tonal Marking 15, 80
Toneme 79
Tongue 105, 111, 122
Trachea 111, 123
transcription 112, 128, 129

U

Uvula 111, 122
uvular 106

V

Velaric airstream 104
Velum 111, 122
Verb 235; *Auxillary Verbs* 236; *Infinitve Verbs* 235; *Linking Verbs* 236
Vocal cord 111, 123
vowel: Regressive Assimilation 47
Vowel: Assimilation 46; Elision 46, 51; Heavy Vowel 43; Light Vowel 43; Progressive Assimilation 46
Vowel harmony 63, 95
Vowels 14, 39, 94, 113, 114; letters 43; Nasalized Vowels 58

W

Word Formation 187
work 69